Six Decades
That
Changed the World

Six Decades That Changed the World

The USSR After 60 Years

Edited by

Marilyn Bechtel, David Laibman
and
Jessica Smith

A New World Review Collection

NWR Publications, Inc.
New York, N.Y.

© NWR Publications, Inc.
156 Fifth Avenue
New York, N.Y. 10010
1978

Library of Congress Catalog Card Number:
77-93161
ISBN: 0-916972-02-X
Printed in the USA

CONTENTS

FOREWORD

The editors of *New World Review* are proud to present this volume illustrating the immense progress the Soviet people have made in every sphere of life in the sixty years since the Great October Socialist Revolution, and the struggles of the whole people against the greatest odds, which have made that progress possible.

Part of this material was published as a special enlarged issue of the magazine (November-December 1977). We are able to provide much greater coverage in this book, more than half of which is devoted to additional material.

In 1917, the working people and peasants of what is now the Soviet Union were suffering not only from the all-pervasive oppression and repression of the tsarist regime, but also from the devastation wrought by the First World War. Those of non-European nationality felt the yoke most acutely, for tsarist Russia was rightly known as "the prison-house of nations."

The story of how the people, under the leadership of Vladimir Ilyich Lenin and the Bolshevik Party, united to overturn first tsarism and then the Provisional Government, which did nothing to benefit the people and which continued the world war, and how they went on to build a great industrial society with a rich material and cultural life based on maximum participation of all its people is one of the greatest epics of all times. In the years immediately following the Revolution, the people of the new Soviet state had to fight off the 14-nation intervention in which the US government participated, as well as counterrevolution aided and inspired by the young state's enemies abroad. At the same time, they had to build a new society from scratch, along lines never before attempted,

The Soviet workers and their allies among the peasantry and the intelligentsia had to restructure the governmental apparatus, to develop new forms assuring the widest possible popular participation, and to learn to make these function. They had to restore the existing primitive technology and catch up with the new technological revolution already developing. They had to overcome the legacy of centuries of racial and national oppression, illiteracy, the backwardness of the countryside. They had to completely reorganize industry and agriculture on a socialist foundation, to learn the skills of managing and develop the science of planning on a nationwide scale. They had to establish a foreign policy based on

9

entirely new lines — equality, sovereignty and the constant quest for world peace.

The Soviet people ended illiteracy and unemployment, raised the level of living in city and in countryside and narrowed the gap between them. They built the giant industrial projects and the great hydroelectric dams to power them. They built great collective and state farms and mechanized agricultural production. They brought the struggle against national and racial oppression to a new stage as they founded the Soviet Union, a federation of nations bound together by common purpose, equality and friendship of peoples. In fact, the USSR can truly be called the world's first "affirmative action" state, because even during the most difficult times, priority has always been given to development of the areas whose people were most oppressed before the Revolution. The people of the Soviet Union developed universal health care where there was none before, and founded a vast network of cultural and recreational opportunities. And all on a foundation of the broadest participation of the people in the decisions which determined their lives.

And then, in 1941, this progress was abruptly and tragically interrupted by the Nazi invasion, which cost the lives of 20 million Soviet people and brought unprecedented devastation to the Western USSR. The Soviet peoples' heroic halt and repulse of the Nazi invaders, through the seige of Leningrad, the battles of Moscow and Stalingrad, and the long struggle to liberate the occupied lands and then the nations of Eastern Europe can truly be said to have saved the world from the tyranny of Nazism, and earned the undying gratitude of all the earth's peoples. Not only the Red Army and Navy, but also the partisans behind the lines, and the women and young people producing on the home front, shared fully in this herculean effort.

After the Second World War, the Soviet people and their government faced enormous tasks of rebuilding, coping with the loss of precious lives, the destruction of 1,700 cities and towns and 70 thousand villages and a third of their national wealth — in effect, building their country twice over. Simultaneously, they continued and strengthened their struggle for peace as the nuclear age began and the US, then in sole possession of the atomic bomb, launched the cold war and the arms race. Despite their immense tasks at home, the people of the USSR gave great assistance to the new socialist countries of Eastern Europe, to the People's Republic of China and later to Cuba, continuing the policy begun three decades before with regard to the Mongolian People's Republic. Their expanded support to liberation movements as the great movement for national independence swept across Asia and Africa helped bring colonialism nearly to an end and found its most striking expression in aid to the Vietnamese people's heroic victory over US aggression.

By the time of the 60th anniversary, the USSR was long established as the world's second industrial power, and led the world in many types of production, including oil, iron and steel, cotton, wool and flax, tractors, locomotives, and mineral fertilizers. Equally important, the people had created and were constantly improving a quality of life which added to satisfaction of material needs the satisfaction of cultural, intellectual and spiritual needs, and in which tens of millions participated directly in political decision-making, economic planning and industrial management.

The peoples of Africa, Asia and Latin America increasingly look to the Soviet Union as a reliable and fair trading partner, as a source of economic assistance with no strings attached in developing their own industrial and agricultural base, as a proponent of international relations promoting world peace, equality and sovereignty for newly emerged states, and as a bastion of help in genuine liberation struggles.

This volume is an attempt to sum up briefly the foreign and domestic policies and present stage of development of the Soviet Union and show the historic roots from which these spring. No one book could fulfill such a broad mandate. Necessarily, much more of great value regarding this vast and diversified land, its people and their multifaceted activities must remain beyond its covers than could find its way within. It is our hope that readers will find here an overview of the nature of Soviet society, which will lead them to further explorations.

We have especially sought to emphasize the broad and intense participation of the Soviet people in political and economic decision-making, which comprises socialist democracy and which is especially exemplified in the new Constitution, and which features nationwide people's discussion of every new measure to be introduced. We have sought to demonstrate a quality of life based not only on such material essentials as improved housing, excellent health care, transport and consumer goods, but also on a rich and growing peoples' culture, educational system, constructive sport and recreational opportunities, and the constant challenge of new frontiers such as the development of the riches of Siberia and the Far North. We have sought especially to emphasize the ways in which Soviet socialist society has overcome the ancient legacy of racism, national oppression and the oppression of women.

Selection and editing has been done by the editors of *New World Review*—Marilyn Bechtel, editor, David Laibman, assistant editor, and Jessica Smith, chairman, editorial board.

Our special thanks are due all the US and Soviet authors who have contributed articles to this collection. And our warmest appreciation to Novosti Press Agency, whose invaluable cooperation helped us obtain the articles by Soviet authors in this volume and other materials.

THE EDITORS

Part One
The USSR and the World

1

WILLIAM POMEROY

Socialism's Sixty Years

Certain historical moments lend themselves perfectly as vantage points for the human perspective, enabling world progress and the prospects for humanity to be seen, past and future, in their broad sweep. One such dramatic moment is November 7, 1977, the 60th anniversary of the revolution that brought into being the world's first socialist state.

Marking a round figure of six remarkable decades of socialist growth and development, this anniversary date is momentous also because of its association with great present-day changes now going on in the world. Those sweeping changes—the crumbling of the last fortresses of colonialism in southern Africa, the casting off of neo-colonialism by developing countries that demand a "new international economic order," the swing to the left in major capitalist countries that flounder in crisis, and particularly the process of detente that is making a reality of peaceful coexistence between countries of different social systems after decades of cold war hostility—are, in fact, intimately related to the social transformation of the world that began in the cities and countryside of the old Russian empire on November 7, 1917.

It may truly be said that from that single day onward the world was never the

WILLIAM J. POMEROY, a frequent contributor to NWR, has written extensively about the theory and practice of socialism and national liberation struggles. Among his many books are *The Forest* (1963), about his life with the Huk guerrillas in the Philippines (where he served ten years of a life sentence for his political activities); *American Neo-Colonialism* (1970), for which he was awarded the degree of Doctor of Science in History by the Institute of Oriental Studies, USSR Academy of Sciences; and, most recently, *An American-Made Tragedy: Neocolonialism and Dictatorship in the Philippines* (International, 1974). He is currently working on a book-length study of Soviet life.

same again. All other eras of social change for humanity—the disintegration of slavery as feudalism arose, the emergence of capitalism to replace feudalism—were processes drawn out over centuries, littered with compromises, without decisive historical dividing moments. November 7, 1917 (October 25 by the old Russian calendar) was utterly clear-cut: on that day for one-sixth of the world capitalism ended, socialist construction began.

From the vantage point of the October Revolution's 60th anniversary it is possible to comprehend the amazing changes that have occurred in the world in that historically brief span of time. The only feature that has not changed, except perhaps in the intensity with which it is carried on, is the campaign of lies and distortions about the Soviet Union, its socialist society and its role in the world that is conducted unceasingly in the capitalist part of the world as it strives to prolong itself by depicting socialism as a system of ineptitude and abuse that is allegedly incapable of real change for the better. With each anniversary of the October Revolution, however, it has become more difficult for its enemies to obscure or to disfigure its accomplishments or its impact.

Lenin wrote in 1921, on the fourth anniversary of the Revolution:

Let the curs and swine of the moribund bourgeoisie and of the petty bourgois democrats who trail behind them heap imprecations, abuse and derision upon our heads for our reverses and mistakes in the work of building up *our* Soviet system. We do not forget for a moment that we have committed and are committing numerous mistakes and are suffering numerous reverses. How can reverses and mistakes be avoided in a matter so new in the history of the world as the building of an unprecedented *type* of state edifice! We shall work steadfastly to set our reverses and mistakes right and to improve our practical application of Soviet principles, which is still very, very far from being perfect. But we have a right to be and are proud that to us has fallen the good fortune to *begin* the building of a Soviet state, and thereby to *usher in* a new era in world history, the era of the rule of a *new* class, a class which is oppressed in every capitalist country, but which is everywhere marching forward towards a new life, towards victory over the bourgeoisie, towards the dictatorship of the proletariat, towards the emancipation of mankind from the yoke of capital and from imperialist wars. . . .

We have made the start. When, at what date and time, and the proletarians of which nation will complete the process is not important. The important thing is that the ice has been broken; the road is open, the way has been shown. (*Pravda*, October 18, 1921; *Collected Works*, Vol. 33)

There have been mistakes and reverses since Lenin wrote those words, since history does not move in a straight line, but they are not the significant aspects of the socialist experience over the past sixty years. What is significant is that, in one way or another, at one pace or another, the majority of mankind has begun travelling down that road opened by the Soviet peoples. The vista that can be seen from the height of sixty years of socialism is a broadening road of transition from capitalism to socialism.

The single most important change for mankind in that time is the division of the world into two contrasting and competing systems, socialism and capitalism. That this actually began with the events of the October Revolution itself was perhaps not so readily apparent, except to the clear-sighted, in the first decades of the Soviet Union, when the capitalist powers maintained a *cordon sanitaire* about its borders and when its relative weakness led the vanguard sectors of the international working class to raise the slogan "Defend the Soviet Union!" A socialist world sector became a fully understood reality only when World War II resulted in the creation of many new socialist states in unity with the Soviet Union.

In 1919, when the Soviet state was fighting for its life against imperialist intervention from all sides, the population of the new socialist part of the world was but 138 million, only 7.8 per cent of the world's total. In 1976 there were 1,317 million people living under socialism, 32.6 per cent of the world's population. The Soviet state in 1922, after the ravages of the interventionist wars, accounted for barely one per cent of world industrial output. In 1976 the socialist countries combined accounted for over 40 per cent of the world industrial output, the Soviet Union itself producing 20 per cent.

It would be erroneous to contend that the multiplying and growth of socialist states has been due wholly to the existence of the Soviet Union. Basically, it has been due to the decline and crisis in the whole capitalist system, and to growth of revolutionary forces for change in each country. However, it is incontrovertible that without the Soviet Union every other single country that has become socialist or socialist-inclined would have had their movements for change defeated and annihilated by the counterrevolutionary forces of imperialism.

There have been no exceptions to this fact. The socialist states of Eastern Europe were protected at their inception in 1945-47 by the Red Army that had already smashed the power of their fascist ruling groups. The Democratic People's Republic of Korea similarly gained its feet at the same time, safeguarded by the Soviet Red Army.

Contrary to Maoist interpretations of history, the People's Republic of China would be absent from maps were it not for the prior victory of the October Revolution. Among the many aspects of Soviet assistance to the Chinese Revolution, from support to Sun Yat-sen's Kuomintang to the handing over to the Communist armies of the armament of the Japanese Kwangtung army that had been crushed in 1945 by the Soviet Red Army, there stands the historical fact that the famous Long March to Yenan that saved the Chinese Communists from annihilation in the 1930s would have been impossible if the old Tsarist empire instead of the Soviet state lay at Yenan's backdoor.

That Cuba has survived and thrived as a socialist state 90 miles from the

United States is indisputably due to the protection and assistance of the Soviet Union. The liberated, socialist states under construction in Vietnam, Laos, Kampuchea (Cambodia), Angola, Mozambique and Guinea-Bissau all owe much of their tremendous victories to large-scale Soviet aid, which has had the form not merely of military means for victory and defense but also of indispensable economic, technical, technological, educational and other means for consolidating and building the new states.

*As the socialist countries of the world have grown numerically and in development, the aid to liberation struggles and to new socialist construction has been more widely shared among them, as the example of Cuban aid to African countries demonstrates today, but the Soviet Union remains the most powerful and most capable source of that aid.

The existence of a socialist system that now embraces over one-third of the world and its peoples is the most important consequence of the October Revolution, but another sweeping change has occurred in close relation with it and has contributed massively to the radical alteration of the world of 1917: the colonial revolution. When the October Revolution took place the imperialist system stood at the zenith of its extent and power. Today, in the broadening wake of that Revolution, the last traces of colonialism are being eradicated, in southern Africa and in scattered outposts of islands and enclaves.

That colonial system would have collapsed as a result of its inner crises and contradictions that have given rise to revolutionary movements for liberation and change was inevitable in due time, but the speed and the character of the colonial revolution have been linked in many ways with the October Revolution.

Occurring as it did in the Tsarist empire that had made colonies of many peoples, the October Revolution was pronouncedly an anti-colonial as well as a anti-capitalist revolution. The 15 people's republics that make up the Soviet Union, and the many autonomous republics and regions within them, are the most remarkable of all examples of developing countries striding swiftly from colonial backwardness to advanced industrial prosperity in little more than a generation, including many that have bypassed capitalism to make the leap from feudal or nomadic existence to socialism.

The very least that can be said is that the October Revolution influenced both the national liberation movements and the international climate in which they occurred and developed. Colonial revolutionaries and national democrats, Communist and non-Commmunist, from virtually all colonies, looked to the Soviet Union as their reliable ally, refuge, base and classroom; eventually, as Soviet strength grew, they could look to it, as did the new socialist countries, as their defender, preventing the old imperialist "gunboat diplomacy" of intervention and aggression from negating their independence victories.

Effects of the Soviet example have been immeasurable. Demonstrating the revolutionary and constructive potential of oppressed peoples, posing a socialist alternative to newly-free countries, and increasingly serving as a non-exploitative reservoir of assistance to their development, the Soviet Union and its socialist allies have literally changed the course of history for new nations. In the three decades that have elapsed since national freedom was attained in 1947 by the first large colonial country to be liberated in the post-World War II period, India, the struggle for the struggle for the future between the world systems of socialism and capitalism has had one of its most dramatic arenas in the 110 or more countries that comprise the "third world."

Whereas at one time national independence, as in the case of the American colonies in the 18th century, would have meant the triumph of national bourgeoisies and a capitalist path of development, the "third world" has in few cases seen such a clear-cut commitment. The step from national independence to social emancipation has been greatly shortened by the existence and example of world socialism. A number of once colonial countries have taken a fully socialist orientation from the outset, others have opted for non-capitalist development that embodies socialist forms, and most of the rest have mixed economies of private and public sectors in which the issue is open between socialism and capitalism.

In the contest between socialism and capitalism in the "third world" a general pattern had developed, in which the Soviet Union and other socialist countries have had policies of trade and aid that have fostered a public sector of basic industries that reinforce independence and genuine economic development, and in which the capitalist countries have fostered a private sector, chiefly non-basic in character, along with neocolonial relations that hamper independence and development. The 60th anniversary period is now witnessing the fruit of this contest: the shattering of the pattern by the developing countries' pressure for a "new international economic order," a set of demands voiced with increasing impatience by the Group of 77 (now grown to 103) countries and by the interlocking Non-Aligned Countries. Basically a trend for freedom from new colonial forms of trade and aid that have featured the capitalist side of the struggle for the developing countries, it is supported by the socialist countries. Along with the heavy swing in the line-up of United Nations members on basic questions, toward unity of the socialist countries with the many developing countries against imperialist positions, this trend is clearly indicative of the forces that are prevailing in the "third world."

Within sixty years the vast majority of mankind has been freed from exploitation, either completely as in the case of the socialist countries or from its most onerous forms as in the case of the once-colonial developing nations. The colonial and semi-colonial countries that won freedom after the October Revolution (not counting those that became fully socialist) contain today 1,981 million people (1974). Together, the socialist and developing countries (in which a large number live under a socialist orientation or non-capitalist forms) now total 3,298 million out of a world population of 4,045 million.

In socialism's 60 years the most critical and decisive period encompassed the years of World War II. Historians are still assessing the colossal impact of that war, which in effect was a tremendous historical catalyst that enormously hastened the process of capitalist decline and of socialist ascendancy. It brought to a powerful head all the revolutionary forces that had been accumulating in the world under the influence of the October Revolution. They delivered a shattering blow to fascism, the most reactionary and aggressive sector of world capitalism, and to the colonial system.

Fascism centered in Nazi Germany, Italy and Japan was a phenomenon that had a dual aim: to conduct an imperialist war for redivision of the world and its colonies, and to destroy the Soviet socialist state that challenged imperialism as a whole. It could have succeeded in the aim of smashing its British and US imperialist rivals if they had not allied themselves with the Soviet Union, but it failed to destroy the Soviet Union with its main blows, and was itself smashed by the powerful Soviet counter-offensives. Millions were able to see clearly the nature and dynamism of a socialist system that could arouse people to such feats of heroism and devotion, and for the first time people of many countries found themselves openly allied in a struggle for democratic interests side by side with a socialist country. Capitalism has since then spent enormous resources and decades of brainwashing to try to remove this understanding and feeling of solidarity that had been generated in whole populations by the clarity of wartime issues.

World War II was a great historical watershed. From an encircled system before the war that had called upon the international working class to unite around the slogan "Defend the Soviet Union," socialism had burst out of the encirclement and was now in a position to defend the struggles and advances of peoples around the globe. Imperialist attempts to restore the former relation of forces, through nuclear blackmail, "containment" and "rollback," and through counterrevolutionary colonial wars, have been to no avail: the world is changed, and history cannot be reversed.

From the vantage point of today's 60th anniversary, a significant lesson of the anti-fascist war stands out clearly. This is the infinite capacity of the Soviet Union to stand in unity with the masses of all countries in struggles against aggression and for liberation. It is a capacity demonstrated repeatedly since then in socialist aid for the liberation struggles of the Vietnamese people, of the Angolan, Mozambiquan and Arab peoples, and currently in support of the liberation and anti-apartheid struggles in Southern Africa. Increasingly, from anti-fascist to anti-imperialist struggles, the unity has grown between the socialist countries, the international working class and its progressive allies, and the national liberation movements.

The capacity of others has been a massive check on the war-making tendencies of imperialism. Socialism has had its main impact on world affairs, however, not through its military might but through its peace policies. Peace was one of the main slogans on the banners of the October Revolution, and peaceful coexistence and disarmament were proclaimed as state polities by the Soviet Union from its inception.

In the past 60 years those policies have vastly influenced the well-being of mankind. The Soviet Union was not yet strong enough before World War II to make that influence decisive; its efforts for collective security to halt war-making fascism were suicidally disregarded by the imperialist rivals and nurturers of Hitlerism. In the postwar period, as the socialist system has grown, it has been a different story. The creation of the United Nations in the form that it took was due principally to the Soviet Union and the anti-fascist forces allied with it, and the growth of the United Nations as a force for peace has been due largely to the work of its socialist members. In addition, the socialist countries have been the moving force of an international mass mobilization for peace, from the Stockholm Peace Appeal to the World Assembly of Peace Forces that met in Moscow in 1976.

Most of all, that World War III has not occurred to dissolve the world in a nuclear holocaust has been due specifically to the firm, tireless efforts of Soviet diplomacy to achieve peaceful coexistence. One of the foremost achievements of that diplomacy, the Helsinki Agreement on European Security and Cooperation signed in 1975, a solid cornerstone of detente, is being extended as the 60th anniversary is celebrated, in its first review conference meeting in Belgrade.

Today, as never before in history, the possibilities of disarmament and of eliminating war from human relations are real and discernable. This is mainly due to the patient, tactful, responsible use of the peaceful negotiating table by the Soviet Union, confident in its strength and responsible and humane in the use of it.

For the international working class the gains have been great. Present-day living standards, social security, semi-socialized medicine, unemployment insurance, and a variety of other benefits in leading capitalist countries were not in existence 60 years ago. In the main, of course, these have been won by the struggles of the working class in each country, but behind the concessions wrung out of capitalism has stood the "specter" of socialist revolution that was carried out by workers and peasants who had been denied concessions.

The New Deal, the Fair Deal, the New Frontier, the Great Society, the British welfare state and other programs have all embodied conscious responses to the socialist challenge. Fascism, it has been seen, may temporarily suppress working class movements, but the revolutionary consequences may destroy capitalism itself. In leading capitalist countries today the ruling class hesitates to carry exploitation or rejection of worker demands to the point of causing revolt, aware that the living example of the socialist alternative is ever-present along with international working class solidarity that is the powerful bridge between the peoples of the two systems.

The felt necessity to compete with socialism permeates capitalist policies both foreign and domestic. Anti-Soviet propaganda dominates capitalist media and culture, keeping the socialist challenge, albeit in distorted form, continually before the people. Social priorities are distorted by gigantic expenditures, comprising the major part of budgets, poured out for a proclaimed military confrontation with socialism. The main aspects of foreign policy and of relations with other states are shaped by fear of socialist strength and of people's movements everywhere that regard socialist countries as friends or allies.

Part of the capitalist response to the rise of the new system has been intensified repression, banning, prohibition, or curtailment of freedom and rights of those in the society who advocate or sympathize with socialism or hail the October Revolution and its anniversaries. This, however, has proved increasingly counterproductive, and today capitalism is caught between its repressive character and the need to appear as a proponent of human rights. The sudden human rights stance by the US and other capitalist governments is not merely an anti-Soviet gimmick but is an attempt to get out from under the fact that the capitalist powers have always been intimately associated with inhumane actions and episodes around the world, while socialist countries have been identified with struggles for freedom and democracy everywhere for the entire past 60 years.

The socialist example, and the demonstrations of socialist solidarity with all who fight against exploitation, oppression and racial discrimination, has had one of its major effects in southern Africa where the Carter Administration is now compelled to take a public position against racism and apartheid, although US-dominated multinational firms continue to profit from investments in apartheid. US spokesmen frankly admit that "Africa will go by default to the Communists" unless the capitalist countries take at least a verbal stand against racism, an acknowledgment that socialism is identified internationally with racial and national equality.

This attempt to respond to the socialist challenge, to its 60 years of enormous achievement and dedication to humane interests, has had other incalculable effects on capitalist society. It has stimulated a greater than normal emphasis on technological development and scientific research. Much of this has been in connection with military aspects of the competition between systems, but the offshoots of this in the electronics, metals and other fields have changed many features of living. The "space race," openly aimed at seeking superiority or military advantage, has been another stimulus of invention and a new range in industry. Culture, sports, sciences, even religion have felt the challenge from a dynamic socialism, and the response most frequently has been one of uncertainty and alarm. The point has been reached where virtually all endeavor and forms of expression under capitalism are measured by and placed in comparison with those under socialism.

Looming over capitalism in the coming period, as a retreat from cold war confrontation occurs, are the psychological effects on a society that has been whipped up for decades to display its superiority but that finds socialism continually abreast or ahead of the best that it can do.

There is a story, perhaps apocryphal, of Lenin dancing in the snow of the Kremlin grounds when the life of the new Soviet state exceeded that of the Paris Commune. The spaces between milestones have lengthened since then for the October Revolution. A decade ago, in 1967, its 50th anniversary was celebrated, a great half-century milestone, hailed as an unparalleled achievement of unflagging revolutionary growth.

The decade since then, from our 60th anniversary vantage point, has all the signs of history being speeded up, like accelerated cinema projection. In that time have occurred the staggering Vietnam defeat of US imperialism, the collapse of the Portuguese colonial empire in Africa and looming demise of racist regimes on that continent, the dissipation of the cold war and its replacement by detente, the development of serious disarmament talks and of nuclear weapon curtailment, the end of fascism in Portugal, Greece and Spain, the four-power agreement on West Berlin, the Helsinki Agreement on European Security and Cooperation, the unimpeded advance of socialist economy while capitalist economic crisis deepens and lengthens, the expansion of trade and of economic exchanges between socialist and capitalist countries.

All of these events have been victories or advancements of the socialist countries' peace policy, demonstrations of their economic strength and growth. Each has involved a retreat by imperialism or an adjustment under pressure of its policies. In some case imperalism has struck back—by fascist coup in Chile, by interventions in Africa against Angola and Ethiopia, by intrigue to reverse the Portuguese revolution—but these are short-term efforts to reverse a peoples' advance on all fronts, as are other imperialist strategies and tactics, of alliance with Maoist-led China and efforts to augment Maoist attacks on the socialist countries, or attempts to divide the Communist movement.

It is in the context of this steady advance of socialism and of the world anti-imperialist forces that the latest tactics of the US and its NATO allies need to be viewed. The magnified fakery of the "dissident" and "human rights" issues have to do not with Soviet or other socialist country weakness but with their strength.

A review of capitalist propaganda over the past sixty years provides an interesting if unwitting study of socialist development. At one time, when the Soviet economy was pulling itself up by the bootstraps of its first five-year plans, the Soviet worker's wages, his working conditions, his housing, the commodities he could buy, were all derided, the Soviet worker made to appear like a tattered slave.

The tremendous growth of the socialist economy, which can no longer be dismissed, has erased the portrait of a Soviet worker "slave." Soviet national income increased by seven times between 1950 and 1975. Monthly wages of factory and office workers rose in that time from 64.2 rubles to 146 rubles.

Anti-Soviet propaganda has the increasingly desperate task of finding a target, and is now switched to intangible, abstract matters like "freedom" and "human rights" which are never really defined or measured. As in the case of the Soviet worker's well-being, the "human rights" propaganda line will collapse as the range of genuine human rights enjoyed by all people under socialism become understood—the right to work, to rest, to leisure, to good housing, to secure old age, to free education, to free health services, to full equality of the sexes, races and nationalities—all embodied in the new Soviet Constitution, and absent from the constitutions of capitalist countries.

Always on the horns of a dilemma, anti-Soviet propaganda tries on the one hand to talk of the weaknesses of socialism while on the other hand it tries to play up the scare image of a Soviet "threat." On this 60th anniversary of the October Revolution the Soviet Union is no longer pictured on the verge of the collapse that has been predicted from the evening that the Winter Palace fell. Instead it is imaged as an expansionist giant, its navies covering the seven seas, its militarily superior armies poised to sweep over western Europe and China, its arms reaching to Africa, the Middle East, South East Asia, Latin America, and to every other corner of the globe. The "threat" propaganda unwittingly points to the strength and uncontestable development of socialism.

What the seventh decade of the October Revolution means for the people of the world could scarcely be imagined but a few years ago: a curtailment and gradual elimination of war as a means of conducting relations between states and systems, an inhibiting of imperialist aggression and intervention, the complete disappearance of colonialism and racist regimes, a socialist system that decisively excels capitalism in production, productivity, and distribution of goods and services, the cooperation of states for the genuine rapid development of the "third world," and for the overcoming of hunger, pollution and major diseases.

Considering the distance that mankind has traveled in the past sixty years, these prospects are not at all unrealistic.   □

2

BORIS N. PONOMAREV

USSR-US Relations: The Soviet View

Mr. Ponomarev is chairman of the Foreign Affairs Commission of the Soviet of Nationalities, USSR Supreme Soviet, and Alternate Member, Political Bureau, Central Committee of the Communist Party of the Soviet Union. In January 1978, he headed a delegation of members of the USSR Supreme Soviet who paid an official visit to the United States at the invitation of the US Congress.

The following are Mr. Ponomarev's remarks to members of the US Senate on January 23, 1978.

Practice shows again and again that every step in the development of Soviet-American relations on a mutually advantageous and equal basis serves the interests not only of our two countries, but also the interests of all nations. It is no accident that the whole world follows the development of Soviet-American relations with such close attention.

This is understandable. The world is going through a very decisive period. Representatives of the highest elective bodies of the USSR and USA are meeting at a time when the thoughts and feelings of all peoples are riveted to questions of war and peace, to the process of detente, and to the things that are counteracting detente.

Unheard-of summits of scientific and technical progress have been scaled, and it is possible to use them for the benefit of a peaceful life for millions upon millions of people. Everybody is concerned over the sharpening of global problems—ecological, demographic, food, energy. They, too, must be solved effectively. And for all this we need peace and tremendous material and intellectual resources. But this is hindered by colossal expenditures on war preparations. Further, in a number of countries these expenditures keep rising from year to year.

We now have a peculiar situation. On the one hand, many fine words are spoken on behalf of peace, and on the other, the arms race continues at an increasing rate. Although in the seventies we have managed a change of course from cold war to a relaxation of international tension, and have paved the way for a positive and salutary process in world affairs, the opposite process—that of perfecting weapons of mass extermination and of piling up armaments—has not been stopped. Indeed, this truly sinister trend has grown even stronger, and keeps threatening the achievements reached in political detente.

The incompatibility of these two processes and the danger implicit in such a situation are legitimately occupying people's minds. Hundreds of millions of people all over the world want to know why they are compelled to pay for the colossal cost of armaments, which threaten people with disastrous consequences, while all this money is so badly needed to meet crying daily needs and requirements in production and labor, in health and housing and food, in environmental protection and in solving other urgent problems.

The Soviet Union fixes the attention of all states, of their elective organs and their people on this dangerous process, and addresses itself to their minds and hearts in order to end this state of affairs. Recently, on November 3, the Supreme Soviet addressed the peoples, parliaments and governments of all countries. "We call upon the peoples, parliaments and governments of all countries," it said, "to do everything to stop the arms race, ban the development of new means of mass destruction and begin a reduction of armaments and armed forces, begin disarmament!"

Everybody understands that the cardinal role in resolving these problems belongs to the Soviet Union and the United States of America. It is no exaggeration to say, therefore, that the whole world has a stake in better Soviet-American relations. Prevention of a world thermonuclear war and bridling of the arms race depends on this to a determining degree.

All countries must make their contribution to preventing war and to developing international cooperation in the name of the very existence and future of mankind. But in this momentous cause a special, heightened responsibility devolves on the Soviet Union and the United States.

It is the imperative of our time to complement political detente with military detente. To ignore this is not simply to "forfeit an opportunity," to scorn the opinion and hope of the peoples of the whole world. In fact, it means putting in danger even that which we have managed to achieve over the preceding years.

Following the Second World War the Soviet Union made more than a hundred proposals aimed at bridling the arms race, banning nuclear weapons, reducing military budgets, and the like. Taking guidance from the foreign policy program adopted by the 24th and 25th Congresses of the CPSU, we have come forward with many new initiatives directed to ending the arms race, launching arms reduction, reducing military budgets, banning nuclear weapons, and destroying their stockpiles. The USSR wants to halt the dismal and cheerless process of building up ever new armaments and wants the positive process of peaceful coexistence and mutually advantageous cooperation to take the upper hand over what are in fact war preparations in order, figuratively speaking, to seal up for good the frightening, all-devouring jaws of the Moloch of armaments.

The turnabout in relations between the Soviet Union and the United States in

1972 was a positive thing. The USSR and the USA signed 61 important documents—treaties, agreements, conventions, joint communiques and statements, and memoranda of accords reached on a number of problems. These include such fundamental documents as the Basic Principles of Relations Between the USSR and USA, in which both of our countries recognized peaceful coexistence as the sole basis of relations between them, the Agreement on the Prevention of Nuclear War, and a number of agreements on the limitation of strategic arms.

Later, relations between the two powers developed in fits and starts. At times they may be said to have ascended to "cosmic heights." The handshake of the cosmonauts and astronauts of the Soyuz and Apollo space vehicles before the eyes of the whole world could be described as symbolic of what peaks Soviet-American cooperation can scale, given desire on both sides.

But there were also other times, when stagnation set in our relations.

This happened against the wishes of the Soviet Union. We stand for further development of Soviet-American cooperation on a jointly established realistic basis. The Soviet Union keeps a firm course toward its further improvement in strict accordance with the letter and spirit of existing agreements. This course is, neither transient nor time-serving. It is a long-term, fundamental policy. This has been stated definitely and firmly by Leonid Brezhnev, General Secretary of the CPSU Central Committee and Chairman of the Presidium of the USSR Supreme Soviet, and also by other Soviet leaders. In his report of November 2, 1977, Brezhnev said: "Life itself demands that considerations of a long-term character, prompted by a concern for peace, be decisive in Soviet-American relations. This is the course we follow, and this is what we expect in return. There is no lack of will on our part to continue developing relations with the USA on the basis of equality and mutual respect."

We have followed and continue to follow this course where Soviet-American relations are concerned. We are convinced that for all the obvious disparity between the social nature and ideology of the two states, there are realistic opportunities to settle differences and disputes by peaceful political means, and not by force and intimidation. We hold that this is the only course that is consonant with the supreme national interests of our countries and the interests of world peace.

This is why, as Comrade Brezhnev put it, "We believe, we firmly believe that realism in politics and the will for detente and progress will finally take the upper hand, and humanity will be able to step into the twenty-first century in conditions of a peace made more dependable than ever before." And we are gratified to note that US President Carter acceded to this optimistic forecast when, responding to Brezhnev on July 21, 1977, he said: "I credit its sincerity.

And I express the same hope and belief that Mr. Brezhnev expressed."

Our line in Soviet-American relations reflects the fundamental course of Soviet foreign policy. A new Constitution of the USSR was adopted recently. Article 28 of this Fundamental Law says: "The USSR steadfastly pursues a Leninist policy of peace and stands for strengthening the security of nations and broad international cooperation." And the next, twenty-ninth, article spells out the ten basic principles of peaceful coexistence as they are set down in the Final Act of the Conference on Security and Cooperation in Europe. In sum, we have given these principles the force of a state law.

Such a course on the world scene flows from the very nature of the Soviet socialist state. It expresses the basic aspirations and interests of all Soviet people, who are engaged in peaceful, constructive labor. Indeed, we have already come to the third year of our Tenth Five-Year Plan which, when completed, will secure a further growth of our country's economy and a further improvement in the life of the Soviet people. So, when our people hear pronouncements emanating from the West about a "Soviet military threat," they are gripped by a sense of legitimate protest. No such threat exists. It is invented by those who want to go on manufacturing armaments endlessly. Far from increasing its defense allocations, the Soviet Union has been reducing them every year since 1972. And in so doing, it is steadily increasing allocations for the most peaceful of needs. In the current five years (ending in 1980) we will spend 70 billion rubles on agriculture, 100 billion on housing, and huge sums on education, medicine and wage increases. What better evidence can there be of our peaceful intentions?

We want to hope that this meeting, like the preceding ones in Moscow and Washington, will turn into a dialogue that will help us to see one another's standpoints and views more clearly, and to exchange opinions on what concretely can be done by the USSR Supreme Soviet and US Congress to further Soviet-American cooperation.

Now let me dwell specifically on a few points.

1. *On the limitation of strategic armaments.* Fairly good prospects have emerged in the present Soviet-American negotiations for concluding a new agreement on the limitation of strategic offensive arms. This assessment was given in L. I. Brezhnev's replies to the questions of a *Pravda* correspondent on December 24, 1977, and in a number of public statements by President Carter.

These opportunities must be translated into practice. Certain efforts will have to be made to achieve this, the more so because there are "guardedly critical" sentiments, sometimes even outright objections, in the United States. Groundless assertions are being made that, seeking to secure strategic superiority over the United States, the Soviet Union is building up armaments behind a screen of talk about detente, and that it is preparing the potential for a nuclear first strike.

Refuting these contentions, Leonid Brezhnev said last year, "The Soviet Union has always been and remains a convinced opponent of this sort of conception. Our efforts are directed precisely to preventing matters from reaching the point of either a first or a second strike, to preventing nuclear war in general." For the first time, the draft treaty envisages important qualitative limitations for MIRV missiles. The Soviet Union has consented to major steps in this direction. And after concluding the treaty we are here prepared to go farther.

When examining this matter we cannot help considering certain factors pertaining to the security of the USSR. First of all, the possession of nuclear weapons by allies of the United States, and also, say, by China. But special mention should be made of the US system of forward-based nuclear vehicles. Tactical US nuclear bombers and ground-based missiles deployed in the region of Europe total some 800 units. And to these should be added the striking power of the aircraft-carriers with their more than 500 bombers, as well as the forward-based missile-carrying submarines. It is also common knowledge that more than 7,000 US tactical nuclear weapons are stationed in Europe at present. Unlike the USA, the Soviet Union has no such forward-based nuclear vehicles in the immediate proximity of the United States. This factor has got to be taken into account in the new agreement when setting quantitative ceilings for strategic offensive arms.

The delegation of the USSR Supreme Soviet hopes that our colleagues in the US Congress will be realistic and take all factors into account when they debate this problem, in whose positive solution both our countries are equally interested. We want the new agreement to be not only a substantial step closer to limiting the strategic arms race, but also that it should set the stage for reducing these arms, and for disarmament in general.

We approach the signing of such an agreement from the standpoint of equality and equal security. We need no superiority over the USA, but we cannot and will not let the other side upset the equilibrium and gain superiority over us.

2. It is proper to deal specially with the *neutron bomb*, which is a new means of warfare. This truly inhuman weapon is being insistently foisted on the world today, though tens of millions of people in all parts of the world are against it. Their protests are understandable. As Senator H. John Heinz rightly said last September, death from neutron radiation is reminiscent of the effects of the chemical or bacteriological weapons, which are rejected by all civilized nations.

Our two countries have achieved the banning and destruction of the stockpiles of bacteriological weapons. Negotiations are now underway to ban chemical weapons. Meanwhile, however, it is suggested that the arsenals be stocked with the neutron bomb, even though, as Congressman Ronald V. Dellums, who studied the question, has stressed, it "makes nuclear war possible" and even "inevitable."

Just consider these words: A weapon is being developed that can make nuclear war not only possible but also inevitable. This was said by your colleague in Congress, but not by him alone. A whole series of such assessments can be cited—by political figures, prominent scientists and public leaders. The neutron bomb is described as, of all things, a "tactical" or "defensive" weapon. Attempts are being made to erase the distinction between conventional and nuclear arms. And this leads to making the transition to nuclear war imperceptible. It is rank hypocrisy and a deception of the nations.

The neutron bomb is being strongly recommended for deployment in Western Europe. Those who live far from Europe can possibly afford to approach the matter so lightly. But many Europeans are of a different opinion.

The Soviet Union is firmly opposed to the development of the neutron bomb. At the same time you ought to reckon with the fact that if this bomb becomes part of the Western arsenal—meaning that it will be directed against us, which nobody denies—we, who are concerned over our security and the security of our allies, will be compelled to accept the challenge. This was true in the case of atomic weapons and the hydrogen bomb, and the Soviet Union did not lag behind in either case.

But we do not want this any longer. This is why last December the Soviet Union proposed agreement on mutual renunciation of manufacturing the neutron bomb. We call on you to treat this highly important proposal seriously and responsibly.

3. *Questions of disarmament.* The present negotiations concerning this problem cover a wide spectrum—from ending all nuclear tests and banning means of chemical warfare to securing military detente in Europe and reducing military activity in the Indian Ocean.

In this connection I should like to call to your special attention the Soviet Union's recent proposal for agreeing on a simultaneous cessation by all states of the manufacture of nuclear weapons of all types, whether atomic, hydrogen, neutron bombs or projectiles—with a simultaneous undertaking by the nuclear powers to begin a gradual reduction of existing stockpiles of nuclear weapons until they are completely eliminated.

Is that a bad proposal? The NATO countries are keeping silent about it. Yet to put this Soviet proposal into practice would be tremendously important for lasting peace. We invite the Senate and the House of Representatives of the United States to consider the proposal with due attention.

We attach much importance to a mutual reduction of armed forces and armaments in Central Europe. Negotiations have been going on in Vienna for all of four years, but, regrettably, there are no concrete results so far.

The socialist countries taking part in the Vienna talks have repeatedly presented concrete proposals directed to reaching agreement. If they had been accepted, armed forces and armaments in Central Europe would have already been reduced by approximately 17 percent. The USSR made a very definite proposal—to "freeze" all arms in Central Europe for the duration of the negotiations. But this, too, was not accepted.

Meanwhile, while the Vienna negotiations are at a virtual standstill, we are witnessing a powerful buildup of the NATO military potential. The military budget of the United States alone for the 1979 fiscal year has gone up again, and has reached nearly 130 billion, a record sum in US history.

NATO troops are being rearmed on a large scale, there are plans to equip them with cruise missiles, and also plans to deploy neutron bombs on the territory of Western European countries. It is even said that the incipient positive changes in the Soviet-American strategic arms limitation talks may, of all things, reduce the military potential of Western Europe, and that, for this reason, it is essential to build up armed forces in Europe.

That sort of development may lead to a destabilization of the political and military strategic situation. This is fraught with great dangers not only for Europe, but also for the rest of the world. The Vienna negotiations must, at long last, get off the ground and stop serving as a screen for a buildup of NATO's military potential.

A special UN General Assembly session on disarmament is scheduled this year. To this we attach great significance. Crucial problems connected with ending the arms race, with military detente, are going to be discussed at this session. These problems have long since ripened, and require an urgent solution. As the Soviet Union sees it, the special UN Session is meant to help break the stalemate in questions of disarmament.

4. *On Security in Europe.* The Soviet Union attaches great importance to the Conference on Security and Cooperation in Europe. The Final Act signed there by the heads of 35 states reflects a thoroughly weighed balance of the interests of all its participants.

I would like to remind you that during the period since the Conference the Soviet Union has done much to translate the Helsinki Accords into practice. Important political documents aimed at reducing the war danger have been signed with France and Great Britain. Cooperation has been expanded in different fields with Italy, Denmark, Belgium, Turkey, Finland, Sweden, Portugal, Ireland. We devote much attention to Soviet-American relations.

The Belgrade conference of representatives of the foreign ministers of countries that participated in the European Conference is now coming to an end. Its purpose is a constructive exchange of opinions on the already available experience of inter-state cooperation and on further efforts to consolidate security and cooperation in Europe, and also on advancing detente in the future. Its participants have made some 100 different proposals. And we would like to hope that in the concluding stage of the Belgrade conference results will be achieved on the basis of these proposals to facilitate the materialization of detente and the implementation of the Helsinki Accords.

5. A few words are in order about the situation in the *Middle East*. The Mid-Eastern knot touches on the interests of both our countries, and has a direct bearing on the outlook for strengthening world peace and security.

As you know, last fall, in the course of Soviet-American contacts, an understanding was reached on the necessity and character of joint efforts directed to a just settlement of the Middle East crisis. A joint document was signed on this score. But the American administration has unilaterally abandoned this understanding in substance, and has begun actively to support the course of separate Egyptian-Israeli negotiations. But this course is an attempt to sidestep the key and pivotal questions that require a solution—those pertaining to the captured Arab lands and to the fate of the Palestinians. The course of events convincingly shows that separate negotiations do not bring closer, but on the contrary delay and subvert, a general settlement. As a result of separate actions, the Middle East problem has not only remained at an impasse, but the whole situation in the region has become substantially more complicated.

As concerns the Soviet Union, its position on the matter of eliminating the Middle East flashpoint has not changed. It provides for the withdrawal of Israeli troops from all Arab territories occupied in 1967; implementation of the inalienable rights of the Arab people of Palestine, including its right to self-determination and to constituting its own state; ensuring the right to independent existence and security of *all* states directly involved in the conflict, and giving them appropriate international guarantees; the aim in view is to end the state of war between the Arab countries and Israel. As recorded in the joint Soviet-American statement, international guarantees of their frontiers could be given to the sides if they so desire, and the USSR and USA are prepared for the sake of securing the terms of the settlement as a whole to participate in these guarantees with consideration for their corresponding constitutional processes.

As before, the Soviet Union is firmly of the opinion that the most effective method of resolving the Middle East problem, on the basis of the corresponding Security Council and UN General Assembly resolutions, is to involve the international mechanism specially created for this purpose—the Geneva Peace Conference on the Middle East—in which all the directly interested sides, including representatives of the Arab people of Palestine in the person of the PLO, must take part.

At present, much attention is focused on the *situation in Africa*. We hold that the struggle of the peoples of the African continent for freedom and independence, for the right to choose their own way of development, is a just struggle, and that kind of struggle our country has always supported and will continue to support. The Soviet Union is firmly opposed to interference in the internal affairs of African countries. We seek no advantages or privileges in Africa. Our policy on that continent, too, is directed to maintaining peaceful and friendly relations with all peoples and to helping them as best as we can to follow the path of their own choice.

6. Finally, a few words concerning *Soviet-American trade and economic relations*.

The Soviet-American trade agreement, signed as far back as October 18, 1972, has not entered into force to this day, and you well know why. Nearly four years ago, speaking in this same hall, we said to you that the amendments to this agreement presented in the Senate, envisioning interference in our internal affairs, nullify the understandings reached and undermine the development of economic cooperation between our countries. Yet the well-known amendment, passed by Congress, has remained in force, and here is the sad result. Our trade with the USA dropped from 2.9 billion dollars in 1976 to 2 billion in 1977.

Yet, if normal trade and political conditions had been created in the USA for the USSR, the volume of Soviet-American trade in just manufactured goods and raw materials, as President Brezhnev noted in addressing the American-Soviet Trade and Economic Council in November 1976, could have passed the ten billion dollar mark in five years.

What has been achieved by those who tried to make the development of trade with us conditional on the right of interfering in our internal affairs? The only thing they have achieved is that profitable orders that could have gone to American firms went to their West European and Japanese rivals.

I would like to say in conclusion that we are still in favor of developing our trade and economic ties on a basis of equality and mutual advantage. And we advocate this development of trade with the United States not because we cannot do without it, but because we consider closer international economic ties an important element in improving international cooperation as a whole.

T hose are some of the problems we are going to discuss. Certainly, the question I have touched upon do not cover the entire range of these problems.

We expect our meeting to help us in our joint search and in finding ways and means for developing Soviet-American relations, extending equal, mutually advantageous and constructive cooperation, and progressing steadily toward peace and the security of all nations.   □

3

MARILYN BECHTEL

Cold War, Detente, and the Future Of US-Soviet Relations

The single most critical relationship between nations today is that of the United States and the Soviet Union. What takes place between these two will determine whether the world must continue to suffer ever-escalating arms race and increasing threat of nuclear disaster, or whether progress toward a genuine and lasting peace will bring all the world's people increasing opportunity to satisfy their basic needs and build a rich, rewarding, humane life.

Six years ago, Richard Nixon and Leonid Brezhnev signed an agreement of great historic significance, for it said that the two countries will "proceed from the common determination that in the nuclear age there is no alternative to conducting their mutual relations on the basis of peaceful coexistence. Differences in the ideology and the social systems of the United States and the USSR are not obstacles to the bilateral development of normal relations based on the principles of sovereignty, equality, noninterference in internal affairs and mutual advantage."

Those agreements were reached as the result of a complex historical process during the previous three decades. They represented the most positive development in American-Soviet relations since the days of the World War II Grand Alliance, when the Soviet people and their government were praised and supported as gallant allies in the struggle to defeat the plague of fascism. They placed US-Soviet relations on a new basis, establishing peaceful coexistence as the norm in international law, and setting the stage for progress not only in arms limitation and toward disarmament, but also for new developments in economic relations, science and technology, and cultural exchange, broadening and deepening contacts between the peoples of the two countries.

Since that time, relations have taken a less favorable turn. Strategic arms limitation negotiations sagged and then were given a rude jolt by the Carter administration's proposals, so one-sided as to be totally unacceptable to the Soviets. Despite some reports of progress, at this writing a new SALT agreement has not been signed. President Carter opened his administration with a salvo accusing the Soviets and the rest of the socialist world of all manner of

MARILYN BECHTEL is Editor of the bimonthly magazine, *New World Review*.

imaginary sins while ignoring the massive human rights violations at home and among many of the US' closest allies. Under a barrage of pressure from the military-industrial complex about Soviet "drive for world domination" and "massive arms build-up," there has been increasing US arms escalation, a turn toward cold war policies and renewed emphasis on first-strike strategy. Despite these ominous signs, the majority of the American people continue to express their concern for better US-Soviet relations.

Matters have reached a critical point. Recapturing the momentum of detente which built up six years ago, and turning the present dangerous course in international relations, is in large part up to the American people, for it is the US government which has failed to live up to the spirit and the letter of the Moscow accords. Looking at the history of US-Soviet relations over the period beginning with World War II reveals the roots of our present difficulties and aids us in considering what is necessary for the future.

In June 1941, the Nazis swarmed to the East in a drive which ultimately overran half a million square miles of Soviet land. The news brought varying responses, many of them hostile, from US government and big business circles. One of the best known was from a future president, Harry Truman: "If we see that Germany is winning the war we ought to help Russia and if Russia is winning we ought to help Germany, and in that way let them kill as many as possible." Senator Robert Taft observed that "a victory for communism would be far more dangerous to the United States than a victory for fascism." Most US officials, whatever their attitude toward the USSR, thought the Soviets could hold out against the Nazi juggernaut for only a few weeks at most.

The Soviet people, however, determined to defend their great gains of the previous 24 years, fought back with a ferocity and determination unmatched in history on so large a scale. Through the blood and starvation of 900 days and more than a million deaths, the heroic defenders of Leningrad held their encircled bastion of freedom. Though disaster threatened Moscow closely, the Nazis were never to engulf the Soviet capital. And at last, and nearly singlehanded, the Red Army and Air Force and the Soviet people turned back the tide of fascism at the glorious and ghastly battle of Stalingrad, and began the long march westward which would free their land and liberate the countries of Eastern Europe from the yoke of the Nazis and their collaborators.

Recognizing the gravity of the fascist threat to the world as a whole, the more farsighted political figures of the West gave their support to the heroic struggle of the USSR in the period soon after the invasion. British Prime Minister Winston Churchill veiled his animosity and called for alliance. President Franklin D. Roosevelt announced within a few days of the Nazi invasion a policy of providing as much assistance as possible without interfering with the prior commitment to Britain. Supplies became available in the fall of 1941, although through 1942 the amount of help remained small.

Actually, although the US government's lendlease assistance was certainly of value, it could hardly be said to have been decisive: through the end of the war, the Soviets supplied 92.5 per cent of the planes they used, 91.5 per cent of the tanks, 98.5 per cent of artillery, 95.5 per cent of shells, 94.5 percent of cartridges and all their rifles.

Large segments of the American people expressed their great admiration and gratitude to their heroic Soviet allies through efforts like Russian War Relief, which involved millions of people and organizations such as religious bodies and trade unions. The sponsors and participants in the great 1942 Congress of American-Soviet Friendship ranged from the Vice President, Secretary of State and Secretary of Commerce, through important members of the diplomatic community, Congress, state and city officials, trade union and religious leaders. From the process it started, the National Council of American-Soviet Friendship developed within months.

Critical to relieve the Nazi pressure on the Eastern Front and speed the liberation of the half-million square miles they had overrun and devastated was the opening of the Second Front. Originally promised by the US and Britain for 1942, it was delayed, primarily because of British stalling, until it was already apparent that the Soviets had not only turned the tide of Nazi advance in their own territory, but were also capable of freeing all Europe single-handed. By the time the long-awaited invasion of France took place in June 1944, the Red Army was well on its way to completing the liberation of Soviet soil.

Winston Churchill, stepping back from his proclamation of alliance early in the war when Britain was still threatened, urged invasion of the Balkans to forestall Soviet influence in Eastern Europe, and after the Second Front was opened in France, he urged a drive on Berlin and advances into the previously agreed Soviet occupation zone of Germany. He even ordered the arms of the surrendering Nazis to be stockpiled in case German troops were to be mobilized against the Soviets in the spring of 1945.

In fact, it is possible to date the beginning of the cold war from 1942. While the British were stalling the Second Front and well before the great conferences at Tehran (late 1943) and Yalta (early 1945) at which the "Big Three" outlined basic agreements on postwar cooperation for a world at peace, Churchill drew up a secret memorandum in which he said, "It would be a measureless disaster if Russian barbarism overlaid the culture and independence of the ancient states of Europe."

Simultaneously, in the US despite Franklin Roosevelt's sincere belief in the necessity of postwar cooperation, Gen. Leslie R. Groves was placed in charge of the Manhattan Project to develop the atomic bomb. He later stated:

... there was never from about two weeks from the time I took charge of the project any illusion on my part but that Russia was the enemy and that the project was conducted on that basis. I didn't go along with the attitude of the whole country that Russia was a gallant ally. I always had suspicions and the project was conducted on that basis.

British scientist P.M.S. Blackett later observed that the dropping of the atomic bomb on Hiroshima and Nagasaki was "not so much the last military act of the Second World War as the first act of the cold diplomatic war with Russia now in progress."

The US emerged from World War II with her industries not only undamaged but much stronger than before. By contrast, the Soviet Union, which had played the major role in beating back the fascist onslaught in Europe, had lost 20 million people, over 1,700 cities and towns and 70,000 villages, and suffered great damage to industry, agriculture and transport in the areas occupied by the Nazis. The US had also improved its position relative to its Western European allies, and most significant of all, it alone had the atomic bomb.

The war had entrenched the arms manufacturers and others benefiting from high military spending firmly in control of the US business community. These most reactionary ruling class elements projected their vision of "The American Century" of world domination. The existence of a social system based on premises of peace and the well-being of its people was an obvious threat to these ambitions. Thus the vigorous attempts of the US and its allies to scuttle decisions taken jointly by the Big Three concerning the necessary shape of a peaceful postwar world—especially decisions about the future of Eastern Europe. This was the meaning of Winston Churchill's "Iron Curtain" speech of March 1947, the meaning of the Truman Doctrine, the Marshall Plan, the growing network of US "forward bases," consolidated and expanded by the NATO, SEATO, CENTO and ANZUS pacts.

The most fundamental issue, however, was atomic energy. In a United Nations almost entirely hostile to the Soviet Union and the nascent socialist world, the US called for all atomic energy developments to be controlled by an international authority whose actions would not be subject to veto. The Soviet plan to ban and destroy the bomb was rejected.

The Soviets were understandably dismayed. They had little reason to trust their erstwhile allies. Their only recourse, as they saw it, was to break the monopoly, which they did in 1949, and seek to ban the bomb and all subsequent mass destruction and terror weapons. Thus was set a pattern which persisted for many years—attempt after attempt by the Soviet Union, assisted by the Eastern European socialist countries as they became UN members, to secure agreement on the principle of commitment to disarm and to destroy nuclear weapons. The West always countered with insistence on exchanging intelligence information first and establishment of "collective security" and control systems before disarmament could begin.

In 1955 the stalemate came closer to being broken than it was to be until 1972. The Soviets accepted British, French and Canadian proposals for a staged reduction in manpower, nuclear and conventional weapons. The US response, in line with John Foster Dulles' dictates, was the "Open Skies" proposal for complete exchange of military information. The relation of this proposal to the theories of "preventive war" endemic in US military circles at the time is obvious.

During this time significant shifts were taking place in the relative position of world forces. By 1950 the Soviets had just about recovered from the war, and a planned, crisis-free economy was yielding stready growth. The peoples of the GDR, Hungary, Romania, Poland, Czechoslovakia, Bulgaria, Yugoslavia, Albania, North Vietnam, North Korea and China were building socialism. The Cuban revolution would follow at the end of the decade. The first great postwar wave of independence and liberation struggles, inspired and aided by the existence of socialism, had freed former colonial possessions including India, Indonesia and the northern part of Vietnam. With this developed the group of "non-aligned" nations which saw their own great need for economic and social development as best served by a world at peace. Soviet aid enabled former dependencies to start building their own industrial base; trade with the socialist countries was developing on a mutually-beneficial basis, in contrast to the neocolonialist policies of the US and its allies. The potential of the non-aligned movement was obvious not only at the UN but also at the 1955 Bandung Conference of 29 African and Asian countries which vigorously protested nuclear testing and called for banning the bomb. This process grew stronger during the 1960s, as dozens of former African colonies won their freedom and several young nations began taking a non-capitalist path of development.

All these factors, plus the regrouping of peace and progressive forces in the US and Western Europe after the wave of postwar repression, combined to make possible the first postwar peace breakthrough. Despite setbacks in US-Soviet relations with baring of US spy-plane flights over the USSR in 1960 and the near-catastrophy over Cuba in 1962, the forces for peace at home and abroad secured in 1963 the signing of the Partial Nuclear Test Ban Treaty forbidding tests in the air, on land and under the sea. (Negotiations are now in progress for a complete ban, and the Soviet Union has just announced a unilateral cessation of underground tests).

The 1960s also brought successes for peace initiatives in Europe. In 1966, President DeGaulle, searching for an independent French role and seeing good relations with the Soviets as important to that process, withdrew French forces from NATO and concluded the first of a series of agreements on peaceful relations and economic cooperation with the Soviets. The same year, the

Warsaw Treaty nations activated a 1955 Soviet recommendation and called for an all-European conference on security and cooperation, thus planting the seed which bore such magnificent fruit nine years later at Helsinki.

In 1970 the Soviet Union and the Federal Republic of Germany concluded a treaty in which, for the first time, two countries with different social systems agreed on the inviolability of post-World War II frontiers. This was followed the same year by a treaty between Poland and the FRG, in 1971 by the Quadripartite Agreement on West Berlin, in 1972 by the treaty between the FRG and the GDR, and in 1973 by the FRG-Czechoslovak agreement which at last nullified Czechoslovakia's dismemberment at Munich. Central to all was the principle of peaceful coexistence.

Impelled by the continued arms escalation of the US and its NATO allies, the Soviet Union had continued developing its own strategic forces. As Richard Nixon put it in 1970:

> The last 25 years have also seen an important change in the relative balance of strategic power. From 1945 to 1949, we were the only nation in the world possessing an arsenal of atomic weapons. From 1950 to 1966, we possessed an overwhelming superiority. . . . From 1967 to 1969, we retained a significant superiority. Today, the Soviet Union possesses a powerful and sophisticated strategic force approaching our own.

Since the early 1960s, the US government had been sinking deeper and deeper into the Vietnam war. The American people's protests cost Lyndon Johnson a second term, and made Nixon try to hide his unprecedented savagery behind talk of withdrawal. The great growth of the peace movement, combined with the emergence of more realistic forces in the business community, caused Nixon also to reopen the strategic arms limitation talks begun with the Soviets during Johnson's time.

Speaking before the 24th Congress of the Soviet Communist Party in 1971, Leonid Brezhnev summed up the situation:

> For more than 25 years now, our people have lived in peace. We regard this as the greatest achievement of our Party's foreign policy. For a quarter-century now, mankind has been safeguarded from world war. This is another historic achievement of the peoples to which the Soviet Union and its foreign policy have made a considerable contribution. However, the forces of aggression and militarism may have been pushed back, but they have not been rendered harmless. In the postwar years, they have started more than 30 wars and armed conflicts of varying scale. Nor is it possible to consider the threat of another world war as being completely eliminated. It is the vital task of all the peaceable states, of all the peoples, to prevent this threat from becoming reality.

There followed a far reaching program for world peace, including peace in Southeast Asia and the Middle East, recognition of postwar territorial changes in Europe, a worldwide conference on disarmament, banning nuclear, chemical and bacteriological weapons, halting the arms race, ending colonialism and developing cooperative relations between nations. Impressive progress was to be made in the next six years in fulfillment of these propositions.

A part of this progress was the signing of the 1972 Moscow agreements between the US and USSR, which ushered in a new stage in the process of strengthening peaceful coexistence. In addition to the historic agreement on the principles of relations between the two states, the two countries agreed to limit anti-ballistic missile systems, decided on interim measures to limit strategic arms, and looked forward to the more definitive second round of strategic arms talks. These provisions were accompanied by an agreement on trade which was immediately rendered inoperative by the Jackson-Vanik amendment, and far-reaching agreements on exchange and cooperative programs in science, technology and culture which have been mutually beneficial.

That May 1972 did not mark a sudden change in the fundamentals of US foreign policy was evident from the continuation of the Vietnam war. Nonetheless, Nixon received Leonid Brezhnev in the US in 1973, and they concluded a strong agreement on prevention of nuclear war. At the Vladivostok meeting between Gerald Ford and Brezhnev in 1974, fundamental outlines of the new strategic arms limitation accord were worked out.

The long-awaited Conference on Cooperation and Security in Europe, in which the US and the Soviet Union participated along with 32 other European countries and Canada, completed its work with the signing of the Final Act at Helsinki on August 1, 1975. The Final Act marked the end of the long, step-by-step struggle of the peace forces of Europe led by the Soviet Union, to establish the basis for a secure peace. Its terms included recognition of post World War II boundaries, respect for territorial integrity and equality of nations, prohibition of the use or threat of force by one nation against another, peaceful settlement of disputes, non-intervention in internal affairs, respect for human rights, and cooperation among nations. The Final Act was an important step to lay to rest the revanchist aims of reactionary forces in the FRG, and set the stage for unprecedented growth of peaceful cooperation between socialist and capitalist countries in science, technology, mutual economic relations and culture. Its role in putting yet another spike in the plans of aggressive circles in the US and Western Europe is proven by the consistent, if contradictory attempts of certain forces in this country to call its conclusions meaningless, and to claim noncompliance by the socialist countries.

Taken all together, the agreements of the 1970s ushered in a new stage in the struggle for peaceful coexistence—the stage of *detente*. Henry Kissinger put it this way:

However competitive they may be at some levels of their relationship, both major nuclear powers must base their policies on the premise that neither can expect to impose its will on the other without running an intolerable risk. The challenge of our time is to reconcile the reality of competition with the imperative of coexistence.

And Leonid Brezhnev:

> We make no secret of the fact that we see detente as the way to create more favorable conditions for peaceful socialist and communist construction. This only confirms that socialism and peace are indissoluble. And when we are rebuked for this, we can hardly help thinking that those who rebuke us are not sure that capitalism can survive without resort to aggression and threats of force, and without encroaching on the independence and interests of other peoples. . . . Faithful to the revolutionary cause, we Soviet Communists are fighting and will continue to fight for peace, the greatest of all boons for all peoples and an important condition for the progress of mankind in our time.

The prime aspect of that struggle for detente, now at the top of the agenda for American people because the most reactionary elements of the US big business community pose the greatest obstacles, is making the process irreversible and extending it to the military sphere. And the most urgent current task is ensuring that the Carter administration returns to the path of the 1972 agreements and proceeds quickly to conclude an equitable new SALT agreement.

The accession to office of the Carter administration in January 1977 brought a number of contradictory trends into focus. Immediately on the heels of the election, an exceptionally open debate began among different segments of US monopoly business circles. Hard-line anti-detente forces rallied around the Committee on the Present Danger, former military officers and government officials, industrialists, educators and trade unionists who claimed the Soviet Union was engaged in a drive for world military domination.

The Committee was quickly opposed by three similarly constituted bodies— the National Policy Panel on Conventional Arms Control of the United Nations Association-USA, the American Committee on US-Soviet Relations and the US component of the US-USSR Trade and Economic Council (350 top business executives representing firms producing a quarter of the US gross national product). These groups' basic positions included calling for an end to the cold war, new and more serious approaches to arms control and disarmament, and increased trade, exchange and cooperation.

Having been elected on the basis of a campaign that promised, among other things, reduction of military spending by $5 to $7 billion, one of the new president's first acts was virtually to adopt his predecessor's arms budget—not only erasing the promised cut but increasing the tab by some $10 billion.

Among his next moves was to initiate a distorted "human rights" campaign which sought to raise the purported plight of a handful of Soviet intellectuals to a height surpassing the importance of the tragedy faced by millions of victims of the most intense repression in Chile, South Korea, Israel, and South Africa, and millions unemployed and deprived of means of bare subsistence in the US itself.

There followed soon after the US submission of totally unacceptable proposals at the March 1977 session of the SALT II talks in Moscow—proposals which violated the Vladivostok agreement that the strategic arms limitation agreement should be finalized in a spirit of equality and undiminished security. The aim of the US administration, concealed behind a facade of making deep cuts in allowable armaments, was actually to insist on cuts which would fall far more heavily on the Soviet Union than on the US. For instance, great emphasis was placed on reducing the Soviets' large land-based missiles, which are of particular importance to them because a great part of their strategic nuclear forces are land-based. But the US raised no proposals for cuts in submarine-based or bomber-carried nuclear warheads, comprising a large part of the US forces, nor did it propose limits on numbers of long range cruise missiles, possessed by the US and not yet by the Soviets. US proposals on range limits for cruise missiles were also inequitable, for these could be launched from US forward bases ringing the Soviet Union, while the USSR lacks such a system ringing the US.

These proposals caused great consternation on the part of the Soviet Union, and peace forces throughout the world, and brought the talks virtually to a standstill for several months.

Two developments during the summer of 1977 stand out as ominous indications of the severity of the Pentagon and reactionary pressure on President Carter, and his willingness to acquiesce to it. In July the existence of the neutron bomb was revealed and the campaign for its acceptance by the NATO governments was begun. And in August, the decision to proceed with mass production of the cruise missile was taken.

The danger of the neutron bomb lies not only in the introduction of *any* new weapon system at a time when SALT talks, negotiations for mutual and balanced force reductions in Central Europe, and other disarmament talks are in progress, but also in the nature of the weapon itself. Though it is referred to as a "bomb," the neutron weapon is a warhead usable with Lance carrier missiles or artillery shells, which makes detection and control almost impossible. Lessened blast renders the warhead less destructive to property, but the intense neutron radiation makes it a people-killer *par excellence*, and threatens an overall amount of death, disease and genetic damage per kiloton far in excess of other current types of tactical nuclear weapons. The neutron bomb blurs the distinction between conventional and nuclear war. In the words of U.S. Representative Ronald V. Dellums, it makes the latter "thinkable" and then "do-able."

The absurdity of announcing mass production of a weapon, the cruise missile, which is a major bone of contention in the SALT talks is obvious. The cruise missile, an updated version of the World War II "buzz bomb," is a small, subsonic unmanned plane capable of carrying either conventional or nuclear warheads, and being launched from the ground, from ships or planes. It skims the ground below the reach of radar detection systems, and because of the great flexibility in its mode of launch, it is virtually impossible to monitor.

These two weapons systems are at present possessed only by the United States.

Following an unproductive period of several months in the SALT talks after the March meeting in Moscow, both the US and the Soviet Union reported progress during the fall of 1977. By early 1978 the momentum had again diminished, amid renewed pressure from cold-war congressmen, Pentagon and CIA spokesmen, concerning alleged attempts of the Soviet Union to achieve military dominance.

In an effort to move the talks in a positive direction, Soviet President Brezhnev made the following proposals on the occasion of the celebration of the 60th anniversary of the October Revolution:

Today as we are proposing another radical step: *that agreement be reached on a simultaneous halt in the production of nuclear weapons by all states.* This includes all such weapons—whether atomic, hydrogen and neutron bombs or missiles. At the same time, the nuclear powers could undertake to start the gradual reduction of existing stockpiles of such weapons, and move toward their complete total destruction . . .

There is another important problem that has a direct bearing on the task of reducing the danger of nuclear war, namely, that of seeing through to the end of the work of banning all nuclear weapons tests . . . Therefore, we state that we are prepared *to reach agreement on a moratorium covering nuclear explosions for peaceful purposes along with a ban on all nuclear weapons tests for a definite period.*

He followed this in late December by a plan for outlawing the neutron bomb:

If such a weapon were developed in the West, developed against us, a fact which nobody even tries to conceal, it must be clearly realized that the USSR shall not remain a passive onlooker. . . . In the final count, all this will raise the arms race to an even more dangerous level. . . . We do not want this to happen and that is why we move to reach agreement on a mutual renunciation of the production of the neutron bomb . . .

A central question in the whole matter of arms control and disarmament, the extension of detente to the military sphere—a key question, indeed in the entire matter of the improvement of US-Soviet relations, regaining and advancing on the high point reached in 1972—is the nature of Soviet attitudes toward war and peace. And one fundamental fact demonstrates the sincerity of the Soviets' constantly reiterated desire for peace. That fact is, there is nothing in the Soviet social system which makes war or the preparations for war desirable. There is no class or group which derives profits from arms manufacture and sale. On the contrary, the spending of billions of rubles for arms (and at 17-plus billion rubles per year it is far less than the $126 billion US arms budget) directly impedes that social and economic progress of its 260 million people which gives the Soviet socialist system its reason for being.

New forces are coming together in the United States in recognition of the necessity for detente and disarmament not only to prevent nuclear holocaust but also to enable the satisfaction of human needs now neglected because of the enormous level of US military spending. Community organizations, trade unions, organizations of Black and other oppressed minority peoples, anti-repression forces, all are joining with the traditional peace forces to call for completion of the strategic arms limitation agreement, reduction of·the US military budget and transfer of funds to jobs, education, housing, schools, health, care for the elderly and other fund-starved social programs.

The next steps involve a mass peace upsurge by this growing coalition of the American people. The Carter administration is in deep trouble with organized labor over the minimum wage and continuing high unemployment and with millions of Black Americans for its refusal to recognize and deal with the legacy of four centuries of racist discrimination and oppression. The task of peace forces in the period ahead is to see that the administration hears just as forcefully from the millions of Americans who are unemployed or under-employed because the arms industry provides substantially fewer jobs than does peaceful production, from the millions whose education, housing, transportation, health, environment and old age benefits are swallowed up in the great maw of ever more destructive weapons of war. There is no segment of the population, other than the arms merchants, Pentagon warriors and CIA, that doesn't have a personal stake in the consolidation and extension of detente and peaceful coexistence.   □

4

LEONID I. BREZHNEV

The Great October Revolution And Human Progress

The following is an abridged version of the speech delivered November 2, 1977, to a joint session of the Central Committee of the CPSU and the Supreme Soviets of the USSR and RSFSR, by Leonid Brezhnev, General Secretary of the Communist Party of the Soviet Union and President of the Presidium of the USSR Supreme Soviet. The translation is courtesy Reprints from the Soviet Press.

Sixty years ago, led by the Party of Lenin, the workers and peasants of Russia overthrew the power of the capitalists and landowners. That was the first victorious socialist revolution in world history.

A new epoch, the epoch of the world's revolutionary renewal, the epoch of transition to socialism and communism, was ushered in.

We were the first. We did not have an easy time. We had to hold out in a hostile encirclement. We had to break out of age-old backwardness. We had to learn to live by new laws, by the laws of collectivism.

We have held our ground, we have stood fast and have won. We won in the stormy, anxious years of the Civil War and armed intervention, when it was a question of the life and death of Soviet power. We won in the teeming years of the first Five-Year Plans, when it was a question of whether the workers and peasants of our country would be able to lay the foundations of socialism.

We won in the grim, flaming years of the Great Patriotic War, when it was a question of whether socialism would withstand the onslaught of world imperialism's shock forces and save mankind from fascist bondage. We won in the difficult, tense postwar years. The ravaged economy was speedily restored and advanced lines of economic, scientific and technical progress were reached, despite the Cold War and nuclear blackmail.

The Soviet Union has been living in peace for more than thirty years now. A developed socialist society, the result of the historic creative work of the masses, has been built, exists, and is being perfected.

We address the warmest, most deeply felt words of gratitude and affection to the veterans of the Revolution. The numbers of those who stormed the old world under the banner of the Leninist Party in October 1917 are dwindling. But

43

the grandeur of their achievements stands out with growing vividness. Honor
and glory to the pioneers of the October Revolution!

During these jubilee days we speak with gratitude of the revolutionary
solidarity with the Land of Soviets unswervingly displayed by our class
brothers abroad. Their determined actions have time and again helped to disrupt
imperialism's aggressive designs.

I. The Soviet Union in the Van of Social Progress

The October Revolution, of course, solved, above all, the problems of our
own country, the problems posed by its history, by the concrete conditions
obtaining in it. Basically, however, these were general problems posed before
the whole of mankind by social development. The epochal significance of the
October Revolution lies in the fact that it opened the road to the solution of these
problems and thereby to the creation of a new type of civilization on earth.

The six decades of socialist construction are the most eloquent demonstration
of what can be achieved by working people who have taken the political
leadership of society into their own hands and assumed responsibility for their
country's destiny. These decades have proved that there never was nor can there
be a road to socialism without the power of the working people, without
socialist statehood.

The victory of the October Revolution gave the working people their first
opportunity of putting an end to exploitation and breaking out of bondage to
economic anarchy. This key problem of social progress was resolved through
the abolition of private property and its replacement with public property.

Within what in terms of history is a short period of time, a huge backward
country was turned into a state with a highly developed industry and collec-
tivized agriculture. It now takes only two and a half working days for our
industry to produce as much as was produced in the whole of 1913. Today we
turn out more industrial goods than was produced by the whole world a quarter
of a century ago. The gigantic economic growth of history's first socialist
country is the result of emancipated labor, the result of the labor of people who
are aware that they work for themselves—for the good of all.

Within the lifetime of a single generation, the Soviet Union rid itself entirely
and for good of the onerous burden of illiteracy. The working people began to
be active in cultural life, becoming the creators of cultural values. A new,
socialist intelligentsia, which brought the country glory through its outstanding
achievements in science, technology, literature and art, came from among the
people. A union that only mankind's finest minds dreamed of, the historic
merging of labor and culture, has taken place.

Among the achievements of the October Revolution a noteworthy place is
held by solution of the national question, one of the most painful questions in
the history of human society.

The peoples of former tsarist Russia were for the first time able to make an historical choice, the right to determine their own destiny. They made that choice. They united voluntarily into a powerful federal state and, relying on disinterested assistance from the Russian people, resolutely embarked upon a new life.

The strength of unity and mutual assistance between nations gave unprecedented acceleration to the development of all the republics. Hostility and mistrust in relations between nations gave way to friendship and mutual respect. Mutually enriched national cultures, forming an integrated Soviet socialist culture, shone with fresh, vivid colors.

The equality, fraternity and unbreakable unity of the peoples of the Soviet Union became a reality. A new historical community, the Soviet people, took shape. Today the mounting process of the drawing together of nations permeates every sphere of life in our society. Such, comrades, is the remarkable result of the Leninist national policy; such is our experience, whose epochal significance is indisputable.

Every Soviet citizen enjoys in full the rights and freedoms enabling him to participate actively in political life. Every Soviet citizen has the possibility of choosing a calling in life that conforms to his preferences and abilities and of being useful to his country and people.

The conditions under which Soviet people live and work are steadily improving. Soviet citizens do not know the humiliating sense of uncertainty about their morrows, the fear of being left without work, without medical care and without a roof over their heads. Society safeguards their rights and interests and protects their civic and human dignity.

A new Constitution of the Soviet Union has recently been adopted. It has reaffirmed that in our country the prime purpose of all transformations, of all change, is to provide every person with conditions enabling him to live like a human being. It has given further convincing testimony that only under socialism do the concepts of human rights and freedoms, democracy and social justice, acquire tangible content.

Never before has our country had such a huge economic, scientific and technical potential for promoting the welfare of the masses, unfolding socialist democracy and furthering the harmonious development of the individual.

Counting from 1967, the fiftieth anniversary of the Soviet power, our country's economic potential has virtually doubled. But the qualitative changes are perhaps just as important. Scientific and technical progress is becoming an increasingly more effective factor of economic development. The most modern industries are developing at priority rates. Labor productivity is growing steadily.

In accordance with the Party's policy, economic development is being increasingly oriented toward improving the conditions of the Soviet people's life and work. To a large extent this is determined by the state of the agrarian sector of our economy. Never before has so much been done in our country to promote agriculture. Within a short period, the material and technical basis and the economy of the countryside have been fundamentally restructured. Land improvement, comprehensive mechanization and chemicalization have been started on an unparalleled scale.

We already see the results of these enormous efforts. In 1967 we took in 148 million tons of grain, 11.5 million tons of meat and about 6 million tons of cotton. This year, which is far from the best and not even average in terms of weather, we expect to take in 194 million tons of grain, nearly 15 million tons of meat and 8.4 million tons of cotton. I believe these figures merit due appreciation, although we are aware that not all the problems of agriculture have been resolved. The Party is making every effort to ensure that this branch fully satisfies the country's growing requirements.

There has also been marked progress in the solution of so difficult a problem as housing, which requires huge outlays. One-third of the housing built since the establishment of the Soviet power has been built during the past decade. Some 110 million of our compatriots have experienced the joy of moving into new housing.

Large resources have been allocated for the expansion of consumer goods. During the past ten years this industry has virtually doubled its output while at the same time substantially renewing and improving it. Retail trade turnover has also doubled. The Soviet people's demand for many durables that only recently were in short supply is now being satisfied.

Economic growth has made it possible substantially to raise wages and increase social consumption funds. During the past ten years, the real income of Soviet people has risen 60 percent. I should like to make special note of the fact that the living standards and the conditions of everyday life of the rural population have improved appreciably.

Comrades, while noting our successes, we are fully aware that we still face many problems and that a vast field of activity lies ahead.

Efficient organization at every level, in every link of Party, state and economic leadership, at every work place, is an indispensable and mandatory precondition for the fulfillment of the tasks set by the 25th Congress.

But these are indeed summits. And the path toward them may be steep and difficult. In order to traverse it at an optimal pace, or regime, to use a technical term, we need to gear even our present plans to fulfilling the tasks of the future.

Orientation not only on current needs but also on the future is a distinctive feature of our agrarian policy in particular. We have been working for the satisfaction of the country's growing needs, under conditions in which the population and its requirements are growing, while the land area remains the same. That is why accelerated and intensive development of every branch of agriculture is part of our plans for the future. That is why we have allocated, and will continue to allocate, large investments for agriculture and for building up facilities in the industries catering to the countryside.

An important role has been assigned to the nonblack-soil zone. This vast area in the very heart of the country must become a zone of highly productive crop farming and animal husbandry. It will add considerably to our food resources.

Other comprehensive programs worked out in the past few years are also oriented upon the future. These are above all the programs for developing Western and Eastern Siberia, building the Baikal-Amur Railway, and extending industrial and timbering complexes in the Far East. They are designed to meet future requirements in oil, gas, coal, ferrous and nonferrous metals, timber and other raw materials. There is much social meaning, too, in the implementation of these programs, since they imply developing many remote regions of the country where dozens of new towns are to be built and new cultural centers established. The very concept of "underdeveloped outer regions" will disappear completely from our usage.

The great construction projects of our day have most forcefully brought out the steadfastness, creative élan and ideological tempering of Soviet young people. Carrying on the fine traditions of their fathers and grandfathers, the young men and women members of the Komsomol have been advancing in the front ranks of the builders of communism, gaining in stature in their labor effort, and learning to manage the economy and govern the affairs of society and the state. The country's future is in their hands. We are sure that it is in reliable hands.

Science will have to make a tremendous contribution to fulfilling the most important tasks of communist construction: the discovery of new sources of energy and substitutes for many types of natural resources; the technical reequipment of the economy to reduce manual, and especially arduous labor to a minimum; the boosting of agriculture; the combating of disease and the prolongation of human life.

The future of our economy lies in ever greater efficiency. There is no other alternative if we are to ensure the successful and dynamic development of the economy. That is why the Party has pursued and will steadily continue to pursue a policy of accelerating scientific and technical progress, perfecting planning and management, enhancing organization and order at every place of work and at every echelon of management.

We have many problems ahead of us, and they are big problems. But the power of socialism lies precisely in the fact that the new social system makes it possible not only to anticipate such problems but also to plan their solution in advance.

But the confidence of the people is exacting. That is why all of the Party's decisions—either political or having to do with organizational, ideological or educational work—have to be such as to consolidate still further its unity with the people and to keep the people's trust in the Party unshakable in the future as well.

II. The October Revolution Has Changed the Face of the World

No event in world history has had such a profound and lasting effect on mankind as the Great October Socialist Revolution.

The most important of the international consequences of the October Revolution that shaped the face of the epoch has been the emergence and development of the world socialist system. At one time the bourgeoisie, terrified at the victory of the October Revolution and its powerful influence on the minds of millions, sought to uncover "the hand of Moscow" in every revolutionary event in the world. Nowadays, few people give credence to such fairy tales. Revolutions start and triumph by virtue of each country's internal development and of its people's will. The series of triumphant socialist revolutions that took place in Europe, Asia and America only signifies a continuation of the ideas and cause of the October Revolution.

As a result, the experience of world socialism has been extended and enriched. Each of the countries that have taken the socialist road in some respects and in its own specific way dealt with the problems of socialist statehood, the development of socialist industry, the drawing of the peasantry into cooperatives, and the ideological reeducation of the masses.

There is no doubt that the transition to socialism by other peoples and countries with different levels of development and national traditions will invest socialist construction with an even greater diversity of concrete forms. However, history provides us with confirmation that the general fundamental and inalienable features of the socialist revolution and socialist construction remain in force and apply everywhere. The sum total of experience in the development of world socialism offers convincing evidence, among other things, of the following:

Power continues to be the main issue in a revolution: either the power of the working class, acting in alliance with all the other working people, or the power of the bourgeoisie. There is no third possibility.

Transition to socialism is possible only if the working class and its allies, having gained real political power, use that power to end the socioeconomic domination of the capitalists and other exploiters.

Socialism can consolidate its positions only if the working people's power proves capable of defending the revolution against all attacks by the class enemy (and such attacks are inevitable, both internal and, most probably, external ones).

But world socialism had also had experience with revolutions of a different kind, which only confirms that deviations from the Marxist-Leninist course, abandonment of proletarian internationalism, inevitably lead to setbacks and hard trials for the people.

It is well known what grave consequences have been brought about in China by attempts to ignore the economic laws of socialism, by deviation from friendship and solidarity with the socialist countries, and by alignment with the forces of reaction in the world arena. The Chinese people's socialist gains have been gravely endangered.

Some leaders in capitalist countries now obviously count on the present contradictions and estrangement between the People's Republic of China and the Soviet Union and other socialist countries continuing for a long time and even growing more acute in the future. We think that this is a short-sighted policy. Those who pursue it may well miscalculate.

There is no point in trying to guess how Soviet-Chinese relations will shape up in the future. I would merely like to say that our repeated proposals to normalize them still hold good.

The new relations that have been established—thanks to the fraternal Parties' internationalist policy—between the socialist countries, above all between the countries of the socialist community, are a great contribution by the world socialist system to the life of the contemporary world.

We can honestly say that our alliance, our friendship and our cooperation are the alliance of sovereign and equal states united by common purposes and interests and held together by bonds of comradely solidarity and mutual assistance. We have been advancing together, helping one another and pooling our efforts, knowledge and resources to advance as rapidly as possible.

We have been jointly tackling the problems of raw materials, fuel and energy, food and transport. We have been deepening our specialization and cooperation, especially in the area of technology, on the basis of the latest scientific and technical advances. We intend to solve these problems reliably, without undue outlays and for the long term; with due consideration for the interests and needs of each fraternal country and the community as a whole.

In the distant days of the 1917 October Revolution, the workers and peasants of Russia came out alone against the old world, the world of greed, oppression and violence. They built socialism in a country surrounded by the hostile forces of imperialism. They built and defended it successfully. Today our country has become part of a great family of socialist states. Can we Soviet Communists and all the other Soviet people cherish anything more in the world around us than this socialist family? To enhance its prosperity and our common well-being we have been doing everything we possibly can.

It is hard to overestimate the tremendous influence that our October Revolution exerted on the development of the national liberation movement.

It was the victory of the October Revolution that truly awakened the political consciousness of the colonial peoples and helped them to score tremendous successes in fighting for liberation from oppression by imperialism. As early as 1919, Lenin wrote that "the emancipation of the peoples of the East is now quite practicable."

Since World War II, since our victory over fascism, more than two billion people have thrown off the yoke of the colonialists and risen to independent statehood. The colonial system of imperialism in its classical forms can, on the whole, be regarded as having been dismantled.

It is of exceptional importance that many of the countries that have achieved liberation reject the capitalist road of development, have set themselves the goal of building a society free from exploitation and have adopted a socialist orientation.

The established socialist countries are staunch and reliable friends of these new states and are prepared to give them utmost assistance and support in their development along the progressive path. This means not only moral and political, but also economic and organizational support, including assistance in strengthening their defenses.

The fighters for freedom are not facing an easy road. They will have to work hard to lay the foundations of the public economy required for socialism. Fierce battles with the exploiter elements and their foreign patrons are inevitable. Now and again these must result in zigzags in the policies of the young states and sometimes even lead to retreats. But the overall trend of development is incontestable. The will of millions of working people who have become aware of their goals and their place in life is a sure guarantee that national independence will be strengthened and that the social system free from exploitation and oppression will ultimately triumph.

None of this means, of course, that imperialism has reconciled itself to such a course of development. Its positions in the former colonies are at times still quite strong and the imperialists are doing everything possible to try to retain them, and to deepen and extend them wherever possible.

It is no longer a simple matter for them to decide on direct armed intervention in the countries that have freed themselves. The latest major act of this kind—the US war against the people of Vietnam—ended in a defeat that was too crushing and ignominious to encourage a repetition of such gambles.

There is growing resistance to the attempts to involve the young states in imperialist military blocs, and the nonalignment movement is one piece of evidence of this.

It is likewise doubtful whether imperialism will be helped by its efforts to make use of the reactionary regimes it has set up or suborned in former colonies.

After all, these regimes cannot offer the peoples anything but new forms of dependence on the same old imperialism.

When the first waves of the peoples' struggle for national liberation were mounting in the countries of the East, Lenin wrote: "No power on earth can restore the old serfdom in Asia or wipe out the heroic democracy of the masses in the Asian and semi-Asian countries." Today we can confidently state: No power on earth can wipe out the results of the heroic liberation struggle of the millions upon millions of people in the former colonies and semicolonies of imperialism. The cause of the peoples' liberation is indomitable, the future belongs to it. The light kindled by the October Revolution shall not fail on this front of world history either.

The building of socialism in the USSR, and then in other countries, helped to foster the political maturity of the proletariat in the capitalist countries. Its ranks became more organized. There arose a force destined to play a great role in history—the international communist movement. The front of the proletariat's allies in the struggle against monopoly domination, for democracy and socialism, grew broader.

Meanwhile, capitalism is ever more clearly showing that it is a society without a future. Its economy is afflicted by chronic fever. Technological progress is pushing masses of workers out of the factories on a scale that threatens to shake the entire sociopolitical system. Prices are continually rising and inflation remains the cardinal problem. Shocking exposures of unsavory political manipulations, corruption, abuse of power, flagrant transgressions of the law by leaders at the highest levels explode like bombshells first in one country and then in another, demonstrating the corruption of the ruling class. A record crime rate completes the picture. All this signifies that the objective economic and sociopolitical preconditions for the transition to socialism have reached a high degree of maturity.

In this situation the communist parties are striving to rally all the democratic forces against domination by the monopolies. Whatever routes may be chosen, the ultimate mission of the Communists is to lead the masses to the principal goal, to socialism. The experience of the struggle for the victory of the October Revolution has shown that changes of tactics, compromises in order to win new allies, are quite possible in revolutionary practice. But we have also become convinced of something else: under no circumstances may principles be sacrificed for the sake of a tactical advantage. Otherwise, as the saying goes, you will keep the hair but lose your head.

The greater the influence of the Communist Parties, the more vigorously does imperialism try to divert Communists from the correct path. This is done both crudely—by pressure and threats—and more subtly. At times Communists inside the bourgeois countries are being promised that their "right to a place in society" will be "recognized." A mere "trifle" is asked of them in exchange; that they give up fighting the power of capital, give up fighting for socialism, and abandon international class solidarity. But the Communists won a place for themselves in society long ago. They won it precisely by their revolutionary struggle. Their role in society is recognized by the people and no one can deprive them of it!

The imperialists would very much like to undermine the solidarity of the communist ranks. That is why, for example, the falsehood is persistently being spread that the Communist Parties in the Socialist countries—and, especially, the Communist Party of the Soviet Union—are imposing upon the Communists in the West their programs for the socialist transformation of society. But this is an obvious fabrication.

Our Party, like all other Marxist-Leninist Parties, firmly adheres to the principles generally accepted in the communist movement: equality, independence, non-interference in internal affairs, solidarity, and mutual support among the Communists of different countries.

The Soviet Government was born under the banner of Lenin's Decree on Peace, and ever since then our country's foreign policy has been one of peace. Objective historical conditions have dictated its concrete content: peaceful coexistence of states with different social systems.

In our day the principles of peaceful coexistence have taken fairly firm root in international affairs as the only viable, realistic and reasonable principles. This is a result of the changed correlation of forces in the world—above all, of the increased might and international prestige of the Soviet Union and the entire socialist community. It is also a result of the successes of the international working-class movement and the forces of national liberation. It is, finally, a result of the acceptance of the new realities by a definite segment of the ruling circles in the capitalist world.

At the same time, it is a result of the tremendous work done in recent years by the Soviet Union and the other countries of the socialist community to reorient international relations toward peace.

The salutary changes in the world, which have become especially appreciable in the 1970s, have been called international detente. These changes are tangible and concrete. They consist of recognizing and enacting in international documents a kind of code of rules for honest and fair relations between countries that erects a legal and moral-political barrier against those given to military gambles. They consist of achieving the first—though for the present only modest—understandings blocking some of the channels of the arms race. They consist of a ramified network of agreements covering many areas of peaceful cooperation between states with different social systems.

The changes for the better are most conspicuous in Europe, where good-neighbor relations, mutual understanding and the mutual interest of the various nations and their respect for one another are gaining strength. We highly appreciate this achievement and consider it our duty to safeguard and consolidate it in every way. Therefore, we attach great significance to cooperation with all European states, large and small, belonging to a different social system.

Naturally, we also attach great significance to relations with the United States. There is much that divides our countries—from the socioeconomic system to ideology. Not everyone in the United States likes our way of doing things, and we too could say a great deal about what is going on in America. But if differences are accentuated, if attempts are made to lecture one another, the result will only be a buildup of distrust and hostility, useless to our two countries and dangerous to the world as a whole. At the very inception of the Soviet state Lenin made it clear to the American leaders of the time that "whether they like it or not, Soviet Russia is a great power" and "Americans have nothing to gain from the Wilsonian policy of piously refusing to deal with us on the grounds that our government is distasteful to them." This was true half a century ago. It is all the more true today.

Life itself requires that considerations of a long-term character, prompted by a concern for peace, be decisive in Soviet-American relations. This is the course we follow, and this is what we expect in return. There is no lack of will on our part to continue developing relations with the USA on the basis of equality and mutual respect.

International relations are now at a crossroads, as it were, which could lead either to growing trust and cooperation, or to a growth of mutual fears, suspicion and arms stockpiling, a crossroads leading, ultimately, either to lasting peace or, at best, to balancing on the brink of war. Detente offers the opportunity to choose the road of peace. To miss this opportunity would be a crime. The most important, the most pressing task now is to halt the arms race which has engulfed the world.

Regrettably, the arms buildup continues and is acquiring ever more dangerous forms. New modifications and types of weapons of mass destruction are being developed, and it is well known on whose initiative that is being done. But every new type is an equation containing several unknown quantities in terms of political as well as military-technical or strategic consequences. Rushing from one type of arms to another—evidently on the strength of the rather naive hope of retaining a monopoly on them—only tends to step up the arms race, deepen mutual distrust and hamper disarmament measures.

In this connection I would like to reiterate, most forcefully, something I said earlier. The Soviet Union is effectively looking after its defense capability, but it does not, and will not, seek military superiority over the other side. We do not want to upset the approximate equilibrium of military strength existing at present, say, between East and West in Central Europe, or between the USSR and the USA. But in exchange we insist that no one else should seek to upset it in his favor.

Needless to say, maintaining the existing equilibrium is not an end in itself. We are in favor of starting a downward turn in the curve of the arms race and gradually scaling down the level of the military confrontation. We want to reduce substantially, and then eliminate, the menace of nuclear war, the most formidable of dangers for humanity. That is the objective of the well-known proposals of the Soviet Union and other socialist countries.

Today we are proposing another radical step: *that agreement be reached on a simultaneous halt in the production of nuclear weapons by all states*. This includes all such weapons—whether atomic, hydrogen, neutron bombs or missiles. At the same time, the nuclear powers could undertake to start the gradual reduction of existing stockpiles of such weapons, and move toward their complete, total destruction. The energy of the atom for peaceful purposes exclusively—that is the call the Soviet state is making in the year of its sixtieth anniversary to the governments and peoples.

There is another important problem that has a direct bearing on the task of reducing the danger of nuclear war, namely, that of seeing through to the end the work of banning all nuclear weapons tests, so that no more such tests should be conducted underground as well as in the atmosphere, in outer space, and under water. We want to achieve progress in the negotiations on this matter and bring them to a successful conclusion. Therefore, we state that we are prepared *to reach agreement on a moratorium covering nuclear explosions for peaceful purposes along with a ban on all nuclear weapons tests for a definite period.* We trust that this important step on the part of the USSR is properly appreciated by our partners in the negotiations and that the road will thus be cleared to concluding a treaty long awaited by the peoples.

The Soviet Union is confidently following the road of peace. It is our active and consistent stand that the contest between socialism and capitalism should be decided not on the field of battle, not on the munitions conveyors, but in the sphere of peaceful work. We want the frontiers dividing these two worlds to be crossed not by missiles with nuclear warheads, but by threads of broad and diversified cooperation for the good of all mankind.

If it should prove possible to solve the world's major problem—that of preventing another world war and establishing lasting peace—new vistas would open for the inhabitants of the earth. The preconditions would emerge for solving many other vitally important problems facing mankind as a whole in our day.

One of them, for example, is that of providing enormous masses of people with food, raw materials and energy sources. It will be borne in mind that, according to available estimates, the earth's population will have increased from four billion to six billion by the end of the century. Another problem is that of ending the economic backwardness left by colonialism in the Asian, African, and Latin American countries. This is necessary for the future normal development of relations between states and for the progress of humanity in general. Last but not least is the problem of protecting man from the many dangers with which further uncontrolled technological development threatens him, in other words, the preservation of nature for man.

These are very real and serious problems. They will become more acute with every new decade unless a rational collective solution is found for them through systematic international cooperation.

In our day the world is socially heterogeneous—it is made up of states with different social systems. This is an objective fact. By its inner development and by its approach to international relations, the socialist part of the world is setting a good example of the lines along which the major problems arising before mankind can best be solved. But, needless to say, it cannot solve them for the whole of humanity. What is needed here are purposeful efforts by the people of every country, broad and constructive cooperation by every countries, all peoples. The Soviet Union is wholeheartedly for such cooperation of the foreign policy course that we call the course of peaceful coexistence.   □

Part Two
The Early Years

5

IVAN KRASNOV and IGOR KRAVCHENKO

The 1905-1907 Revolution and Its Echo in the United States

The 1905-1907 revolution in Russia played the historic role of the first people's revolution in the epoch of imperialism.

After the 1861 emancipation from serfdom, Russia was steadily turning into a capitalist state with a growing working class exploited no less than the peasantry. The working people were subjected to a double pressure: that of the Russian landlords and capitalists and of the foreign capital which had penetrated the leading branches of the country's economy. Russia was turning into a focal point of the contradictions of the world imperialist system.

The tsarist autocracy, obsolescent and impeding social development, had been impaired by the 1901-1903 economic crisis in Russia, the defeat in the war against Japan, a powerful strike movement of the workers in the country's capital and industrial centers, and the aggravation of antagonisms among the ruling classes, as well as between the exploiters and the exploited.

The revolution broke out with the events of January 9, 1905, in St. Petersburg. On that day which came to be known as "Bloody Sunday," the tsar's troops shot down the workers who peacefully marched to the tsar to hand him a petition on their vital needs.

That act evoked a storm of indignation and protest. A wave of anti-government demonstrations, meetings, and strikes swept across the country. Under the leadership of the Bolsheviks, general strikes broke out in industrial

IVAN KRASNOV is Senior Research Associate of the Institute of History of the USSR Academy of Sciences.
IGOR KRAVCHENKO is a Candidate of Historical Sciences specializing in the international labor movement.

cities and regions of Russia and barricades were erected. The working masses of Russia came out in open battle against tsarism.

In the revolution the working class fought for the Bolshevik minimum program. This envisaged the establishment of a democratic republic and the eight-hour working day, and the confiscation of landlords' estates. Under the influence of the proletariat a wide movement developed among the peasantry and unrest in the army and navy increased. Side by side with the Russians, the struggle against tsarism was waged by workers and peasants from the various national minorities.

In the course of the revolution, which was bourgeois-democratic in its aims and proletarian in content and methods of struggle, there appeared, for the first time in history, political organizations which were called the Soviets of Workers', Peasants', and Soldiers' Deputies. They became the prototype of Soviet power. Subsequently, the correctness of Lenin's conception of the Soviets as the most representative bodies of genuine people's power was corroborated by reality.

The climax of the revolution was the uprising of December 1905 in Moscow where the struggle was especially stubborn and violent. The insurgents fought against regular troops and artillery. Although tsarism succeeded in putting out the flames of revolution in Moscow, the uprisings spread to Krasnoyarsk, Perm, Novorossiisk, Sevastopol, Nizhni Novgorod and other cities, to Georgia, Finland, the Ukraine, Latvia, and Estonia. Later on reactionary forces took the upper hand there, too.

The first Russian revolution ended in defeat for a number of reasons. The organizational activity of the workers was insufficiently concerted, because there was no proper unity in the actions of the workers and peasants. The greater part of the army remained on the side of tsarism whose position was helped by the treacherous conduct of the liberal bourgeoisie. The victory of the reactionary forces was also made easier by the substantial aid from international imperialism which helped tsarism conclude peace with Japan and receive a loan of 2,500 million francs.

The working class had to bear the brunt of struggle in the 1905-1907 Russian revolution. Although it ended in failure for the progressive forces, it dealt a heavy blow to autocracy, undermined the rule of the landlords and the capitalists, and aroused the masses of the people for a further struggle against their exploiters. On the whole, the revolution brought nearer the collapse of tsarism, and was, as Lenin put it, "the dress rehearsal" for the two subsequent and triumphant revolutions in Russia.

The first Russian revolution was also of great international significance. Lenin noticed this as early as the first days of the revolutionary fight. Mentioning its tremendous influence on the destinies of the international working class movement, he wrote: "The proletariat of the whole world is now looking eagerly towards the proletariat of Russia. The overthrow of tsarism in Russia, so valiantly begun by our working class, will be the turning-point in the history of all countries; it will facilitate the task of the workers of all nations, in all states, in all parts of the globe."

The 1905 revolution did indeed, evoke a lively response among progressive sections of the US proletariat. Conducive to that was an aggravation of class antagonisms in the United States. The latter had entered the imperialist stage of development by the turn of the century. An upsurge of the working class and trade union movement in the country at that time called forth violent reaction from the capitalists. Researchers subsequently noted that around 1905 the attitude of employers towards unions had become one of increasing hostility. Antiunion tendencies led them to such aggressive actions as employing spies, agents-provocateurs, and strike breakers; and using city, state and federal troops, privately paid deputies, local police officials, and company guards. A vigorous movement was often accompanied by bloodshed.

Progressive America was shocked by the reports about "Bloody Sunday" in Russia. Participants at meetings adopted resolutions of protest against the tsarist terror, and launched a campaign of raising funds to aid the Russian revolutionaries. The US press, especially socialist newspapers and magazines, published many articles about the beginning of the revolution in Russia. Their authors urged support for the Russian workers.

In many US cities, Boston and San Francisco among them, Friends of the Russian Revolution societies were set up. Their members, workers and representatives of the progressive intelligentsia, published bulletins, newspapers, and did their utmost to open the eyes of Americans to the tremendous significance of the events in Russia.

Especially noteworthy were the greetings to the Russian revolution from the participants in the First Convention of the Industrial Workers of the World (IWW) which opened on June 27, 1905 in Chicago. Addressing the audience, which packed the hall, Lucy Parsons, the widow of Albert Parsons, executed for heading May-Day activities in 1886, urged the strengthening of proletarian solidarity and the following of the example of the revolutionary workers of Russia. "Those who raise the red flag," she said, "it matters not where, whether on the sunny plains of China, or on the sun-beaten hills of Africa, or on the far-off snow-capped shores of the North, or in Russia or in America—know that they all belong to the human family and have an identity of interest."

The Convention enthusiastically passed a resolution specially devoted to the question of the 1905 Russian revolution:

WHEREAS there is in progress at the present time a mighty struggle of the laboring class of far-off Russia against unbearable outrage, oppression and cruelty, and for more humane conditions for the working class of that country; and

WHEREAS the outcome of the struggle is of the utmost consequence to the members of the working class of all countries in their struggle for their emancipation; . . .

RESOLVED, that we, the industrial unionists of America in convention assembled, urge our Russian fellow-workmen on in their struggle, and express our heartfelt sympathy with the victims of outrage, oppression and cruelty, and pledge our moral support and promise financial assistance as much as lies within our power, to our persecuted, strruggling and suffering comrades in far-off Russia."

William Haywood, Eugene Debs, Daniel De Leon and other leaders of the working class and socialist movement in the United States called upon the masses of the working people to support the Russian revolutionaries, and to cement the solidarity between the workers of Russia and the United States. The *International Socialist Review* issued a call to help the Russian proletariat with money and arms. The presence of Maxim Gorky, the proletarian writer, in the United States was important in bringing US progressives over to the side of the Russian revolution. In his lectures and articles on the events in Russia, Gorky exposed the atrocities of tsarism, and called for international solidarity. That was all the more timely as the bourgeois press, prone—then, as now—to discoursing on the "people's democratic rights," since the December armed uprising in Moscow, which became the culmination of the revolution, openly declared itself against the people and for tsarism. The press was frightened by the remarkable strength of the awakened proletariat.

As to the US progressives, the Bolshevik tactics helped them to assess their methods of struggle against the monopolies anew, and to understand the harm of opportunism and theories of "class harmony." When, on May 1, 1906, the Socialist Labor Party organized a mass meeting in New York, its participants passed a resolution pointing out that the Russian proletariat was in the front ranks in carrying out the historic role of the working class in the struggle for socialism. The Russian revolution was conducive to the growth of the class-consciousness of the US proletariat and showed the irreconcilability of the class struggle. The speakers at the meeting held in Buffalo on June 29, 1906, branded as infamy the bloody repressions in Russia and, specifically, the pogroms of Jews in Belostok. The Americans who remembered, from their own history the reprisals against strikers, the anti-Black massacres and the tyranny of the exploiters, could not keep silent when the tsarist government went over to reactionary terroristic acts.

At the same time US workers were growing increasingly militant in defending their interests. In the summer of 1907, the workers succeeded in freeing William Haywood and Charles Moyer, leaders of the Western Federation of Miners, who had been jailed under a false accusation of murdering the ex-Governor of Idaho. The strike movement intensified as well. In the course of 1907 the IWW headed more than 20 strikes.

Generally, the year was marked by militant action of US workers. A strike of miners in Goldfield, Nevada, started in the spring, had grown so acute by autumn that Governor Sparks even called in troops. The workers' unity prevailed with the strikers obtaining the required minimum wage for all workers and an eight-hour working day.

Thus, the influence of the Russian revolution on the working class and the socialist movement in the United States was extremely important. However, it should be neither underrated nor overrated. Objectively, it was weaker than in Europe or Asia for a great number of reasons. Of importance in this was the fact that before World War I practically nothing was known in the United States about Bolshevism in Russia and Lenin's works. Only the immigrants from Russia knew about the struggle for a party of a new type waged by the Bolsheviks under the leadership of Lenin. The US socialists were strongly influenced by opportunism. The Right-wing and the Centralist leaders of the Socialist Party did quite a lot to fence the US workers off from the revolutionary events in Russia and the rest of the world. As a result of this, as William Z. Foster put it, "Even the Russian Revolution of 1905, filtered as it was through the interpretations of the opportunistic leaders of the Second International, impressed few major lessons upon the American Socialist Party." A realistic estimate shows that even the best representatives of American socialism underestimated the role of a party, were carried away by syndicalist ideas, did not fight for independent political action of the proletariat, and reduced class struggle merely to an economic plane.

Nevertheless, the Left-wing elements in the US working-class movement from then on markedly increased their struggle against reformism, opportunism, and "business trade unionism." Herein, again, is a resonance of the first Russian revolution.   ☐

6

IVAN KRASNOV

The Road to October (1907-1917)

After the revolution of 1905-07 the development of imperialism in Russia proceeded at a comparatively rapid pace. A long period of industrial stagnation was succeeded by a boom. Output in all industries grew from year to year. New large industrial centers were springing up in the Ukraine, the Baltic area and Transcaucasia. The number of wage workers increased greatly since the beginning of the century, and the percentage of workers in the population was growing. Russia was ahead of all the other countries in the degree of concentration of workers in large industrial enterprises. For example, plants with 500 and more employees accounted for about one-third of all workers in the United States, whereas in Russia they employed more than half of the industrial work force.

Foreign capital was flowing on an ever bigger scale into Russia's principal industries (oil, coal, ore mining and metallurgical). And yet, Russia was lagging ever further behind the advanced capitalist countries. In 1913, she had only one-fourth as many modern machines as Britain, and one-tenth as many as the United States.

A handful of Russian and European industrialists were growing richer, while the people were growing poorer. The cost of living was rising, and the condition of the workers was going from bad to worse. Poverty and misery reigned in the countryside. The tsarist government's new agrarian policy had brought about a forcible break-up of the traditional peasant community. The kulaks (rich peasants) who had detached themselves from it were ruthlessly exploiting the bulk of the peasantry. Impoverished peasants were leaving the dying villages together with their families, swelling the ranks of the industrial proletariat. Hundreds of thousands of destitute people were trying their luck abroad: in the first decade of the 20th century, over 1.5 million left Russia to seek wage labor in Europe, Canada and the United States.

As the Bolsheviks had predicted, new revolutionary struggles began. The working class was the first to take the offensive. The years of revolution and

IVAN KRASNOV is Senior Research Associate of the Institute of History of the USSR Academy of Sciences.

reaction had taught it a great deal. Its political awareness had grown, and its ranks had become stronger. The economic struggle of the workers was increasingly turning into political struggle. Mass strikes spread throughout the country. Up to one million people went on strike every year.

Political actions by the workers, the peasants' struggle against landowners, the democratic youth movement, the outbursts of discontent in the army and navy—all were signs of an imminent new revolution.

On April 4, 1912, tsarist troops fired on a peaceful procession of workers at the Lena goldfields in Siberia. Demonstrations and strikes were held in many cities to protest against the massacre. "The Lena shootings," Lenin pointed out, "led to the revolutionary temper of the masses developing into a revolutionary upswing of the masses."

The mounting revolutionary battles posed sharply the question of strengthening the Marxist party of Russia's working class and of new tasks in the leadership of the mass revolutionary movement.

After the defeat of the 1905-07 revolution all parties that called themselves opposition or revolutionary parties capitulated to reaction and renounced the revolution. The Bolsheviks alone retained their party (an illegal Marxist party), continuing to win over the proletariat and struggle against bourgeois influences. Combining the activity of the legal party press and their deputies in the State Duma (parliament) with clandestine work among the people, the Bolsheviks organized and headed the struggle of the proletariat. Everywhere—during strikes and political demonstrations and at factory-gate meetings—they spoke of revolution as the only way out of the catastrophic situation in which Russia had found herself. The Bolshevik slogans expressed the most cherished aspirations of the people: a democratic revolution, an eight-hour working day, confiscation of landlords' land for the peasants.

Along with preparing the working class and the peasantry for the overthrow of the autocracy, the Bolsheviks urged them to resist in every way its preparation of a new war. They argued that the way to revolution through war would be too gruelling for the working people, of whom great sacrifice would be demanded: millions of them would lose their lives. They said that a revolution was possible in peacetime as well. Noting that no true Marxist had "ever linked expectations of a revolutionary situation exclusively with the 'beginning of a war,'" Lenin referred to the experience of the revolutionary situations in Russia in 1859-61, 1879-80 and 1901, when no wars were being waged by the country.

The revolutionary situation that shaped up in Russia in the summer of 1914 was interrupted by the outbreak of the First World War. Lenin's party lost no time in calling upon the people to fight against the war or for converting it into a civil war against tsarism, against the bourgeoisie and landowners. Lenin's stand, at once revolutionary and realistic, was designed to bring into the struggle for putting an end to the war all sincere champions of peace, regardless of their attitude to the ideas of scientific socialism. Lenin wrote in October 1915 that if a revolution made it the ruling party in the current war, the party of the proletariat would offer peace to all the belligerents. A year later Lenin repeated this statement. And one more year later, when the 1917 October Revolution did make the Bolsheviks the ruling party, they fulfilled their promise.

The world imperialist war of 1914-18, which killed ten million people and crippled 20 million more, aggravated all the contradictions of imperialism and augmented the objective prerequisites of a socialist revolution. In Lenin's words, that war had become an almighty producer of revolution.

In the war years, basing himself on an analysis of imperialism, Lenin evolved the theory of socialist revolution: in the new conditions, when the unevenness of development of capitalist countries had grown sharply, the victory of a socialist revolution simultaneously in all countries was impossible, but it was possible in one single country.

The objective course of history confirmed the correctness of the Bolsheviks' conclusion that the war was creating a revolutionary situation in Russia. All the contradictions of imperialism were manifesting themselves there more sharply than anywhere else. Russia's proletariat was headed by a tested Marxist party, and its revolutionary spirit was particularly high. Two years of war sufficed to exhaust the strength of tsarist Russia. All this made her the weakest link in the world chain of imperialism.

In January and February 1917, Russia was swept by a powerful wave of strikes. Workers' meetings and demonstrations were held in Petrograd, Moscow, Baku (Azerbaidzhan), Kharkov and the Donets Coal Basin in the Ukraine. They were predominantly of a political character. Their chief motto was, "Down with the autocracy!"

Alarmed by the approach of the revolution, the tsarist government entered into secret negotiations with Germany on a separate peace so as to be free to fight the revolution. This alarmed both Russia's allies—Britain, France and the United States—and the Russian bourgeoisie. The allies feared the loss of the help of the Russian army; and the Russian bourgeoisie, the loss of the profitable war orders. Supported by the Entente, the Russian bourgeoisie decided on a palace coup to save the monarchy and prevent the revolution. But its plan was foiled by an uprising of the Petrograd proletariat supported by the whole people.

On February 27, a bourgeois-democratic revolution was accomplished in Russia. Tsarism was overthrown. On the initiative of the Bolsheviks, Soviets of Workers' and Soldiers' deputies began to be set up all over the country. The Soviets voiced the interests of the joint struggle of the workers and peasants against the autocracy, for the soldiers were predominantly of peasant stock.

Fear of the people compelled the bourgeoisie to give up the counterrevolutionary plan for preserving the monarchy and to agree to the establishment of a Provisional Government. The result was a dual power, an interlacement of two dictatorships. Real power was in the hands of the Soviets as organs of the revolutionary-democratic dictatorship of the proletariat and the peasantry. At the same time, there was the Provisional Government, functioning as the organ of the dictatorship of the bourgeoisie. That expressed, as Lenin pointed out, a transitional phase in the development of the revolution, "when it has gone farther than the ordinary bourgeois-democratic revolution, but has not yet reached a 'pure' dictatorship of the proletariat and the peasantry." The February Revolution won very swiftly, because the people, and the proletariat especially, had gone through tough schooling in political struggle during the first Russian revolution. The working class exercised hegemony in the February Revolution. It was not the bourgeoisie, which had gone in for a deal with tsarism, but the working class, headed by the Bolshevik Party, that provided leadership in the struggle against the autocracy to the millions of peasants and soldiers, to the multinational people of Russia. That was what brought the revolution to victory.

Yet, the bulk of Russia's population was made up of petty bourgeois elements—landowning peasants, urban and rural handicraftsmen—who followed the Socialist-Revolutionaries and the Mensheviks. They determined the composition of the Soviets, giving the petty-bourgeois parties a predominant influence. This explains why the victorious workers and peasants, represented by the Soviets, surrendered power to representatives of the bourgeoisie. While the Bolsheviks were fighting tsarism at the head of the masses, the Socialist-Revolutionaries and Mensheviks hastened to take advantage of the people's victory and seize leadership of the Soviets.

As a result of some bourgeois-democratic reforms Russia became the freest of the world's bourgeois countries. The February Revolution brought about an abrupt change from the lawlessness and terrorism of tsarism to broad political freedom. Tens of millions who had previously taken no part in politics and were not versed in them, suddenly found themselves drawn into political activity. But the central problems of the life of the country were not solved. The peasants did not receive land; the workers were not freed from capitalist exploitation; the war was going on. The discontent of the masses with the policy of the bourgeois Provisional Government was rising. The situation made the speediest possible development of the revolution a vital necessity. Only a socialist revolution and proletarian dictatorship could bring to the people what they had aspired for: put an end to the war, turn over the landlords' land to the peasants, make the factories the property of the whole people, lead the country out of the economic crisis, abolish national oppression and the inequality of the peoples.

The February Revolution had wide repercussions in the world. Numerous meetings and other actions to demonstrate solidarity with the working class of

Russia were held in France, Italy and Germany. The gains of the people of Russia were hailed by progressives in the United States. The ruling circles of the US, however, like those of the Entente, regarded the February Revolution from the point of view of their military interests. They egged on the Provisional Government in every way to actively continue the war and supported the pro-bourgeois parties in the Soviets, trying to neutralize the growing influence of the Bolsheviks. They depicted the imperialist war as struggle of the democratic Entente against monarchical regimes. The reactionary circles in the United States even set about raising a "Russian freedom fund" to purchase a replica of the Statue of Liberty for Russia.

Returning from emigration to Petrograd on April 3, Lenin called for continuing the struggle for the second, socialist stage of the revolution, "which must place power in the hands of the proletariat and the poorest sections of the peasants."

Lenin determined also the political form of state power. Taking into account the experience of the Soviets created by the revolutions of 1905 and 1917, he concluded that a republic of the Soviets of Workers', Soldiers' and Peasants' Deputies would be the optimal *state form* of the dictatorship of the proletariat. The slogan "All power to the Soviets!", proclaimed by the Bolshevik Party, signified elimination of the dual power with the placing of all power in the hands of the Soviets, the dismantling of the old machinery of state standing above the people, and the establishment of a new state apparatus wholly serving their interests.

The economic program provided for the nationalization of the land, enterprises and banks and the setting up of model farms on the estates of the nobility. Regarding these measures as transitional to socialism, Lenin insisted that the task was not to "introduce" socialism, but to carry out those transitional measures, which would make possible "further progress towards socialism in Russia."

The situation in Russia at that time was such, in Lenin's opinion, that the transition to socialism could be accomplished in a peaceful way, without armed insurrection. But the bourgeoisie had recourse to violence (in its most brutal forms at that), disregarding morality and law.

In July 1917, through the fault of the bourgeoisie, the development of events in Russia took a non-peaceful form. On July 4, the Provisional Government shot down a demonstration of workers, soldiers and sailors of Petrograd that had unfolded spontaneously under the peaceful slogan, "All power to the Soviets!" About 400 people were killed or wounded.

The bourgeois government proceeded to repressive measures. Wholesale searches started in the working-class districts. The regiments which had taken part in the demonstration began to be disarmed. The Bolshevik newspaper *Pravda* was banned. The order was given to find Lenin and detain him at all costs. Lenin went into hiding.

This repression put an end to the dual power. In effect, a counterrevolutionary dictatorship of the bourgeoisie and the military was established in the country. The Menshevik and Socialist-Revolutionary Soviets became an obedient appendage of the military dictatorship. The peaceful development of the revolution was paralyzed. Now the working class could take power only in an armed way. A new effective tactic was needed, and it was worked out by Lenin without delay. He proposed the temporary withdrawal of the slogan "All power to the Soviets!", but that did not mean the renunciation of a Soviet republic. The point was that the Soviets as they were then composed, and led as they were by the Socialist-Revolutionaries and Mensheviks, could not be organs of people's power.

At the same time Lenin warned against an immediate action against the government. A resolute assault was possible only given a new revolutionary upswing, which would be accelerated by the war and economic dislocation.

The Sixth Congress of the Bolshevik Party, which was held in conditions of semi-legality in Petrograd in July-August, 1917, endorsed Lenin's new tactics of struggles for power—a line for a socialist revolution.

The pace of revolutionary developments continued to quicken after July. The discontent and impatience of the masses were growing; the contradictions between the proletariat and the bourgeoisie were sharpening; the masses were losing faith in the Socialist-Revolutionary and Menshevik parties and inclining in favor of the revolutionary program of the Bolsheviks. All this frightened the Russian counterrevolution, the bourgeoisie. It decided to impose a civil war upon the people, and made preparations for setting up a military dictatorship. The role of military dictator was assigned to General Kornilov, who was promised help by the United States, Britain and France. On August 21, traitorously withdrawing troops from the front, Kornilov surrendered Riga to the German troops, and opened the road before them into the heart of Russia. Then he launched a counterrevolutionary march on Petrograd. The situation was complicated by the fact that Kornilov had started the revolt supposedly against the Provisional Government headed by Alexander Kerensky. And that is how the Socialist-Revolutionaries and Mensheviks tried to present the matter. They called for defence of the Provisional Government. But the Bolshevik Party organized struggle against Kornilov, all the while continuing to expose the Provisional Government.

The workers of Petrograd responded to the Bolsheviks' call to take up arms. New Red Guard detachments were hurriedly formed. The Kornilov revolt was crushed by the workers, soldiers and sailors organized by the Bolshevik Party. At the insistence of the people, Kornilov and his fellow-conspirators were arrested. The attempt to undermine the revolution failed.

The rout of the Kornilovites at the walls of Petrograd opened up a new stage in the struggle of the proletariat for state power. "The whole course of events," Lenin wrote, "all economic and political conditions, everything that is happening in the armed forces, are increasingly paving the way for the successful winning of power by the working class, which will bring peace, bread and freedom and will hasten the victory of the proletarian revolution in other countries."

The utter hopelessness of the situation in the country inexorably induced the workers and peasants to fight for their vital rights, for the overthrow of capitalism as a social system. And although Russia's proletariat was comparatively small (there were about 12 million industrial and agricultural workers and day-laborers, including approximately four million wage workers employed in industry and rails), it was concentrated as in no other country in industrial centers and large enterprises. Its role in the revolutionary movement was far bigger than its share of the population. It was allied with the semi-proletarian masses of working people, the poorest peasantry and the progressive section of the intelligentsia. All this determined the vanguard role of the proletariat in the fight for the vital rights of the working people, against exploitation and wars of conquest and plunder, for socialism.

In Lenin's words, the very course of her socioeconomic and political development confronted Russia with a choice "between perishing or entrusting its fate to the most revolutionary class for the swiftest and most radical transition to a superior mode of production. Perish or forge full steam ahead."

By its strikes and other actions, especially in 1917, the working class of Russia showed in practice that it was capable of mass revolutionary action and could lead the working people in the assault upon capitalism.

Between February and October 1917, the revolutionary activity of the proletariat manifested itself in the toppling of tsarism, in the subsequent powerful strike movement, in the fight for the establishment of workers' control over production, in the July events, in the crushing of the Kornilov revolt in August, and in the mighty political strike movement that spread to all of Russia's major industrial centers in September and October. It showed up in the highest-ever rise of the peasant movement beginning with the summer of 1917, and in the growth of the national liberation movement of the peoples of the borderlands of Russia. And when, in October 1917, the Central Committee of the Bolshevik Party headed by Lenin adopted the historic decision on armed insurrection, the proletariat and its party, which already had at least 400,000 members, had the support of the majority of the politically active population of Russia.

All the while, the economic position of the country was fast deteriorating. In 1917, gross industrial output fell by more than 35 per cent compared with 1916. Hundreds of enterprises were closed down; the army of the unemployed was growing. At the front, the Russian troops, poorly armed and often led by inefficient commanders, were suffering tremendous casualties. By the autumn of 1917, a general revolutionary crisis had ripened in the country. The "upper strata" could not rule Russia in the old way any longer, while the "lower orders" refused to live in the old way. "The crisis has matured," Lenin wrote at that time. "The whole future of the Russian revolution is at stake. . . . The whole future of the international workers' revolution for socialism is at stake."

On October 7, Lenin secretly returned to Petrograd, where a detailed plan of an armed uprising was worked out. At a sitting of the Party Central Committee on October 10, he stated this plan, stressing insistently that the political situation was ripe for a revolution, for the transition of power to the proletariat and the village poor, and that now practical preparation of the insurrection was the order of the day. The Central Committee endorsed Lenin's resolution, which became the Party's directive to prepare for armed insurrection immediately.

Only two Central Committee members, Zinoviev and Kamenev, opposed the resolution. They asserted that the working class was incapable of carrying out a socialist revolution, and championed the bourgeois republic.

At that meeting of the Central Committee Trotsky did not vote against the resolution on the insurrection. But he insisted on its being postponed until the Second Congress of Soviets was convened, which was tantamount to wrecking the insurrection. The adoption of the plan of the insurrection at the congress would deprive it of the factor of surprise.

At an enlarged meeting of the Central Committee on October 16, Lenin proposed reaffirming the resolution on resolute preparation for the insurrection, leaving it for the Central Committee and the Petrograd Soviet to decide when to launch it. The resolution was reaffirmed by nineteen votes to two (Kamenev and Zinoviev), with four abstentions.

On October 17, Lenin wrote in his "Letter to Comrades:" "There is no power on earth apart from the power of a victorious proletarian revolution that would advance from complaints and begging and tears to *revolutionary action*. . . . In insurrection delay is fatal."

In the early hours of October 18, Lenin met with the leaders of the military organizations of the Party and instructed them to make more painstaking preparation for the insurrection and establish closer contacts with revolutionary units at the front. In the morning he learned about the dastardly crime of Zinoviev and Kamenev, who had betrayed the Central Committee's secret decision on preparing the insurrection to the non-party newspaper *Novaya Zhizn*. That was a monstrous piece of treachery.

Forewarned by the traitors, the Provisional Government took immediate steps to crush the revolution. Special units were summoned from the front, the whole of Petrograd was divided into districts, and these were patrolled by mounted detachments. Kerensky declared boastfully: "I have more forces than needed. The Bolsheviks will be smashed for good." By that time, however, the correlation of political forces in the country had changed tremendously in favor of the revolution.

Under Lenin's direction the Party Central Committee took the most resolute steps to mobilize Red Guards, sailors and workers for the immediate launching of the revolution.

On October 20, the *New York Herald Tribune* correspondent reported from Petrograd: "The Maximalists [Bolsheviks] continue their preparations for a demonstration, the date of which is being kept secret, but is believed to be set for November 4. It is persistently rumored that they intend to take armed action to seize the supreme power. The government is receiving offers of help from all quarters and will prevent the proceedings by force, if necessary."

Kerensky's government decided to strike first. At 5:30 a.m. on October 24, troops were dispatched to wreck the offices of the Bolshevik newspapers *Rabochy Put* and *Soldat* and arrest Bolshevik leaders, but they were prevented from doing so by Bolsheviks aided by revolutionary soldiers. In such a situation armed action could not be delayed.

In the evening of October 24, still in hiding, Lenin sent an urgent letter to the Central Committee members in which he demanded: "Under no circumstances should power be left in the hands of Kerensky and Co. until the 25th—not under any circumstances; the matter must be decided without fail this very evening, or this very night." The letter ended with the warning: "To delay action is fatal."

After dispatching the letter Lenin, accompanied by the Finnish worker Eino Rahja, went to the Smolny Institute to assume direct leadership.

With Lenin's arrival at the Smolny the beat of the heart of the revolution became still more energetic. The Red Guard detachments, sailors and Petrograd's workers were put on the alert.

In the evening of October 24, and in the night, the Red Guards, supported by Baltic Navy ships, occupied the railway and power stations, the telegraph office, the central telephone exchange, the State Bank and a number of government buildings. Events were developing swiftly and successfully.

By the morning of October 25, the Provisional Government had been deposed. At 10 o'clock in the morning there appeared the manifesto "To the Citizens of Russia!" written by Lenin. It stated, in part: "The Provisional Government has been deposed. State power has passed into the hands of the organ of the Petrograd Soviet of Workers' and Soldiers' Deputies—the Revolutionary Military Committee, which heads the Petrograd proletariat and the garrison."

The government which had been deposed remained in possession only of the Winter Palace, garrisoned by officer cadets and a woman's "shock battalion." Lenin gave orders for this last stronghold of the bourgeois government to be taken by storm. From the Neva River, the cruiser *Aurora* fired a shot, giving the signal for attack. That shot heralded the birth of a new world. On the night of October 25, the Winter Palace fell; the ministers were arrested. The head of the Provisional Government, Alexander Kerensky, escaped arrest by fleeing from Petrograd in a US embassy car. He still hoped to muster up troops loyal to him and launch a war upon insurgent revolutionary Petrograd.

In the evening of October 25, the Second All-Russia Congress of Soviets of Workers' and Soldiers' Deputies assembled in the Smolny. At it Russia proclaimed a Republic of Soviets of Workers', Soldiers' and Peasants' Deputies, and the program of activity of Soviet power was outlined. The Congress of Soviets formed the first Soviet government, with Vladimir Lenin at the head, thereby legislatively initiating a new epoch, that of socialism.

In contrast to the dismay expressed by the US capitalist press at the accomplishment of the October Revolution, representatives of America's working people enthusiastically hailed the birth of the world's first state of workers and peasants. John Reed, an outstanding journalist and writer, a witness of the Great October Revolution, began his article "Red Russia—the Triumph of the Bolsheviki" with these words: "The real revolution has begun . . . For the first time in history the working class has seized the power of the state, for its own purpose—and means to keep it."

The dream of countless generations of fighters for the happiness of mankind finally became a near prospect. The victory of the Great October Socialist Revolution inaugurated a new epoch, when "man himself, with full consciousness," started to "make his own history."   □

7

NINA CHASOVNIKOVA

The Birth of a Socialist State

O n October 25, 1917, by the old calendar (November 7 by the new one), the Great October Socialist Revolution overthrew the power of the capitalists and landed aristocracy in Russia. The working class and the Communist Party, headed by Lenin, founded the world's first socialist state, a state of workers and peasants.

Administration of the vast country, occupying one-sixth of the globe, was taken over by Soviets of Working People's Deputies, elective bodies of people's power. "We have a right to be and are proud," wrote Lenin, the organizer of the Communist Party and the founder of the Soviet state, "that to us has fallen the good fortune to *begin* the building of a Soviet state, and thereby to *usher in* a new era in world history."

It was a very complex task to destroy the old state apparatus and create a new one. In practical terms it meant immediately doing away with the bodies of oppression of the masses and replacing them with bodies having entirely new functions—to serve the interests of the working people and direct the economic and cultural life of the nation. These were the Congress of Soviets, the All-Russia Central Executive Committee, and the Council of People's Commissars.

The Second All-Russia Congress of Soviets, held on October 25 and 26, 1917, proclaimed that all state power had passed into the hands of the Soviets, and approved the Decree on Peace and the Decree on Land, prepared by Lenin. The Decree on Peace appealed to the governments and peoples of all countries participating in the First World War to cease hostilities immediately and begin talks for concluding a universal and democratic peace. The Decree on Land abolished private ownership of land and land was proclaimed the property of the whole people; the land of the monasteries and big landowners was handed over to the peasants without recompense.

Between the congresses of Soviets, the All-Russia Central Executive Committee was the supreme body of legislative and executive power and control. The Congress of Soviets invested it with the authority to enact laws, to appoint

NINA CHASOVNIKOVA holds the degree of Candidate of Science in History.

and replace members of the government, and to approve, repeal or amend decrees and decisions of the government.

Upon its formation the All-Russia Central Executive Committee comprised 62 Bolsheviks, 29 Left-wing Socialist-Revolutionaries, six Menshevik-Internationalists, three Ukrainian Socialists and one Socialist-Revolutionary Maximalist. The Council of People's Commissars included 11 Bolsheviks and seven Left-wing Socialist-Revolutionaries. The latter party had representatives in many local Soviets. But when the leaders of the Left-wing Socialist-Revolutionaries began to oppose the Soviets, which represented the interests of the working people, and to take up arms against Soviet power, they lost what support they had had from the people. Like other petty-bourgeois parties the party of Left-wing Socialist-Revolutionaries disintegrated, and by the early 1920s had hardly any representatives in the Soviets. Thus, owing to specific historical conditions, the political system of the Soviet state became confined to a single party.

From its formation, the All-Russia Central Executive Committee functioned as both a legislative and executive body. The members of the Committee worked in the Soviets, trade unions and other organizations. Sittings of the Committee were frequently attended by representatives of factories and army units.

The Second All-Russia Congress of Soviets elected a workers' and peasants' government—the Council of People's Commissars, headed by Lenin. The Council of People's Commissars had the task of smashing the old state machine and building a new one, and carrying out the domestic and foreign policy of the world's first proletarian state.

The fifteen commissars headed the People's Commissariats set up for directing the activities of the state: internal affairs, agriculture, labor, trade and industry, public education, military and naval affairs, finance, etc.

Sabotage by civil service officials of the old regime was a serious obstacle to organizing the new state apparatus. Soon after the victory of the Revolution the personnel of fourteen former ministries of the Provisional Government went on strike.

There were different forms of sabotage: attempts were made to conduct "business" independently of the Soviet apparatus, waste time while at work, muddle up business correspondence, steal documents and keys to safes, etc. When the people's commissars came to the ministries to take control of them and to organize the work, they found empty rooms and locked cabinets. State bank officials refused to issue money to the Soviet government, while liberally supplying opponents of the Revolution with funds. The counterrevolutionaries were confident that such sabotage on the part of the officials would prevent the proletariat from using the old state apparatus. Without trained and experienced personnel, the Russian bourgeoisie thought, the Soviet government would fail.

Shortly before the victory of the October Revolution these hopes of the Russian bourgeoisie were expressed by the reactionary newspaper *Novoye Vremya* (New Times): "Let us imagine for a moment that the Bolsheviks will win. Who will come to rule us then? Maybe cooks, these connoisseurs of cutlets and beefsteaks? Or maybe firemen, stable-men, or stokers? Or perhaps they'll have nannies rushing to a meeting of the Council in between washing the diapers? Who will they be, these statesmen? Maybe locksmiths will take charge of the theaters, plumbers will deal with diplomatic work and joiners with the post and telegraph? Will this be the case? No. Is this possible? History will give the Bolsheviks its authoritative answer to this mad question!"

History did give its answer.

"We have a 'magic way' to enlarge our state apparatus *tenfold* at once, at one stroke, a way which no capitalist state ever possessed or could possess. This magic way is to draw the working people, to draw the poor, into the daily work of state administration," Lenin wrote.

On behalf of the Party Lenin called upon the workers and peasants: "Comrades working people! Remember that now *you yourselves* are at the helm of state. No one will help you if you yourselves do not unite and take into *your* hands *all affairs* of the state."

The staff of the People's Commissariat for Internal Affairs was filled with the help of the workers of the Putilov plant (now the Kirov plant in Leningrad). The sailors of the Baltic fleet and the workers of the Siemens Schuckert plant (now "Electrosila" in Leningrad) sent representatives to the People's Commissariat for Foreign Affairs and the railway men of Petrograd and Moscow, to the People's Commissariat for Railways. Revolutionary soldiers—Red Guards and sailors—formed the backbone of the People's Commissariat for Food Supply. The personnel of the People's Commissariat for Labor was formed of industrial and office workers belonging to the steel workers' union, trade union committees at factories and employees of insurance companies.

A large number of progressive-minded students were drawn into the work at the People's Commissariats. Students of the Mining Institute cooperated with the Peoples's Commissar Anatoly Lunacharsky and his deputy, Nadezhda Krupskaya (Lenin's wife), to set up the People's Commissariat for Education.

Those who came to work at the People's Commissariats often had no experience in state affairs, but they were full of revolutionary enthusiasm. Together with old employees who sided with the Soviets, they formed the backbone of the personnel of the People's Commissariats. However, it took some time to develop effective forms and methods of work, to achieve uniformity in their structure and to coordinate their clerical work.

The military apparatus and its leading bodies underwent drastic changes. A

Commissariat for Military Affairs was established, which took measures to smash the old army apparatus and create a new workers' and peasants' Red Army.

Other Commissariats were beginning to function effectively. The People's Commissariat for Nationalities played an important part in building and consolidating the Soviet Republic, the new multinational state. Its structure differed from that of other commissariats. Its departments and commissariats were set up on a national basis, since each nationality had its own particular way of life which called for specific methods of work. Commissariats of the Polish, Lithuanian, Byelorussian, Armenian, Jewish and other nationalities were formed within the system of the People's Commissariat for Nationalities.

The People's Commissars met daily for the sittings of the Council of People's Commissars. "That was the first university, and the only one in the world at that time, where the people's commissars learned how to build a workers' and peasants' state," wrote Grigory Petrovsky, the first People's Commissar for Internal Affairs.

All questions raised at the Council of People's Commissars were settled by vote. Decisions were adopted if more than fifty per cent of the People's Commissars or their deputies present voted in favor. It is noteworthy that Lenin never claimed his opinion should be considered decisive. Despite tremendous authority, Lenin always abided by the principle of collective leadership.

Anatoly Lunacharsky, the first People's Commissar for Education, described the meetings of the Council of People's Commissars thus: "Under Lenin the atmosphere at the Council of People's Commissars was lively and businesslike. It was also at that time the procedure for considering various questions was established: rigid time-limits were set for speakers, both our own and those invited from other places. Lenin required that every speaker be brief and to the point. The mood that prevailed was one of intense concentration, so that time itself seemed to be packed with facts and ideas, with decisions squeezed into every minute. Not a hint of red tape, of bureaucratic 'superiority'; no visible tension in those people doing unbearably hard work."

The activities of the Council of People's Commissars were made known to the people. By decision of the Council of People's Commissars of December 23, 1917, special reports on the proceedings of all government meetings were published. The results of the Council's work were covered by national and local newspapers and magazines.

Defending the Revolution

"No revolution is worth anything," wrote Lenin, "unless it can defend itself." The Party summed up the experience of the Paris Commune which "fell only because it did not make proper use of armed force at the right moment."

In the very first weeks after the victory of the October Revolution the people smashed the hateful bourgeois state apparatus of violence and coercion: the police, gendarmery, bourgeois courts and offices of public prosecutors. The army was democratized and placed under the command of soldiers' committees and Soviets. The working people rose to fight counterrevolution and crime.

Revolutionary order could be ensured and the gains of the revolution preserved only by enlisting as widely as possible the efforts and initiative of the people and drawing them into the building of a new state under the guidance of Lenin's Party.

The Military-Revolutionary Committee set up by the Petrograd Soviet of Workers' and Soldiers' Deputies on the eve of the October Revolution became the first Soviet body for combating counterrevolutionary and criminal acts.

When revolutionary battles were still being fought in the streets of Petrograd the first Soviet committee of inquiry consisting of workers, soldiers and sailors, recommended by public organizations, was set up under the Military-Revolutionary Committee. They arrested and prosecuted enemies of the revolution, criminals and profiteers. Dangerous criminals and counterrevolutionaries were imprisoned.

Despite the determined efforts of the Soviet government to achieve peace, the German imperialists continued the war. One hundred and fifty-eight German and Austrian divisions were fighting on the Russian front. The Soviet government could not use the old army against them: sick of war and anxious for peace, the troops were demobilizing on their own and leaving the front.

The army consisted chiefly of peasants and they hastened from the front fearing that they might be too late to take part in the distribution of the land confiscated from the landowners. It was impossible to hold them back and stop the mounting spontaneous demobilization.

While demolishing the old army the Soviet Government began to organize the socialist army and navy. The Red Guards were the nucleus of the new army. They had been formed during the revolution, played an active part in carrying it through, and constituted the foundation of the armed forces of the Soviet state in the first few months of its existence. In October 1917, the Red Guards—the front-rank fighters of the revolution—numbered about 200,000.

However, the Red Guard alone was not enough to withstand imperialist aggression. On January 15, 1918, the Soviet Government issued a decree on the organization of a Workers' and Peasants' Red Army, and on February 14, a decree on the organization of a Workers' and Peasants' Navy.

The Red Army was formed of workers and peasants on a voluntary basis. It was the only basis on which the army could be formed in those days when the Soviet Republic had no laws on compulsory military service, no registration or drafting bodies.

But it was impossible to create a large army in this way. By the end of April

1918, the Red Army consisted of 196,000 volunteers—obviously not enough to combat the foreign interventionists and the White Guards. In the summer of 1918, when many areas of the Soviet Republic were engulfed in the flames of civil war, compulsory military service was introduced throughout the country.

The Red Army was based on the principles of equality and friendship of the nationalities of which it was composed; it opposed all forms of slavery, oppression and exploitation. The working people of the Soviet state regarded it as a reliable defender of their class interests. Trained and led into combat by the Communist Party, its officers and men displayed exemplary discipline, great courage and high political consciousness.

In the first six months of 1918 more than 40,000 Communists joined the army as volunteers. In the years of the Civil War nearly half of the Party's membership was in the army. At least 50,000 Communists gave their lives in the struggle against the interventionists and White Guards.

While Red commanders were being trained for the army, on Lenin's initiative former military specialists and officers who possessed valuable knowledge and experience were drawn into the work of the Red Army. During the years 1918-20 more than 48,000 former officers were enlisted in the Red Army. They held different command and staff posts under the control of Red Army commissars. Most of them performed their duties honestly and conscientiously. Later, Lenin wrote: ". . . if we had not accepted them in our service and made them serve us, we could not have created an army."

In fierce battles against the numerous enemies of Soviet power the newly-formed Red Army defended the gains of the October Revolution and demonstrated its superiority over armies of the bourgeois type.

The Main Sphere of Struggle for Socialism

Along with the creation of the new state apparatus and the armed forces, the Soviet government tackled the most difficult and complicated task of the proletarian revolution—the organization of a socialist economy.

The first and most important step towards transforming the economy along socialist lines was the introduction of workers' control over production and over the distribution of food supplies. Workers' control had been introduced in many factories and plants immediately after the bourgeois-democratic revolution in February 1917. After the victorious October Revolution, workers' control became a school of economic management for thousands of front-rank workers and was the first step towards the complete transfer of all factories and plants to state ownership. The Decree on Workers' Control was adopted by the All-Russia Central Executive Committee on November 14, 1917.

Those who were elected by their fellow-workers to exercise control became responsible to the state for the maintenance of law and order, and for discipline and the protection of property at their enterprises. Their decisions were binding on the owner of the given enterprise and could be cancelled only by trade unions.

The bodies of workers' control were active in many fields. Together with the Soviets of Working People's Deputies they switched military plants over to peacetime production and launched a drive for raising labor productivity and strengthening labor discipline.

The deposed exploiter classes bitterly opposed workers' control and did everything in their power to evade it. The bourgeoisie resorted to wide-scale sabotage of the measures undertaken by workers' control bodies. For instance, they closed down their enterprises and laid off workers, sold their enterprises to foreigners, and illegally transferred their capital abroad in their efforts to force the working class to admit that it was incapable of managing the country's economic life.

The fierce opposition of the bourgeoisie to workers' control was finally broken. The industrial census of 1918 carried out in thirty-one provinces in the European part of the RSFSR showed that 87.4 per cent of all plants and factories with more than 200 workers had factory committees responsible for workers' control.

Workers' control bodies enabled hundreds of thousands of workers to acquire the knowledge and experience necessary for managing the work of plants and factories, thereby providing the Soviet state with its first executives for industry.

While nationalizing the key industries by confiscating the private property of the big capitalists, the Party did not immediately set out to put an end to capitalist relations in the economy in their entirety. It tolerated the temporary survival of capitalist property under state control and was prepared to pay compensation to proprietors, particularly owners of small enterprises, for facilities nationalized. However, the bourgeoisie rejected the opportunity for cooperation afforded by the proletarian state and opposed its policy of control. This fact considerably speeded up the process of nationalization.

On June 28, 1918, the Soviet Government decreed the nationalization of all industrial enterprises.

In this period the Soviet state concentrated on achieving planned control and management of the national economy. Local and central bodies concerned with management of the economy began to map out short-term production plans for enterprises, separate industries and whole areas.

In the spring of 1918 a draft of the first national economic plan for the Soviet Republic was worked out. It elaborated measures for the rehabilitation of the devastated economy and the building of new facilities. The construction of new enterprises was begun on a small scale.

The Land to the Peasants

Revolutionary changes in the countryside began with the adoption of the Decree on Land (October 26, 1917) whereby the private ownership of land was abolished. Besides the landowners' estates, approximately 19 million dessiatins* of land belonging to factory owners and merchants, and more than 60 million dessiatins of privately owned mortgaged lands were taken over by the state.

Great attention was given to explaining the government's land policy to the peasants. In Lenin's opinion this policy could prove successful only if it was understood by each peasant. The Decree on Land was published in all the newspapers, and put out as a special booklet in several editions and sent out to all the *volosts* (small administrative territories comprising several villages).

To help the Soviets with the implementation of the Decree the government delegated land specialists to the guberniyas; simultaneously it sent propagandists to the villages to explain the land policy to the peasants.

The local Soviets set up special commissions from among the local authorities and peasants to confiscate the landowners' estates. They investigated the estates and decided whether they were to be preserved as particularly efficient agricultural units or distributed among the peasants. Of the 1,427 private estates in Novgorod region 92 were singled out to be model farms and the Soviets appointed special representatives to take charge of them. According to the People's Commissariat for Agriculture, by the end of 1918, a total of 3,101 Soviet state farms had been established on the basis of these estates.

By transferring the land to those who tilled it, it became possible to do away once and for all with the exploitation of the peasants by the landowners and to strengthen the alliance between the workers and peasants—which was essential for the establishment of the young Soviet state.

Culture for Millions of Working People

The October Revolution ushered in radical changes, not only in the political and economic sphere, but also in the cultural life of society. It laid the beginning of a cultural revolution in the Land of Soviets.

The object of the cultural revolution was to raise the cultural and educational level of the people on a nation-wide scale, to make the achievements of science and art accessible to all, and to ensure the development and progress of science, technology and art so that in this sphere the country could emerge in a leading position in the world.

The country's cultural heritage was extremely uneven. Advanced social thought, scientific discoveries, technical inventions and immortal works of art and literature existed side by side with mass illiteracy, ignorance and back-

---

* One dessiatin = 1.09 hectares = 2.7 acres.

wardness of the population. More than 75 per cent of the population were illiterate. Illiteracy was even higher among women, in the rural areas and among the non-Russian peoples in the outlying areas.

A People's Commissariat for Education was set up in place of the pre-revolutionary Ministry of Education to direct the country's cultural and scientific development. It took charge of all aspects of the cultural revolution, from the preschool education of children to the work of scientific institutions, theaters and museums. It comprised 17 departments, many of which were entirely new.

Local management of public education was put in the hands of the Soviets of Workers' and Peasants' Deputies that immediately began to set up local education bodies. As a rule, all organizational matters were settled at the congresses of Soviets.

The People's Commissariat for Education was faced with the major task of creating a new Soviet school, and many difficulties had to be overcome before this could be achieved. The Soviet Republic inherited a poor legacy from tsarist Russia. Nearly 80 per cent of all children of school age had received no education. Lenin described the schools of prerevolutionary Russia as "nothing but an instrument of the class rule of the bourgeoisie. They were thoroughly imbued with the bourgeois caste spirit. Their purpose was to supply the capitalists with obedient lackeys and able workers."

Even in the first year of its existence the Soviet government found considerable funds for public education. In 1918, it allocated 3,000 million rubles to the People's Commissariat for Education. This represented 6.8 per cent of the total state budget.

Illiteracy among the adult population was eradicated in the first years of Soviet power. To achieve this task 7,134 schools for adults and 101 people's universities were organized. There the working people were taught Russian and arithmetic and the fundamentals of the social and natural sciences. Between 1917 and 1920 seven million persons learned to read and write.

Local Soviet Government

After the overthrow of the bourgeois Provisional Government and the victory of the Socialist Revolution, Soviet power began to extend throughout the whole of Russia. This was the time of the revolution's triumphal march. The working people welcomed the revolutionary changes introduced by the dictatorship of the proletariat. In the first months of Soviet power it was apparent that the resistance of the bourgeoisie (which still retained in its possession certain material resources and which had at its disposal experienced military leaders and forces) and of its right-wing socialist allies was futile: the reactionary forces were overpowered by the more numerous forces of the people. Only in the outlying areas of the country (the Don region, the Southern Urals, the Ukraine,

Central Asia and the Transcaucasus) were the counterrevolutionary forces able to resort to armed attacks, but they too were suppressed by the working people.

The Communist Party and the Soviet Government attached tremendous importance to encouraging the people's initiative with regard to forming new government bodies. The newspaper *Izvestia* wrote at the time: ''Political power has passed to the Soviets. In the provinces many comrades have not yet got down to business, and even those who have, are not doing their work as well as this great historical moment demands of us. The class of landed aristocracy and capitalists has been replaced in government, but in the provinces the old-time officials still reign supreme.

''Workers, soldiers and peasants must realize that all power at every level now belongs to them. They can exercise this power through the Soviets of Workers', Soldiers' and Peasants' Deputies. . . . Do not wait for instructions from the top, comrades, do not wait for directives, but use this power in practice. . . .''

The first results of the efforts of the Soviet government to consolidate the gains of the Great October Socialist Revolution were summed up at the Third All-Russia Congress of Soviets in January 1918.

At this Congress the highest bodies of government accounted to the working people. The reports of Lenin and of Sverdlov, the first Chairman of the All-Russia Central Executive Committee, summed up what had been achieved in forming the new state.

Lenin began his report to the Congress by saying that the Soviet Republic had now been in existence for two months and 15 days, that is, five days longer than the Paris Commune, the first historical experience of workers' power. He expressed his firm belief that the Soviet state, unlike the Commune, was invincible, for its indestructible basis was the alliance between the workers and poorest peasants. Lenin emphasized that the workers, soldiers and peasants had succeeded in creating the apparatus of a new state power that enjoyed the wholehearted support of the majority of the people.

This is how Lenin described the significance of the Third All-Russia Congress of Soviets: ''There are incontestable grounds for saying that the Third Congress of Soviets has opened a new epoch in world history. . . . It has consolidated the organization of the new state power which was created by the October Revolution and has projected the lines of future socialist construction for the whole world, for the working people of all countries.'' □

8

JESSICA SMITH

The American People
And the Socialist Revolution

> There is nothing in all the struggle of the oppressed people of the earth
> for freedom that begins to compare in historic importance to the signifi-
> cance of the sublime spectacle that the Soviet Republic presents to the
> world. . . . The Russian Revolution will be chronicled in history as the
> greatest and most luminous and far-reaching achievement . . . a beacon
> light of hope and promise to all humanity!

Thus spoke Eugene V. Debs, beloved and outstanding working-class leader in November 1922, the fifth Anniversary of the Socialist Revolution. His faith remained firm to the end of his days. Let these words stand as his greeting to the 60th anniversary.

Despite the hostility of US Government and big business circles (with a few rare exceptions), hostility based on their fear of the challenge of socialism to the capitalist system; despite the vicious anti-Soviet lies and slanders of the reactionary press, large sections of the American people hailed the Revolution with enthusiasm and sympathy. Among the first to make the truth known were such eyewitnesses of the Revolution in its early days as John Reed, Louise Bryant, Albert Rhys Williams, Bessie Beatty, Raymond Robins, Lincoln Steffens, Jerome Davis. Many thousands followed them.

The more advanced workers and rank and file trade unionists, with millions of their brothers and sisters in other countries, were quick to show their solidarity with the world's first working-class state. And a considerable number of labor leaders were friendly, undeterred by the implacable hostility of AFL President Samuel Gompers, Vice-President Matthew Woll and William Green after them.

In the beginning, practically the whole radi movement, despite different ideologies, was for the Revolution, including many right- as well as left-wing Socialists. (The Communist Party was formed only two years later.) Liberal opinion, in different degrees, was largely pro-Soviet in the early days. The Revolution was hailed by our foremost artists, writers, musicians and other

JESSICA SMITH, chairman of *New World Review*'s editorial board, was editor of NWR and its predecessor, *Soviet Russia Today*, 1936-1976. In 1976, the Supreme Soviet awarded her the Order of Friendship Among the Peoples, one of the USSR's highest honors.

cultural and public figures. however misled later by anti-Soviet propaganda, and some far-sighted businessmen glimpsed the huge market that lay ahead.

The tremendous impact of the Revolution on Black people is described in some detail elsewhere in this book, by Professor Gerald Horne. No one could see so quickly the meaning of the Revolution for ending the colonial system and racism. No voices spoke so clearly of this, then and later, as those of the great figures of Dr. W.E.B. Du Bois, Paul Robeson and, happily still among us at 87, William L. Patterson.

The most popular mass expression of the peace movement at that time was the People's Council, representing 300 radical groups in 32 states. It was suffering serious persecution after our country entered World War I in April 1917, and gained new momentum from Lenin's Appeal for Peace as did the Women's International League for Peace and Freedom and other more conservative peace organizations.

As the hatred and hostility of the US Government mounted, the sympathy of the people grew. Attempts to disrupt the Soviet Government from within failed and the United States joined thirteen other capitalist nations in armed intervention to overthrow the Soviet state.

This aroused a storm of protest from the American people. Dozens of organizations and committees sprang up in defense of the USSR, many ''Hands Off Russia'' demonstrations, meetings and marches against intervention and blockade took place. Resolutions of support and sympathy poured out of trade union organizations. None were more active than the Seattle workers.

When hundreds of cars filled with crates for Vladivostok marked ''sewing machines'' arrived at Seattle, the workers became suspicious and let one crash on the dock. Huge stacks of arms for Kolchak's counterrevolutionary government in Siberia fell out. The longshoremen refused to load the evil cargo and workers all along the coast followed suit. In the East, the Marine and Transport Workers Union struck against shipping arms to Wrangel.

The intervention failed of its purpose though it caused much misery and destruction. But the Red Army and the Soviet people and their leaders stood firm against their foreign enemies and the White Generals they armed and paid for. The US troops sent to the North on the pretext of guarding Allied supplies found their purpose was something quite else. They were mainly workers and did not want this job. Through their families word of the people's protests at home reached them. They mutinied and were soon recalled. Major General William S. Graves was sent to take command of the US troops in Siberia, ostensibly to help Czechoslovak troops join their allies in the West. When he found the Czechs playing a counterrevolutionary role, he refused to have anything to do with the dirty business and soon withdrew with his troops.

While the defeat of the intervention belongs to the Soviet Government and people themselves, credit must also go to the people who opposed US policies, at the cost of vicious persecution, and especially the workers who refused to ship arms to aid counterrevolution and the soldiers who refused to fight the revolutionary government. There is a lesson in this today on what can be accomplished by mass pressure in restraining the Administration from the influence of the Pentagon and rightist circles in its dealings with the USSR.

Even during all the period of intervention, Lenin lost no opportunity to talk normal relations, peace and trade with US business men and important public figures trekking to Moscow. He appointed Santeri Nuorteva, a Finnish socialist living here, to open an information bureau in New York City to start things going. When he was deported, Ludwig C. A. K. Martens, a Russian engineer in the United States, was appointed as the first representative of the Soviet Government in this country, who opened a Technical Aid Bureau for jobs for Russian-Americans wanting to go home, or for Americans drawn by the Revolution. The mouths of more and more businessmen watered at the thought of the Soviet market. The US, however, would deal only with the representative of the non-existent Provisional Government which the US had continued to recognize.

Early in 1919 the first national conference was held to form the American Labor Alliance for Trade Relations with Russia, officered by leading trade unionists (see article by Prof. Gerald Horne) and supported by labor bodies all over the country who recognized that trade with Soviet Russia would mean jobs for American workers, already feeling the crunch of the coming unemployment crisis. This led to the first resolution in Congress to establish US-Soviet diplomatic relations, introduced by Senator William Borah and carried on by a group of leading Senators for sixteen years until finally won.

While mass pressure from the people was a major factor for recognition, great credit should be given to Col. Raymond Robins, head of the US Red Cross Mission, who was sent to the USSR to keep Kerensky in power and then became a passionate partisan of Lenin and the Revolution and worked indefatigably for the rest of his life for establishment of normal relations.

A new wave of sympathy swept our country at the time of the great Volga famine, a disaster intensified by the years of imperialist and civil war, armed intervention and blockade.

Herbert Hoover, then Secretary of Commerce under Harding, headed the American Relief Administration. He saw food as a weapon, had used it to destroy Bela Kun's revolutionary government in Hungary and hoped he might use food to control the situation in Soviet Russia.

Hoover failed to carry out his designs. The Soviet authorities made sure that what happened in Hungary would not be repeated. Hoover found political capital in getting Congress to appropriate $20 million to buy up corn and some other products to send to the Russians, from US farmers who had a surplus crop that year. Numerous religious and other groups raised funds for food, medical and other needed supplies, all of which were deeply appreciated by the Soviet Government and people.

My own first visit to the land of Soviets was as a relief worker with the American Friends Service Committee. It was the old village we lived in, devastated by the famine. We saw the first sprouts of socialism come to the village, heard Lenin speak on a vacation trip to Moscow, saw the amazing transformation of the country in a two-year period—but all that's another story. I was simply one of the young Americans of that period whose whole life was changed by working in Soviet Russia during those early years of the Revolution.

With peace at last in their land (all but for some Japanese interventionists in the Far East) the time had arrived for the Soviet people to get at the reconstruction of their country they had longed for so long, to plow their earth with tractors instead of tanks, and sow it with seeds instead of bullets, to restore their ruined mines and factories, to put up new homes to live in—to start *building* socialism instead of fighting to defend it!

Thousands of people in America who had been defending the Revolution from afar with words and banners and slogans were caught by the same dream of helping to build the New World, tightening our bonds of friendship with it and spreading its word of peace. Space permits using only a few examples of the projects developed. In the United States an extensive people's organization, Friends of Soviet Russia—which had become an umbrella for a group of organizations, with branches all over the country—raised a million dollars the first year. Harold Ware,* agricultural engineer and practical farmer, asked the FSR officials about using some of that money to buy tractors and provide skilled drivers to demonstrate their use to Soviet peasants to help prevent famines in the future. The project was carried out successfully on the State Farm in Toikino, Siberia. Lenin watched it closely, and told the FSR, ''Not a single kind of help by Americans has been so timely and important.'' Ware followed this up by bringing over a larger group of farm specialists and their families and modern machinery and set up a model state farm and school that worked out many methods useful in the collectivization campaign that came later.

In that period and later various other US groups set up agricultural projects. Tremendous help was given by 16 Black agricultural specialists who worked in an experimental cotton selection station near Tashkent and were honored by the Soviet Government. Only recently, at the Soviet Embassy in Washington, John Sutton, a member of this group, received an official letter award commending

---

* Harold Ware's story, told by Lement Harris, will soon be published by the American Institute for Marxist Studies as an Occasional Paper.

his notable contribution in the early years of the USSR (See NWR, July-August 1977). George Tynes and the late Oliver John Golden became Soviet citizens and raised families in the USSR. Articles by Slava Tynes of Novosti, and by Dr. Lili Golden, of the staff of the Institute of Africa of the USSR Academy of Sciences, have appeared in *New World Review*.

Immigrant Russian workers, driven to these shores by tsarist oppression, wanted to take their skills back to their native land to build up its industry. Many American workers were also drawn to help. Thousands of workers became involved in forming groups to raise money for machinery and tools to take with them to help rebuild the ruined mines and mills and factories. While some came back, resentful that life after the Revolution was not all bread and roses, many others who did not seek Utopia remained and made a most valuable contribution.

In June 1977, the Soviet press carried the story of the 84-year old John Pinter who had come to the Soviet Union with a group of 32 coal miners to work in the Don Basin, had remained, was decorated and eventually retired. A considerable number of American technicians and engineers offered their services, or were hired by contract, as Lenin's great GOELRO plan for the electrification of the whole country (forerunner of the five-year plans) got under way.

Charles P. Steinmetz, the legendary American engineer, scientist and socialist, consultant to the General Electric Co., corresponded with Lenin and offered to help carry out his electrification plan. He wrote of the Soviet Union and Lenin in glowing terms in US publications. Lenin welcomed the offer enthusiastically. Only the death of Dr. Steinmetz prevented his carrying out his offer of assistance.*

Col. Hugh L. Cooper, builder of great hydroelectric projects in the US such as Muscle Shoals, acted as planner and consultant in the building of Dnieprostroy—the hydroelectric station on the Ukraine's Dnieper River, first of the great series of dams which have made Lenin's dream a reality. In 1920, Soviet Russia produced a little over 500 million kwh of electric power (about what is produced by one small power station today). Today the Soviet Union has over 50 power stations with a capacity of one million kwh and more; in 1976 actual output was 1,111,000,000 kwh.

The Amalgamated Clothing Workers of America, after its President, Sidney Hillman, had several conferences with Lenin, in 1922 set up the Russian American Industrial Corporation which established several experimental clothing factories to bring American methods of mass production where primitive, handicraft methods still prevailed. The Soviet clothing industry later paid back the investment in full.

* *Charles P. Steinmetz: Scientist and Socialist (1865-1923)*, by Sender Garlin. AIMS Occasional Paper No. 22.

One of the largest and most important of these undertakings was the Kuzbas industrial colony.

The Kuzbas Industrial Colony

Among the many US workers eager to give technical aid in building up the new Soviet state, was a young IWW foreman at the Detroit Ford works, Herbert Spencer Calvert. He had come there in 1919 to learn the skills needed.

He had studied metallurgy and become expert in the operation of blast furnaces, foundry and heat treatment and other machine processes in the steel industry. In 1921 a chance came to join the US delegation to the first Congress of the Profintern (Trade Union International) in Moscow. With his union's blessing and some important steel formulas in his bag, he embarked on a North Atlantic liner with a group of young Russian-Americans returning home.

This was an auspicious time for his project. Stimulated by Lenin's writings on the Soviets' need for reconstruction and new building and the possibility of foreign concessions, Calvert sat down and wrote a paper on Economic Reconstruction, embodying his plan for utilizing the skills of US-trained workers. Many of the returning Russian-Americans were already skilled workers, he wrote. Along with some 20,000 skilled workers and technicians already registered with Martens' Bureau for Technical Aid, here was the basis for a production army which could set up a complete industrial unit based on the modern technology for which America was famous.

Calvert had become friendly with Mikhail Borodin (later famous for his work in aid of the Chinese Revolution) and showed him his plan. Borodin was impressed and sent it on to Lenin, who returned it almost immediately. Written diagonally across the first page with a heavy red pencil was Lenin's comment, "A good idea, give us something definite."

Calvert distributed copies of his plan to various delegates to the trade union Congress. Among them was Big Bill Haywood, the IWW leader recently deported from the US, ready at once to take part. Another was Sebold G. Rutgers, a Dutch Communist noted for construction of the Port of Rotterdam and engineering projects in the Dutch East Indies and the US. He took fire at once and joined an informal committee to go ahead with the project, of which he was eventually to become the leader.

After much research, the Committee selected Kuznetsk Basin in Western Siberia, 2,400 miles from Moscow, a region where basic raw materials—iron and coal—and food supplies were available, and, they learned later, foundations of a steel plant designed like those of Gary, Indiana. Calvert wrote ecstatically:

Imagine the Kemerovo coal veins on barge and railroad! Five years of development work had been done! A chemical plant was almost completed! A sawmill! Housing for several hundred people! A big university at Tomsk! Virgin black-earth meadows and timber up river! Food surplus! Surplus peasant labor!

Soon a detailed plan was ready for Lenin for the development of Kuznetsk Basin with exhaustive reports on its history and resources and proposing that a colony of foreign skilled workers each contributing $200 plus transportation be sent there.

In two days, Lenin gave his support to the plan on condition that the American workers and colonists would bring with them 1) provisions for two years; 2) clothing for the same and tools; 3) a practical proposition formulated in 20 lines and addressed to STO (Council of Labor and Defense). "Please answer by bearer," Lenin concluded.

On June 22, 1921 STO endorsed the projects, instructing the appropriate government departments to start negotiations immediately. By June 28, Calvert with a group of qualified specialists, was off on an exploratory trip to make sure Kuznetsk Basin was the best location for a foreign labor colony. (Among the group was A. A. Heller, one of the founders of *Soviet Russia Today*, NWR's predecessor.)

The delegation made a thorough survey of the region and its industries, which would become a part of their enterprise. They spent eight days working with the Siberian Revolutionary Committee, which was unanimously in favor of the plan. "I have never met a more competent group of men and women than the members of the Sibrevkom," Calvert wrote.

After signing the agreement, to the Americans' amazement a couple of sacks of jewelry were dumped out on the table. A. A. Heller was asked to select some $200,000 worth of jewels to provide *valuta* with which to buy machinery and equipment. Royalty fleeing eastward loaded with treasure amassed at the cost of the people's misery had been relieved of their burdens which would now help build modern socialist industry.

The 50-page report on the delegation's findings was presented to STO September 13, 1921. The report proposed that STO guarantee adequate facilities to transport 4,000 American and other foreigners from port of entry to Kuzbas, reducing all formalities and red tape to a minimum; that STO contribute one dollar for every dollar spent by American colonists for the purchase of tools, machinery, etc., and grant a credit of 200,000 dollars for this purpose; that H. S. Calvert's expenses to the US be paid to arrange for workers, their equipment and transportation, and to purchase tools and machinery. A preliminary unit of 200 workers would be sent to Kuzbas; grain for the first year to be guaranteed for American workers in addition to foodstuffs for two years they would bring with them; and mechanized farms started to secure food for the future.

Monday, September 19, 1921, Rutgers, Haywood and Calvert, were called to an interview with Lenin. Lenin used no translator. Declaring it was a good idea, he asked "Who is going to do it?" His main concern was whether they really could recruit in America the skilled workers who would be willing to endure the hardships they would face. The group assured him they could.

That same day Lenin wrote to V. V. Kuibyshev of the Supreme Economic Council, outlining the plans. He suggested that a representative of the Kuzbas group attend the STO meeting the coming Friday. He proposed that about half of the 200 American lumberjacks in Moscow, itching to get to work, be sent at once to Kuzbas, fully equipped, to start building log cabins for the colonizers. He suggested that an extremely precise contract be drawn up.

Greatly concerned about the ability of foreign workers to fit into the harsh conditions of Soviet life in 1921, Lenin proposed that all workers coming from America should sign the following pledge:

1. We pledge to arrange and *collectively guarantee* that only men willing and able consciously to bear the hardships inevitable in the rehabilitation of industry in a very backward and incredibly devastated country will arrive in Russia.

2. Those coming to Russia pledge to work with maximum intensiveness and productivity of labor and discipline on a higher level than capitalist standards, otherwise Russia will be unable to outstrip or even catch up with capitalism.

3. We pledge to refer all conflicts without exception to the final decision of the Supreme Soviet power in Russia and to conscientiously abide by all its decisions.

4. We pledge to bear in mind the extreme nervousness of the starved and exhausted Russian workers and peasants in the vicinity of our enterprises and to help them in every way to establish friendly relations and overcome suspicions and envy.

L. C. A. K. Martens, now back in Moscow, was skeptical of the plan, as were some others. Lenin insisted that the plan should be corrected, not rejected. Pending STO's decision, Lenin was checking out all the angles, giving careful attention to every detail. On October 12 Lenin wrote to the Politbureau, calling attention to the risks involved:

I propose, first, that the Central Committee decide the political question. The Politbureau is necessarily involved because of the expenditure of gold. It is a difficult question.

Pro: If the Americans carry out their promises, then the gain will be gigantic. Then it would be a mistake not to spend 600,000 rubles.

Con: Will they carry out their promises? Rutgers might fall into leftism. Calvert is too talkative. We have no guarantees. Impulsive people in an atmosphere of unemployment can be a group of adventurers and we'll lose the 600,000 rubles in gold we give. The risk is not small.

For: I.W. Smirnov and Maksimov (from the Urals).

Against: Martens, who should know the Americans well, is against.

Because of the hesitation of some of Lenin's comrades, Rutgers' proposal

was rejected in its original form. A decision of the Central Committee signed by
Lenin suggested that the plans be reworked as follows:

a) Change the composition of the leading group of initiators, by co-opting five to eight
prominent members of the American trade union movement or other labor organizations;
b) reduce our government's expenditures to a maximum of $300,000; c) reduce and
specify our expenditures in the event the contract is cancelled.

The members of the group were anxious to accept any proposals made by
Lenin, and Rutgers notified Lenin and STO that the changes would be made.
The agreement between the Council of Labor and Defense and the initiating
group of American workers was signed October 21, by both sides.

The day after the agreement was signed, the *Organization Committee of the
Autonomous Industrial Colony Kuzbas* was officially formed.

Calvert ended his chapter on the events recounted above: "When I left
Moscow the query Lenin made during our interview was still ringing in my
ears—'Who is going to do it?' The query lives today as then to one and all of us.
We have the idea—the world is ours to possess by action as creator, conser-
vator, consumer and educator!"*

In an article in the British *Labour Monthly*, April 1970, Tom Barker (then
82—he died soon after) added a few interesting details. He had traveled with
Calvert and Haywood to Kemorovo to take over officially the tools, machines
and other equipment already on hand. They discovered a great store of equipment and non-ferrous metals in the Simonovsky Monastery grounds, some of
which, such as mine hoists, would be of great use to the colony. Such dumps of
valuable stores were formed to free rail wagons for the transport of Tsarist
troops in World War I.

When it became apparent that the load in the US would be too heavy for
Calvert alone, Barker was asked to accompany him (expenses of both to be paid
by the Soviets). But meantime he had fallen in love with a Soviet girl, Berta
Isaakovna, whom he expected to marry, and there was a rule that delegates
could not take Soviet wives with them. As soon as Lenin heard of this he made
arrangements for Barker to take his wife along. Barker and Calvert were both
non-Party, and some on the Moscow Committee felt they should join the Party.
"But Lenin would have none of this," wrote Barker. "He agreed with Calvert
and myself that our hands would be more free and to some extent we would be
better positioned in our recruiting program as non-members."

Calvert and Barker set up offices in mid-Manhattan and formed a distin-

*The story up to this point is based on material by H.B. Calvert, furnished us by courtesy
of Mrs. Mellie Calvert, his former wife and secretary in the Kuzbas Colony.

guished American Committee. They contacted local unions and other labor bodies across the entire country and in a few weeks nearly 30 Kuzbas locals were established. In the application forms the harshness of Soviet living conditions at that time was stressed and the four pledges written by Lenin (quoted above) given prominence. (And a good thing too. One disgruntled family who had left the colony swore out summonses against members of the Kuzbas Committee on reaching New York. The New York Grand Jury, on seeing the pledges on the application form they had signed, threw out the case.)

"Our plans moved forward," wrote Barker, "and parties of workers began to leave. Kuzbas had caught the imagination of the American left at that time. Many prominent people such as Charles P. Steinmetz, supported us."

Tom Barker edited the monthly *Kuzbas Bulletin* which kept an increasing number of people abreast of developments in this great venture. "I remained on organization work at the New York end from 1921 to 1926," he wrote. "When I returned to the Soviet Union and made my first exciting visit to the Kuznetsky Basin colony, I carried in my portfolio the plans for the construction of the great steel mill of Novokuznetsk; the authors were the Freyn Engineering Company of Chicago, which later was responsible for the first two sections of the plant. Of course by now the old backwardness of Western Siberia has gone forever. Who would have rejoiced more than Lenin himself if he could see what had come out of his office in the Kremlin in the hard days of 1921!"

"Wanted, Pioneers for Siberia!" was the heading of an article by Mike Gold in the *Liberator* calling for recruits for the great adventure. He quoted Calvert on the reasons the Kuzbas colony was so important to the Soviet Union:

Russian industry, based upon one-sixth of the land mass of the globe, and necessary to the life of 130 million human beings, was slowly sinking even below the primitive level of the Tsars' medieval regime.

The industrial workmen started production under revolutionary control, but the demands of the Revolution called them from the factories. Some went to the front in charge of the Red Army and died on the battlefields of the Revolution. Others, with the formation of the government of workers and peasants, became administrators. The less conscious workers returned to the villages to till their acreage of free land. These three movements from the factories continued—to the army, to the government and to the villages, until at last the factories had to close down for want of skilled proletarian labor. This labor, because of the backwardness of Russian industry, and the enormous losses of the Red Army, could not be replaced. Tens of thousands of class-conscious Russian workers died on the battlefields against Kerensky, Kolchak, Korniloff, Denikin, Wrangel and the rest. Today their machines are idle.

And what manner of man was this Calvert, who saw these things happening and put his whole being into finding a way to help? Barker described him:

Calvert is a new kind of intellectual. He speaks of castings, coal seams, iron ore, chemical plants, stone quarries, concrete shafts, acid reservoirs, large scale farming, saw mills and jack hammers with the same sacred, loving enthusiasm with which poets discuss the great sonnets and lyrics, and believers the miracles of their saints. Calvert has a creative imagination about these things. He fired others with his vision. He sees the race of man with these mighty tools in his hands, throwing itself like a disciplined, singing army upon the earth and conquering her at last, building at last the free society of peace and plenty and brotherhood and creation in the midst of the primeval, unmoral Chaos. He is a poet of power, of real things, of forces and control.

Much of the story of the subsequent operation of the Kuzbas colony appeared in *New World Review* in the Fall of 1971 (Vol. 39, No. 4), in a groups of articles by Nemmy Sparks, Ruth Epperson Kennell and Anna Preikshas. We shall not therefore retell their stories here.

Nemmy Sparks (who died in 1973) pulled no punches in telling some of the problems the colony faced. Many of the thousands who applied in New York had to be weeded out and altogether only about one thousand went, some taking their families. Among these, according to Sparks, were many first class miners, construction workers and mechanics, who made important contributions with their skills, but there were also too many nondescripts seeking Utopia.

Arrived at Kemerovo the colonists found the work had been hampered by the fact that under the Tsar the concession for the mines and coke plant had been granted a Franco-Belgian corporation. After the Revolution most of the foreign engineers departed, taking the plans with them. During the civil war the local government, between Red, and White, and successive engineers, had made new plans and alterations. An intensive search turned up duplicates and work got under way. Lenin's illness during this period, however, left many problems unsolved, and a number of Tsarist specialists still around tried to sabotage the whole operation. Some of the Americans caused trouble by their chauvinistic attitude that they had come to bring the blessings of an advanced culture to a backward native population. But there were some whose quiet, efficient and unassuming methods helped bring about cooperation all around. Among them was Anton Struik from Holland, brother of the distinguished mathematician and sometime contributor to *New World Review,* Dr. Dirk Struik.

Despite all problems, the project was a great success, pacing the magnificent achievements of the Soviet Union as a whole.

Sparks and Harry Kweit had been put in charge of the chemical plant operations. Amid many dramatic crises (no such by-product coke plant had ever before been set up in such a severe climate in the dead of winter) the plant went into operation in February 1924. There was greater progress than expected in getting the mines into operation and preparing to get the steel mill underway. The Soviet economy had been recovering at a rate beyond expectations. The Soviet Government had so far been able to appropriate two million gold rubles for the Kuzbas enterprise instead of the 600,000 Lenin had been prepared to risk in the beginning.

The American colonists had passed on their skills to the local peasants and workers. New Russian forces had been arriving and it was clear the Americans could easily be replaced. The plans for the specifically American contribution in skilled workers, engineers, etc. had, indeed, been only partially fulfilled. "But the plan itself," wrote Sparks, "had called forth similar latent abilities among individual Russian workers, or brought into the locality Russians with outstanding ability. . . . We returned to New York with $60 between us, but with the priceless experience of having participated and worked in the early stages of a revolutionary society." Back home, Nemmy Sparks held many leading posts in the Communist Party USA, until his death.

Ruth Epperson Kennell* had arrived at Kemerovo with her husband at Kuzbas in August 1922. She became secretary and librarian, doing the typing, handling mail and correspondence for all departments. In one of her numerous articles about the stirring experience of helping to build the new socialist society, she told abut receiving the May 21, 1970 issue of the Kemerovo paper *Kuzbas*. It carried a full page of photographs of the American colony members, and described their work:

A shining example of proletarian solidarity was manifested in the creation, under Ilyich's initiative of the Autonomous Industrial Colony of Kuzbas. The people of our country recollect with warm feelings the foreign workers who came in that difficult time to help our native land.

Anna Preikshas was twelve years old when she arrived at Kuzbas with her parents and brothers. Her father was a miner from West Virginia. After the colony was dissolved the family continued to work in Kemerovo. Having moved to the Ukraine, Anna still keeps in touch with Kemerovo. Her article dealt with the amazing growth of all its industries and social institutions, and she still corresponds with American friends about it.

A beautiful photo album "Kuzbas," published recently in the USSR, depicts the region today. Text and photos make one gasp with astonishment after reading the experiences of the early pioneers, who would scarcely recognize the place where they worked in 1922. The name Kuzbas is applied not only to the coal basin itself but to the whole surrounding region covering 95,000 square kilometers. Following the reconstruction period, its legendary upbuilding began with this first five-year plan in 1929.

In addition to the flourishing main city of Kemerovo, over 40 new industrial towns have sprung up. The not yet uprooted trees of the Siberian taiga grace all the towns and their surroundings. All around are lovely vistas of both heavily

*Mrs. Kennell, who died in February 1977, was the author of *Theodore Dreiser and the Soviet Union* and a number of children's books.

wooded and flat meadowlands rising into the gently sloping Ural Mountains. The River Tom and its tributaries add beauty, opportunities for fishing and sport. Three million people are digging into fabulous wealth of coal and iron. Every industry from metallurgy to children's toys can be found here. Over a billion rubles worth of goods supplies the needs of the region and the rest of the country and is exported abroad each year. Kemerovo is full of trees and parks, wide asphalted boulevards with masses of flowers of every variety in wide swathes down the center. Large trees from the primeval forests were spared the crashing bulldozers in order to beautify the city, and new ones were planted where none grew before. Here is "Mayakovsky Place," here "The House where Dostoyevsky lived."

A hundred thousand boys and girls attend educational institutions of all kinds from day nurseries to scientific institutes. There are dozens of new workers' apartment houses, museums, theaters, movies, libraries, hospitals, youth cafes, restaurants, stores of all kinds.

Set in little parks of their own are impressive buildings with legends over the doorways: "Miners' House of Culture," "Metallurgists' House of Culture," "Aluminum Workers' House of Culture," and others. All these have numerous facilities for the workers in amateur circles, under the supervision of trained teachers, in drama, dance, music, painting, sculpture, nature study, photography, various sciences. They have their own auditoriums, their own ballrooms, gymnasiums and sport grounds. For sport and leisure too the lovely River Tom runs through the town with shores beautifully laid out for walks, for sun-bathing and swimming, yacht clubs for the workers. There are sport grounds and soccer fields outside the town, too, for local use or regional competitions. And further beyond great forest areas still stand for wandering, picnicking, hunting and mushroom picking—beloved sport of all Soviet people. And in the flatlands numerous state and collective farms are providing food for the people and building their own new life.

The streets of Kemerovo are adorned with statues and monuments. A monument "Glory to the Miners' Labor," another to the Heroes of the Civil War, an obelisk to the dead of the Great Patriotic War (as World War II is called in the USSR). Statues to their beloved pioneers—and among them, there is a statue to Rutgers on a street called Rutgers. The leader of the Kuzbas colony is honored to this day along with Calvert and the others who gave part of their lives to a great pioneering project which has become a leading center in the new socialist life of the USSR today.

No country has ever faced such obstacles in establishing a new state, a new form of society. With armies hurled against them from East, West, North and South, the people prevailed against the ruinous world war, against armies and famine, blockade, refusal of normal relations and trade. The Soviet Union played a major part in the victory against Hitlerism and after two world wars, rebuilt their country twice over, with little help from the outside and created a mature socialist society with an ever ascending quality of life for its people. It is the greatest force for peace in the world today.

This article has dealt mainly with the role of the American people during the early years of the Revolution, before the beginning of the first five-year plan in 1929.

But let us heed again the lesson of those early years for today. The mass pressure of the American people, especially the workers, was an important factor in preventing our government from destroying the young socialist state. Today the anti-Soviet campaign is again in full swing, threatening the peace of the world. The overwhelming majority of the people want normal relations with the Soviet Union, the key to peace. Mass pressure of the people on the administration today for friendly instead of hostile US-USSR relations, for a SALT agreement, for an end of the arms race, for abolition of nuclear weapons, for disarmament, can save the world from destruction.   □

9

IGOR VITUKHIN

Soviet Power: The First Decade

R ussia's proletariat began to build a new life in a precarious situation. The socialist revolution had been accomplished, but its gains still had to be consolidated. Devastated and exhausted by the four years of war, Russia was exerting its last strength to suppress the resistance of the overthrown classes supported from outside. The Russian counterrevolution was knocking at the doors of the Allied embassies more and more insistently, clamoring for help.

But Lenin and the Bolshevik Party were confident: history could not be reversed, and the victory of the revolution was final. The revolution was spreading to Russia's towns and villages and out-of-the-way provinces. The nation craved peace.

On assuming power the Bolsheviks immediately proposed to the warring peoples to put an end to the world war They did not mean ceasing hostilities unilaterally and letting troops "stick their bayonets into the ground" and go home. The Soviet government's Decree on Peace called on the belligerent nations to conclude a universal and democratic peace.

The Entente and the United States, however, were in accord in opposing the Soviet peace policy and branding it as a "German intrigue." On November 20, 1917, heeding the will of its people, the Soviet government entered into the peace talks with Germany on its own. Simultaneously it published the tsarist government's secret agreements with the Allies, which plainly indicated that both sides participating in the war harbored aggressive intentions. That was a severe blow to the prestige of President Wilson, who had justified US involvement in the war by claiming it was in pursuit of noble ends.

The prospect of Russia's withdrawal from the war was extremely disturbing to the Allies. Although drained of blood, the Russian army was still engaging one-third of the German and Austro-Hungarian troops at the eastern front, who would immediately be moved to the western front in the event of an armistice. But what the Allies dreaded even more was that peace would strengthen the Soviet Republic; their opposition to the Soviet peace policy was actually an attempt to crush Soviet power.

IGOR VITUKHIN holds the degree of Candidate of Science in History.

The United States went as far as threatening to cut short its deliveries of food and ammunition to Russia should the Bolsheviks insist on a peace with Germany. Soon that threat was taken up by all the participants in the anti-peace campaign.

German imperialists regarded the Soviet peace policy as no less dangerous, fearing the impact of the Russian Revolution on Germany and its army. At one moment they even planned to attack revolutionary Russia, but gave up since Germany was too weak to fight on two fronts. They chose another way to fight the Bolsheviks: Germany would sign a peace with them, smash the United States, Britain and France in the West, and in the meantime, set the stage for the overthrow of Soviet government in the East. That was why they accepted the Russian proposal for peace talks with such amazing haste: the armistice was signed by December 2. 1917.

The cease-fire was not yet peace, but Russia was closer to it than ever before. While the Provisional Government had been cheating the people with vague promises of peace all the eight months it had been in power, it took the Bolsheviks only a little more than one month to put a stop to hostilities. After the armistice had been signed, the Bolsheviks continued urging the belligerents to accede to the peace talks, but the Entente and the United States ignored Soviet Russia's peace initiatives. Thus it was still alone at the talks in the enemy-occupied Brest-Litovsk.

Soon after the opening of the negotiations it became plain that the German Alliance was determined to force exceedingly hard peace terms on Soviet Russia. It wanted to keep Poland, Lithuania, a part of Latvia and Byelorussia, which it had occupied, and demanded the separation of the Ukraine. In the event the Soviet Government declined those terms it threatened to resume hostilities.

Continuation of the war was fraught with the danger of the fall of Petrograd and the defeat of the Revolution. Exhausted, the old army was not fit to fight and the Party had not yet formed a new army which would be capable of defending the gains of the Revolution. It needed time. The Bolsheviks were compelled to accept the peace terms.

Meanwhile Trotsky, who headed the Soviet delegation at the peace talks in Brest-Litovsk, acting unscrupulously, in defiance of Lenin's instructions, refused to sign the peace on German terms. At the same time he declared that the Soviet Republic was withdrawing from the war with the German Alliance and dissolving its army.

The German Government seized upon the opportunity that thus materialized and, violating the armistice, on Debruary 18 launched an offensive along the entire length of the front from the Baltic to the Black Sea. Lenin's message accepting the German terms, which had been sent immediately, remained unanswered for a long time.

The dispatches from the front reported on the spread of the German offensive. The remains of the old Russian army wavered and within a few days the enemy, encountering no serious resistance, had been able to occupy all of Latvia and Estonia, a considerable area of the Ukraine, and was rapidly approaching Petrograd.

Mortal danger hovered over the socialist republic. On the call of the Party, Red Army contingents, which had only just been formed, were being sent to the hottest sports at the front. The whole nation rose to fight the invaders. The repulse at Pskov and Narva stopped the German advance on Petrograd. Germany was now forced to quit the Eastern front and sign the peace, having grabbed a good hunk of Soviet territory.

On March 3, 1918, the Peace of Brest-Litovsk was signed on humiliating terms. However, it pulled, in Lenin's words, "the first hundred million" people on earth out of the imperialist war and gave Russia the respite it had so longed for.

Defending the idea of the Brest Treaty before his critics, Lenin said in particular that in 1776. "In their arduous war for freedom, the American people also entered into 'agreements' with some oppressors against others for the purpose of weakening the oppressors and strengthening those who were fighting in a revolutionary manner against oppression."

As a matter of fact, just as Lenin had expected, the Brest Peace was short-lived—just a little over eight months. The revolution, which had broken out in Germany itself in November 1918, made an end of Kaiser Germany, and its defeat in the world war enabled the Soviet Republic to wrench itself free of the burdensome Brest Peace, and annul all its clauses.

Short as the Brest respite was, it did help the Party to set up the Red Army, complete the nationalization of the key sectors of the economy, solve the problems of procurement of grain and foodstuffs, in short, to prepare the country for the hard and long-drawn-out struggle against the intervention which had not been long in coming, unleashed by the Entente and the United States. Foreign capital could not put up with the existence of a proletarian state in the world. Western monopolies were unwilling to lose their billions' worth of loans out of which they had been coaxed by the tsarist and provisional governments, or to part with the vast profits they were pumping out of Russia.

When the prospect of Germany strangling the young Soviet Republic for them had vanished, the Entente and the United States launched their own intervention against it. In the spring of 1918, the United States, Britain and France landed their troops in Murmansk in the north of Russia. Somewhat later Japan and Britain moved their armies into the Soviet Far East and further on, Siberia. On June 29, they were joined by 9,000 US marines under the command of General William S. Graves in Vladivostok.

Murmansk and Vladivostok became the outposts of the intervention for good reason. Ever since the world war, an Allied squadron had been under steam in the waters of the Murmansk port. Murmansk, with its concentration of ammunition and material that was originally to be shipped to the tsarist army, was a great arsenal, which made it easy for the Entente to turn the city into a strong base in the struggle against Soviet power.

US Ambassador David R. Francis, followed by ambassadors of other powers, moved from Petrograd closer to Murmansk—first to Vologda and then to Arkhangelsk—to be in the vicinity of the areas to be occupied. They settled there in spite of the Soviet government's suggestion for them to move to Moscow where the national capital had been transferred. From Vologda and Arkhangelsk the ambassadors contacted enemies of Soviet power, encouraging and supporting them and giving them the money they needed.

As for Vladivostok, it was a place where the interventionists' financial interests were represented extensively. Economically, the region was largely dependent on the United States and Japan. Before the revolution American goods had made up 23 per cent of all the imports brought in through Vladivostok. In 1917, there were over 50 branches of trading firms and companies there, for the most part American or Japanese. The American industrialist Herbert Hoover had appropriated tremendous ore deposits in Eastern Siberia; the British owned practically all of Siberia's gold output; American companies had extended their feelers as far as the Kuznetsk coal basin with its vast reserves of coking coals. Surely *The New York Times* was rather hypocritical when it wrote in its issue of June 13, 1918, that "it is the duty of the Allies to intervene and save Russia from herself." Fearing the ultimate victory and consolidation of Soviet power, the interventionists were saving not Russia, but the profits of their bosses, the stock exchanges of New York, London and Paris.

At the end of May 1918, the Entente and the United States provoked the 60,000-strong Czechoslovak Corps stationed in Russia to move against the Soviets. The rebellious Czechs and Slovaks were joined by the White Guards formed by Russian officers and the Cossack top brass. The move of the rebel corps encouraged internal counterrevolutionaries. The overthrown classes had unleashed a civil war. Kulaks rose in Siberia, the Urals and the Volga Region. Intervention ships entered the White Sea. Arkhangelsk fell. Japanese and American troops helped White Guards to capture the whole of Russia's Far Eastern regions. They took part in putting down popular resistance, persecuted and murdered civilians, robbed the country, and carted away timber, furs and gold. Germany had violated the Brest Peace Treaty and seized the southern parts of Russia and Georgia. The British had invaded Turkestan and the Transcaucasus. The seizure of Baku completed the enemy encirclement of the Soviet Republic, which now found itself cut off from the major food and raw material reserves: the oil of Baku, the coal of the Donets Basin and the grain of the Ukraine and the Don. Many plants and factories were idle. The cities had no electricity. The population was starving. Bread rations had been cut to an eighth of a pound a day. Riots were brewing throughout the country, acts of subversion and plots were in the making.

Summoned by the Party, Russia's workers and peasants rose to defend Soviet power. The Red Army was becoming battle-hardened. The pooling of efforts of all the peoples of Russia had built up its strength, but the grip of the economic blockade and diplomatic isolation was growing tighter and tighter. The counter-revolution picked that moment for its heinous stab in the back of the Party and people: the Socialist Revolutionary Fania Kaplan made an attempt on Lenin's life, gravely wounding him with two poisoned bullets.

The news of the attempt aroused a wave of wrath which swept the country, rallied the armed forces and brought the people even closer together. Workers and peasants increased their aid to the Red Army which was able to assume the offensive and rout the joint Czechoslovak and White Guard force at the eastern front. Heavy fighting broke out along the Volga and in the central regions of the country. To retaliate against counterrevolutionary terror the Soviet government launched the Red Terror.

While repulsing the attacks of home and foreign enemies by force of arms, the Soviet government did not give up its attempts to terminate the war by diplomatic means, proposing to the Entente and the United States to hold peace talks. But silence was all it received for an answer.

After the end of the civil war the peoples of Soviet Russia were faced with enormous problems. It was essential to make good the losses incurred during the struggle against the foreign intervention and domestic counter-revolutionaries as soon as possible. The damage which had been inflicted was estimated at more than 50 billion gold rubles. The country lay in ruins and industrial production had slumped to a critical level. Moreover, the country had been afflicted with a terrible famine caused by two successive periods of drought. Crops failed throughout a vast territory with a population of 30 million. Driven by hunger, many workers fled to the villages. The working class was becoming dispersed.

War Communism, an emergency economic policy wholly subject to the interests of national defense, was no longer fit for the new conditions of peacetime. The political and military alliance of the working class and peasantry rested on a weak economic basis. The peasantry were dissatisfied with the State confiscating all surplus (and sometimes more than that) of food and fodder which they could sell in the open market.

The 10th Party Congress, held in March 1921, announced the adoption of a

New Economic Policy (NEP). The taxation of peasants was now fixed and assessed in kind, and peasants were free to sell the surplus. That measure provided an incentive to expand the sown area and raise production; this spurred a rapid development of agriculture throughout the country, which the Party considered to be of prime importance. The development of agriculture would make it possible to boost industry, particularly heavy industry, and lay a basis for the transfer of agriculture onto industrial lines.

The NEP meant the development of free trade and the opening of small private shops, and allowed for a certain revival of capitalism. The socialist system was not threatened, however, since the State continued to own the land, industry, banks and transport, and to control foreign trade.

The conclusions reached by the 10th Congress proved correct. Already by the spring of 1921, in some regions peasants began to increase the sown area. The position of workers had also improved and many were returning to their plants and factories, which were rising from the ruins. The nation was pulling through the economic dislocation. The Donets Basin was being restored. The restored oilfields of Baku and Grozny were beginning to supply fuel to industry.

The international working class was giving fraternal help to the Soviet people. Although the US rulers were still opposed to the economic revival of Soviet Russia and establishment of business contacts with her, ordinary Americans—workers, farmers and engineers—were volunteering to go to Russia to work. In reply to the American agronomist Harold Ware's question—"will we send food or tractors to Russia?"—farmers organized the shipping of a train of Fordson tractors to peasants in the Urals. Many Americans arrived with the train and, putting up with hardships and want, taught the peasants how to handle the machines, and introduced them to advanced methods of farming to increase their crops.

When Ware was going back to the States Lenin sent with him his reply to Charles Steinmetz. A prominent specialist in electrical engineering and a leading engineer of the General Electric World Company, Steinmetz had studied Lenin's plan for the electrification of Russia and had offered his help to the Soviet government. He was invited to Moscow and was preparing to leave when he died.

The selfless effort put in by the Soviet people under the leadership of the Party was bringing fruit: the work of rehabilitation of the national economy was nearing completion by 1924 Created in 1922 to unite the Russian Federation, the Ukraine, Byelorussia, Azerbaidzhan, Armenia and Georgia (the latter three then united in the Transcaucasian Republic), the Soviet Union was growing stronger. The hopes of the world bourgeoisie for the Soviet system to grow into capitalism under the impact of the NEP were dashed. The West was gradually expanding its economic relations with the Soviet Union. It was becoming clear that the policy of non-recognition of the USSR could not be counted on as a means of arresting the process of this country's consolidation and successful advance. Furthermore this policy was detrimental to capitalist countries themselves as it hampered the development of quite profitable economic ties with the Soviet Union.

Not everyone believed that Lenin's plan of social measures, later termed GOELRO, could be carried out. In 1920, when the plan was still on paper, the British writer H.G. Wells visited Russia. The famous author, who had conquered a vast readership by his incredible imagination, was not so imaginative this time. In his talk with Lenin he commented on the electrification project ironically, and called it a Utopia.

In the history of Soviet foreign policy 1924 stands out as a year of recognition of the USSR by other states: diplomatic relations were established by Britain, Austria, Norway, Greece, Sweden, Denmark, Mexico and France. The United States was the only great power in the 1920s which had stubbornly refused to grant the Soviet Union recognition. The US Government had repeatedly declined all Soviet proposals that could lead to establishing normal relations and settling disputed questions. A major overhauling of the Soviet socioeconomic system was the only price American rulers would accept for US recognition.

US business circles were of a different opinion and continued their attempts to establish commercial contacts between the two countries. In 1926, having visited the Soviet Union, a group of American businessmen headed by Edward Sherwood, sent a letter to President Coolidge urging him to waste no time in recognizing Russia.

Between 1924 and 1925, the Soviet Union had established diplomatic relations with 13 countries in different continents. It concluded trade agreements with them and granted them concessions, thereby increasing its foreign trade. Thus the policy of isolation of the Soviet Union had been ruptured. Still the West did not lift its economic blockade, denying it loans and forcing it to restore the national economy almost by its own means.

The second half of the 1920s was a period of especially turbulent political events and economic shifts in the Soviet Union. The restoration period had ended and the 14th Party Congress inaugurated its policy of transformation of old agrarian Russia into an industrial power. The quiet of yesterday's backwoods was disturbed by the tumult of huge construction sites. The face of the earth was changing, and changing with it were the people themselves. Exerting every effort, the nation was taking its first, but even then gigantic, steps along the road of socialist transformations, in an atmosphere of unprecedented mass labor enthusiasm and of difficult, and at times painful, breaking up of old ways and customs, conceptions and relationships.

The Bolshevik Party was translating its policy of industrialization into concrete reality on a grand scale, having put into motion masses of people who were leaving their out-of-the-way places to work on the construction of new projects — mines, power stations, etc. The world was stunned at the scope and pace of construction in the Soviet Union. Old plants and factories were being reconstructed and new ones built. By the end of 1927, industrial production had topped the prewar level. Heavy industry was developing at a particularly high rate, much higher than that in the leading capitalist countries. The share of the socialist sector in the economy was constantly increasing — industrialization was obviously socialist in nature. An increase of more than 11 per cent was registered in the national income in 1927, whereas it was not more than two to four per cent in the United States, Britain and other industrial powers. The Soviet Union was rapidly advancing to socialism.

Agriculture, the largest and vital sector of the economy, which was lagging behind, was the source of the Party's concern. There was not enough grain — the demand for it was steadily rising with the growth of the working class and the urban population. The small, scattered peasant husbandry had practically exhausted its potential, turning out the barest minimum of produce, and especially of grain. Another crop failure in the south of the Ukraine and in the Northern Caucasus, the principal grain-growing areas, made matters even worse. The kulaks, who possessed enormous stocks of grain, would not sell it to the State at fixed prices.

In December 1927, the 15th Party Congress discussed the grain problem and passed a resolution on an immediate collectivization of agriculture and the transfer of farming onto a socialist basis. That was the only way of supplying the nation with the foodstuffs it needed, of delivering millions of toiling peasants from kulak bondage, poverty and ignorance.

At the same time the Congress arrived at the conclusion that it was high time the kulaks should be driven out of the national economy even though they produced a fifth of the marketable grain. Supported by the masses, the Party and the Soviet Government defeated the kulak resistance.

Another major event at the 15th Congress, an event of great importance for the future, was the adoption of the directives on the first five-year economic development plan. Lenin's words in one of his last articles were coming true: "we now have an opportunity . . . of ascertaining the period necessary for bringing about radical social changes; we now see clearly *what can be done in five years, and what requires much more time.*"

Thus passed the first decade in the life of the world's first state of workers and peasants. The difficulties were gradually falling behind and the wounds inflicted by the civil war and intervention were healing. The Soviet people were winning their right to a new, worthy life through the utmost exertion of their strength and will, confident of the justice of the ideas proclaimed by Lenin's Party in the days of the October Revolution.   □

10

GERALD C. HORNE

US-Soviet Relations: A View from History

Contrary to many interpreters, the socialist revolution in Russia was not at odds with Marxist theory—or with the views of Marx and Engels themselves for that matter. The correspondence of these two giants is filled with references to their belief that Russia could become the first nation to achieve a revolution. For example, on September 1, 1870, Marx wrote to F.A. Sorge, a US Marxist, of the "inevitable social revolution in Russia," and again, on September 27, 1877 he wrote to him: "This time the revolution will begin in the East, hitherto the unbroken and reserve army of counter-revolution."

The first legislative act of the Soviet government was the famous Decree on Peace. Issued on November 8, 1917, this proclamation called for immediate world peace, on terms "equally just for all peoples," without seizure of territory or oppression of any nation; a peace in V.I. Lenin's words, "in accordance with the sense of justice of democracy in general and of the toiling classes in particular."

Characteristically, the response of the powers of the capitalist world to these lofty phrases was to launch a 14-nation invasion from all sides; the purpose being, in Churchill's now ignominious phrase "to strangle the baby in its cradle." Unfortunately, the US government played a pivotal role in this foul scheme. Two contingents of US troops landed at Vladivostok in August 1918. A month later two thousand more soldiers arrived under the command of General William S. Graves. By late 1918, the US had 7,000 soldiers in Russia in a vain attempt to stifle socialism. With such bountiful assistance, anti-Bolshevik forces were able to set up at least eight counterrevolutionary governments throughout Russia. Large supplies of war material were sent to

GERALD C. HORNE is a lawyer now working toward a Ph.D. in US history at Columbia University. He formerly represented the National Conference of Black Lawyers at the United Nations, and is active in the National Anti-Imperialist Movement in Solidarity with African Liberation. His current research concerns Dr. W.E.B. DuBois and international affairs.

Admiral Alexander Kolchak; many private banks in the US helped to finance these ventures; the US government allowed the payment of $1.239 million accredited to the Kerensky government for printing currency to be used by Admiral Kolchak's "White Russian" reactionary forces. Presiding over this mockery of international law was Woodrow Wilson, the pious racist who had accelerated the segregation of the nation's capital, who had approved heartily the inflammatory film "Birth of a Nation," and who had penned his deceptive "14 Points" in direct response to the world-wide appeal of Bolshevism.

But this Canute-like effort to roll back the socialist wave was destined for failure. Protest in the capitalist world and especially the US was instantaneous and widespread. The Land of Lenin was hardly without friends in the West. The liberal *New Republic* hailed the Bolshevik Revolution. The Industrial Workers of the World, under increasing attack because of their militant labor stance, nonetheless stood shoulder to shoulder with the young republic. The American Federation of Labor, the largest national labor organization in the US, initially applauded the revolution and the new-found "freedom in Russia." Eugene Debs, the old socialist so popular that he could receive close to a million votes while running for president from a prison cell, declared: "from the crown of my head to the soles of my feet I am a Bolshevik and proud of it."

Progressive forces in the US had a tough row to hoe in acclaiming solidarity with the Soviets. The investment of US financial circles in Baku oil, Urals timber and minerals in Siberia was huge. Herbert Hoover, subsequently US president, had interests in no less than eleven Russian oil companies. In conjunction with British multimillionaire Leslie Urquhart he controlled 2,500,000 acres of land, including vast timberlands and waterpower; estimated gold, copper, silver and zinc reserves of 7,262,000 tons; 12 developed mines, 2 copper smelters, 20 sawmills, 250 miles of railroad, blast furnaces, rolling mills, sulphuric acid plants, gold refineries, and huge coals reserves. The total value of these properties was estimated at $1 billion. After the Revolution these concessions were abrogated and properties confiscated by the Soviet government. Little wonder that Hoover was later to say, "Bolshevism is worse than war." He remained an unflinching foe of diplomatic recognition and cooperation with Moscow.

Thus, in calling for "Hands off Russia," progressives in the US were indeed sailing into a bitter wind. The now infamous Palmer Raids, which anticipated the Gestapo in midnight raids, mass arrests and deportations without due process, were the answer of the ruling class to this campaign of solidarity.

Yet the campaign against US intervention continued and gathered steam. Senators like Hiram Johnson, William Borah and Robert LaFollette (later to lead in 1924 one of the more successful third party efforts in US history) all spoke out. The central trade union bodies of Portland, Cleveland and Akron demanded a withdrawal of US troops along with granting of diplomatic recognition. The General Strike in Seattle was a direct response to the intervention. This firestorm of protest at home coupled with the withering defeats inflicted on the battlefield by the Red Army finally caused Washington and Wall Street to come to their collective senses and US troops sailed home. The venture was costly. The Archangel expedition alone cost US taxpayers more than $3 million, not to mention 240 killed and 305 wounded.

With the withdrawal of US troops—a signal victory—as so often happens the battle had not ended but had just shifted to a new front. For still outstanding were the matters of the blockade of Soviet Russia and normalization of diplomatic relations by the US followed by trade relations. Once again the US working class stormed to the front on these issues. Early on the Pennsylvania Federation of Labor, the major labor body of the state, called for lifting the blockade. At the 14th convention of the International Ladies Garment Workers Union (ILGWU) in May 1918 resolutions opposing the intervention and blockade were passed with substantial majorities. The ILGWU's sister union, the Amalgamated Clothing Workers, followed suit and then went a step further. Sidney Hillman, a leader of the ACW, visited Soviet Russia in 1921 and heartily praised the effort to construct socialism. Hillman, later a leader of the Congress of Industrial Organizations (CIO) and adviser to Franklin D. Roosevelt, helped to found the Russian-American Industrial Corporation, which assisted in developing the clothing industry in Russia. The American Labor Alliance for Recognition and Trade was able to get the first resolution for the establishment of US-USSR Relations introduced in the Senate, through Senator Joseph France of Maryland. Other unions which came out for recognition were the United Mine Workers of America, Painters, Locomotive Engineers, Machinists, and Stationary Firemen.

Not surprisingly, US Blacks played a crucial role in beating back the anti-Bolshevik campaign. Dr. W.E.B. DuBois, a founder of the National Association for the Advancement of Colored People (NAACP), remained a friend of the Soviet Union until his death in 1963 at the age of 95. In the May 1919 issue of *The Crisis,* organ of the NAACP, he termed the Bolshevik Revolution "the one new idea of the World War—the idea which may well stand in future years as the one thing that made the slaughter worthwhile." DuBois added that unfortunately some might obtain a distorted vision of the new socialist state because of "the maledictions hurled at Bolshevism" by the ruling class and its minions of the mass media.

Afro-Americans, subjected to Jim Crow and lynch-law at home, were naturally attracted to the Bolshevik Revolution because of its systematic efforts to end national oppression against non-Russian national minorities—the Uzbeks, Georgians, Tatars, etc. W.A. Domingo, radical and long-time leader of the Caribbean community in New York, continually emphasized this point. He noted especially the hypocrisy of the ruling class which shed buckets of crocodile tears about alleged deprivation of human rights and civil liberties in Soviet Russia while not lifting a finger against the brutal machinations of the Bilbos, the Hoke Smiths and the Cole Bleases right here at home. As Domingo succinctly put it:

> In Russia the franchise, the right to vote, is based upon work, upon the performance of useful service. . . . If approval of the right to vote, based upon service instead of race or color is Bolshevism, count us as Bolshevists. . . . If the demand for political and social equality is Bolshevism, label us once more with that little barrack behind which your mental impotency hides when it cannot answer argument.

So worried were Wall Street and Washington about Black attraction to Bolshevism, that one investigative committee after another analyzed this issue. The New York State Legislature, which earlier had unceremoniously and illegally expelled its only Socialist members, authorized the so-called Lusk Committee to explore the matter of Blacks and Bolshevism, among other ''seditious'' activities. After a hefty expenditure of taxpayers' dollars, they arrived at the none too surprising conclusion that: ''The very fact that the Negro has many just causes of complaint adds to the seriousness of (radical) propaganda.'' They added auspiciously: ''The Communist Party will carry on agitation among the Negro to unite them [sic] with all class conscious workers.''

Progressives in the Black community recognized that the very existence of Soviet Russia would not only lead to a situation where concessions could be more easily wrung from the ruling class but also that liberation of Africa from colonial domination would finally emerge on the historical agenda. This was stated repeatedly in *The Messenger*, a radical Black publication put out by Chandler Owen and A. Philip Randolph, subsequently head of the Brotherhood of Sleeping Car Porters and leader of the March on Washington Movement.

Meanwhile, the State Department and Administration remained adamant about lifting trade restrictions and granting diplomatic recognition. Secretary of State Charles Evans Hughes sanctimoniously demanded in March 1923 that before the Soviet Government could be recognized it had to abrogate the decree annulling foreign loans, compensate US citizens for property nationalized and cease the ''destructive propaganda of Soviet Power.'' Subsequently, it was stated that recognition would not be granted because Soviet Russia was not a government but merely a bunch of revolutionists and that ''communism'' was unworkable and recognition would encourage it to pursue its folly. In any event, the State Department has rarely won awards for historical prescience.

Recognition was not a mere diplomatic courtesy or academic issue but fraught with material consequences. Lack of recognition allowed the so-called

"White Russian" counterrevolutionaries to bring suit in US courts in the name of the Russian Government and collect damages. For example, in 1927 this motley group received $984,104.62 from the Lehigh Valley Railway Company for an explosion occurring in 1916. That this was merely another method to fund reactionary efforts need not be elaborated upon. By contrast, the Soviet Government could not bring suit in US courts for recovery of, say, unfulfilled contracts but they could be sued by others in US courts!

Thus lack of recognition plus trade restrictions placed barriers in the path of normal US-Soviet relations and especially hindered commercial relations. In 1912 US exports to Russia amounted to $27,315,137, while imports totaled $28,346,870. During the war year of 1916, US exports totalled a phenomenal $470,508,254 to Russia while imports amounted to $8,618,695. But by 1923 exports had plummeted to $10,066,726 and imports constituted a paltry $1,515,779. And it should be added that the export total for 1923 includes famine relief supplies.

The Soviet Government consistently attempted to reverse this abnormal situation. L.C.A.K. Martens, the Soviets' official representative in the US, on March 18, 1919 sent a memo to the State Department stating, "the Soviet Government wishes to take up trade relations with other countries and the USA especially." He was pointedly ignored. Although at least 941 firms in 32 states expressed willingness to enter into trade relations with Soviet Russia, reactionaries blocked the way.

Once more the strength of organized labor, this time combined with realistic elements in the business community, prevailed. Martens was subjected to continued persecution by the Justice Department and finally was forced to leave the US, but not before tens of thousands of workers bade him farewell from New York harbor. This spurred the efforts of the American Labor Alliance for Trade Relations with Russia, organized in November 1920 by New York labor and representing 800,000 workers. Alexander Trachtenberg of the ILGWU was secretary. Their efforts were endorsed by twelve international and national unions, scores of state federations and central labor unions of 72 cities in 29 states, representing a membership of 2.5 million workers (the American Federation of Labor at the time represented four million members). James Walker, president of the Illinois State Federation of Labor, endorsed trade relations with the Soviets as did the International Association of Machinists. The Schenectady Trades Assembly (home of the massive General Electric plant), representing 20,000 workers, called for trade. The Central Labor Union of industrial Hartford backed trade relations. Even the union of American Federation of Labor chief Samuel Gompers, the Cigar Makers, joined the campaign for trade. Clearly US workers recognized that trade with the first land of socialism translated into jobs.

Certain businesses also came to recognize the mutual advantage of US-

Soviet commercial relations. As early as January 1920 the American Commercial Association to Promote Russian Trade was organized. The very next month Senator Joseph France of Maryland introduced a resolution looking toward the re-opening of trade. Senator Henry Cabot Lodge, chairman of the Foreign Relations Committee attempted to bury it. Finally on July 7, 1920 the State Department lifted certain trade restrictions, while other remained in place.

One barrier to normal trade relations was the claim put in by US firms for property formerly held. US investment in pre-Soviet Russia was not especially huge, 117,750,000 rubles ($58.875 million) or 5.2 per cent of total foreign investment. The problem was that these investments weren't scattered but held by ten concerns, including such giants as International Harvester, Otis Elevator, Singer, Babcock Wilcox, NY Life Insurance, Equitable Life and National City Bank. The other problem was that total US claims including investments and debts privately held, bonds, etc. amounted to a hefty $658 million. But the Soviets counter-claimed for damages caused by the intervention. These financial matters were to remain a bone in the throat of US-Soviet relations; this problem was solved eventually but not without immense difficulty.

However, such outstanding issues did not prevent commercial intercourse altogether. As early as November 1919 E.P. Jennings, president of Lehigh Machine Company of Pennsylvania, one of the largest machine shops in the US, came out for trade relations. One of the largest financial deals completed was with W.A. Harriman and Co. of New York, which was able to obtain a concession in the Chiatouri manganese mines of Georgia; these mines supplied 50 per cent of the total world output of manganese before the war. By the terms of the contract signed June 12, 1925, the company secured the exclusive right to prospect and work the Chiatouri deposits for twenty years. The concession district contained 12,492 acres believed to hold 80,000,000 tons of ore valued at $1.6 billion. Armand Hammer was able to secure a contract for the manufacture of pencils, pens and similar articles. As is well known, Harriman and Hammer, now head of Occidental Petroleum Corp., have been in the forefront of US ruling circles who have adopted a more realistic policy toward the socialist camp; this illustrates the value of trade as a bridge to peaceful relations.

Subsequently, the American Russian Chamber of Commerce was reorganized in June 1926 after years of inactivity with Reeve Schley, vice-president of Chase National Bank as president. Thus a statement of the major Soviet foreign trade concern, the Amtorg Trading Corporation, based on the data of September 1, 1927, indicated that the US was second only to Germany in the number of concession agreements signed with Soviet authorities.

As a consequence, there was an obvious powerful tide pushing for normal relations; but it would be a gross oversimplification to present only this side of the picture. Certain news organs resorted to every threadbare slander, shopworn distortion and retreaded lie in order to forestall diplomatic recognition. Such activities forced Senator Robert LaFollette of Wisconsin to declare: "Whatever comes to the American people through the censored channels of the press regarding the Soviet Government ought to be subjected to pretty careful scrutiny before it is accepted as stating the whole truth. The great organized wealth of all the established governments of the world at this time fears above all things on earth the principles attempted to be established by the Soviet Government of Russia." Helen Keller, militant suffragist and foe of imperialism, addes: "But have not our people been deliberately supplied with falsifications appealing to their fears and their prejudices to make them hostile to Russia and its present government." Sherwood Eddy of the International Committee of the Young Men's Christian Association (YMCA) after a visit to Russia in the summer of 1926 felt that the Soviet Union was "a challenge to the rest of the world, to nations ruled by swollen, selfish capitalism" and that its government should be recognized by the US."

Little wonder that progressives complained about media coverage of socialism. A few headlines from the New York Tribune on Soviet affairs gives an inkling of what LaFollette, Keller and others were talking about:

SOVIETS FIGHT FAMINE AS GRAIN MYTH EXPLODES (October 26, 1925)
CLAIM STARVING POOR THREATEN DOOM OF SOVIET (June 15, 1925)
RUSSIANS FREE! TO ROB, STARVE, MURDER AND DIE (November 15, 1925)
SIBERIA TRIES TO SHAKE OFF MOSCOW'S YOKE (November 26, 1925)
RUSSIA UNLOADS JEWELS TO SAVE SOVIET REGIME (February 10, 1926)
SECRET REPORT SHOW RUSSIA NEAR COLLAPSE (March 20, 1926
UNCOVER SECRET TERRORIST PLOT TO SEIZE RUSSIA (July 30, 1926)
RUMANIA HEARS OF WIDESPREAD RUSSIAN REVOLT (August 7, 1926)
SOVIET PARTY IN CHAOS AS TRADE, INDUSTRY TOTTER (August 4, 1926)
ODESSA TROOPS MUTINY AGAINST MOSCOW REGIME (August 9, 1926)
RUSSIA FERMENTS AS RED FACTIONS GRASP FOR POWER (August 10, 1926)
REDS REINFORCE KREMLIN FORT AS MUTINY GROWS (August 13, 1926)
ECONOMY REGIME IN RUSSIA FAILS; CRISIS IMPENDS (August 21, 1926)
REPORTS REVOLT AGAINST SOVIET BEGINS IN RUSSIA (April 9, 1927)
RED ARMY FIGHTS WITH SOUTH RUSSIANS (April 19, 1927)
RUSSIA CALLS SOLDIERS HOME AS REVOLT RISES (April 21, 1927)
FAMINE STRIKES RUSSIA; POLAND FEARS INVASION (July 27, 1927)
MOSCOW TRAPS CASH OF FOREIGN BUSINESS FIRMS (October 16, 1927)
INDUSTRY FACES SWIFT DISASTER IN RED RUSSIA (October 23, 1927)
TROTSKY'S CLAN FIGHTS SOVIET POLICE; 18 DIE (November 23, 1927)
HUNDREDS DIE IN UKRAINE RIOTS, RUMANIA HEARS (November 26, 1927)

So much for claims for "objectivity" and "non-partisanship." The Hearst and Scripps-Howard newspaper chains to their everlasting shame were especially responsible for the nationwide distribution of such putrid effluvia. They were aided and abetted by the American Legion, the National Civic Federation (a big business outfit), fascist groups like the Silver Shirts, and reactionary clerics. Many are familiar with Father Charles Coughlin and his frequent anti-communist appeals; but he was only echoing the sentiments of his mentor Pope Pius, who acknowledged the "obvious advantages" of Italian fascism.

Nonetheless, those who set out to isolate the Soviet Union wound up being isolated themselves. February 1924 saw the British Government, pressed on all sides by labor militancy, grant *de jure* recognition to the Soviet Government. Italy followed on February 7; Norway on the 13th; Austria on the 20th. March saw Greece, Danzig and Sweden join the ranks. China, Denmark and Mexico followed shortly thereafter. France and Japan were not far behind. Consequently, it was merely a matter of time before the US bowed to the inevitable. D.F. Fleming, leading US historian of the Cold War, points to the Great Crash of 1929 and the world political situation as crucial factors in bringing on US recognition. The collapse of Wall Street led to exports falling from $5.2 billion in 1929 to $1.61 billion in 1932. One of every four employable men was out of work; a quarter of the people did not have adequate incomes to live on. In the Soviet Union, on the other hand, unemployment had been eliminated and industry was humming. The demand for goods was great. It is therefore hardly surprising that in 1932, during the election campaign, the next president of the US, Franklin D. Roosevelt, was studying a memorandum calling attention to Soviet markets. Senator Robert Wagner (Dem-NY) was to say later: "I would vote for recognition purely for trade relation purposes." Thus 16 years of sustained, mass people's campaigns culminated in diplomatic recognition of the Soviet Union on November 16, 1933.

Tensions were rising between the capitalist countries. US apprehension about a Japanese challenge to their hegemony in the Philippines and other parts of Asia was heightened by the Japanese seizure of Manchuria in 1931—an event deemed by many as the opening shot in World War II. At the same time definite groupings in the capitalist world were attempting to provoke Japan to attack the Soviet Union.

This brings to the fore a central point: it is impossible to understand international relations and US foreign policy in the period after 1917 without an understanding of the role of the Bolshevik Revolution. October 1917 marked the onset of capitalism's general crisis, its irreversible decline, and this was recognized subliminally by some, overtly by others. At the Versailles Peace Conference which had as its purpose the final resolution of World War I, the presence of the Soviets was felt although they were not invited. The centerpiece of Versailles, the attempt to create a League of Nations, was seen by Britain's Lloyd George as a direct "alternative to Bolshevism." Yet inter-imperialist contradictions and the desire by the US to have the League subjected to Washington's hegemony foiled these anti-Bolshevik plans. At the same time, France's desire for a dismembering of Germany crashed on the reefs of the US-Britain scheme for a strong Germany to serve as a bulwark against Bolshevism.

These anti-Soviet machinations were carried forward at the Nine-Power Conference in 1922, convened on US initiative, and designed to consolidate Washington's dominance in the Far East. Once again the Soviet Government was not admitted though the conference debated issues which directly affected her interests. Nevertheless, inter-imperialist contradictions prevented the capitalist countries from seeing eye to eye on anything—besides anti-communism—and this helped to thwart their immediate plans for an invasion and overthrow of the Soviet Government. Britain and France were at odds over the former's plan to build up a strong German state. Britain and the US were bitterly contending over the Middle East and oil. Japan was seething over US efforts to prevent her from exerting influence in Asia and thus refused to ratify the Versailles Treaty and the League of Nations covenant. France similarly abjured ratification. Italy felt she had been cheated of her share of the plunder. And progressives and working people in all of these countries were blocking the path of an anti-Soviet front.

Yet Washington kept trying to bring this imperialist dream to fruition. The Dawes Plan was an effort to lessen the crucial French-German antagonism via an international loan of 800 million marks to Germany, which was supposedly to help Germany pay reparations to France. Repaying of this loan was through taxes on consumers' goods, which put the ultimate burden on the backs of working people. The Plan offered many opportunities for an influx of foreign investment; and much of this capital went into the revived German arms industry, viewed as essential for the eventual confrontation with the Soviets. This tendency was observed further at the Locarno Conference of 1925, which declared Germany's western borders as inviolable while her eastern borders were not declared so. Why? Giving Germany maximum "freedom of action" in Eastern Europe was seen as the goal.

As can readily be seen, responsibility for the rise of the Nazis must be placed at the door of US and British imperialism; they undertook immediately after World War I to rebuild Germany's industrial and military potential. These Western powers did nothing to counter Germany's military occupation of the left bank of the Rhine, her introduction of compulsory military service and other acts in defiance of Versailles. Between 1924 and 1930 credits and loans to

Germany totaled an astronomical 21 billion marks. Indeed in 1935 the British government concluded a naval agreement with Germany giving an official sanction to revival of German sea power. The US was little better. The notorious I.G. Farben Co., which represented an amalgamation of 177 German corporations, which carried out poison gas experiments on inmates at Auschwitz, which employed 63,000 foreign slave laborers, also developed close ties with DuPont and was connected with Standard Oil, Ford and Mellon interests through interlocking directorates.

All the while, the Soviet Union and other peace forces were calling for the international equivalent of the united front—collective security to isolate the aggressors. Their appeals were repeatedly scorned in Washington. However, the role of the Soviets' peace offensive was not unappreciated in the US. W.E.B. DuBois in particular recognized that it was the social system itself of the Soviet Union that allowed it to come to the Disarmament Conference in Geneva "with clean hands and a real desire for peace." Similarly, DuBois, as well as other peace forces, recognized that it was the Soviet Union that stood virtually alone in "open objection to this high-handed program of theft, lying and slavery" that Italy wished to foist upon Ethiopia.

Meanwhile economic warfare continued as the US forced its exports on "allies" that could not pay, since the US closed its doors to imports. The Smoot-Hawley Tariff of 1930 led the way in protectionism with Britain and France following in 1932. This was accompanied by heightened armaments spending as capitalist countries sought an outlet for surplus that would at the same time help in extending political, economic and military influence.

The attempt by Franco and his band of mercenaries to overthrow the duly elected regime in Spain was a watershed and turning point on the path to World War II. On the one hand, there were Hitler and Mussolini sending weapons and troops and generally using Spain as a testing ground for further aggression. On the other hand, there was the Soviet Union, heeding the Spanish Republic's call for assistance, along with other progressive forces worldwide, including the Abraham Lincoln Brigade of volunteers from the US.

Three weeks after the rising against the Republic the US State Department announced a "moral embargo" against shipping of arms to either side. This was allegedly based on the Neutrality Act of 1935 which, however, applied to *countries* at war. Hence, there existed no legal basis to interrupt or modify the exchange of goods between Spain and the US. Thereafter Vacuum Oil, a US Corporation, refused to service ships of the Republic's Navy. Five hours after the revolt five Standard Oil tankers were on their way to Spain but changed course and sailed to a port occupied by the rebels. This was an act of war. Thereafter the State Department told any company seeking to sell war materiel to the Republic to cease and desist—though these sales were perfectly legal. The US went so far as to try to prevent Mexico from aiding the Loyalists. By the same token, the rebels never lacked US oil, gasoline, etc. The German and Italian planes that bombed civilians in Guernica, Barcelona, etc. were all powered by US fuel. Moreover, though the rebels received 1,700 trucks from Italy and 1,800 from Germany, they obtained 12,000 from the US (principally GM and Ford). US consulates were maintained in rebel territory. Bombs from US companies were sold to Germany, then re-exported to the rebels. Somehow Franklin Roosevelt was able to muster enough gall to term all this "perfectly legal."

Soviet foreign policy was forced to operate under these difficult conditions of capitalist encirclement and aggression. Despite the US provocations, US-Soviet relations showed some improvement. The economic crisis in the US was abated somewhat by Soviet purchases in 1935, which more than doubled the volume of 1934. The USSR-US commercial agreement of August 4, 1937 accorded most favored nation treatment to the Soviets.

A great deal of the credit for improvement in US-Soviet relations must be given to peace forces in the US, especially those grouped around the fledgling publication *Soviet Russia Today*. Their ceaseless, untiring efforts served as a welcome antidote to the attempts by the Coughlins, the Fords and the Lindberghs to poison peaceful relations. A milestone in this process was the massive rally of thousands in New York in 1937 which welcomed the Soviet pilots who had negotiated the first transpolar, non-stop flight. Representatives of Mayor LaGuardia were present at this celebration, along with Sidney Hillman of the Amalgamated Clothing Workers. Sending greetings were Governor Herbert Lehman of New York and such Senators as Claude Pepper, Robert Bulkeley and William McAdoo.

But the process of egging Hitler on to attack the Soviets continued. Time and time again Stalin, Litvinov and other leading Soviet officials warned Britain, the US and their allies that they were merely cutting their own throats, but the warnings went unheeded. Slyly using the bogey of anti-communism and promising to drive those "dirty Communists" into the sea, the Axis powers and their fifth column took over country after country. Collective security could have halted them in their tracks but this sensible proposal was repeatedly rejected. Thus in September 1938 the dream of all anti-communists had seemingly reached fruition—the infamous Munich Pact which knocked together Germany, Italy, Britain and France in an anti-Soviet Holy Alliance. The intended victim of Munich was the Soviet Union, though its first victims were the peoples of Europe; once more anti-Sovietism covered betrayal of democracy for as a result of Munich the Sudetenland was gobbled up, Czechoslovakia ceased to be independent, Lithuania surrendered its only port, Memel, to Germany and Italy invaded Albania.

What now for the Soviets as the cordon sanitaire tightened? As US Ambassador to Moscow Joseph Davies later conceded, the Soviets in the Spring of

1939 had agreed to join with Britain and France against Germany if the latter attacked Poland and Rumania. British and French delegations sent to Moscow were not even empowered to negotiate, and refused to accept the Soviet proposal. Knowing—and understanding—that no effective arrangement could be made with the Western powers, the Soviets had no other choice than to sign a non-aggression pact with Germany. It was not an alliance as it has sometimes been called. This move gave the Soviets a critical breathing space and time to fortify against inevitable attack; equally important, it insured the break-up of the anti-Soviet front as Hitler in his plan for world domination preferred to mop up weaker Britain and France first then move on to the stronger USSR.

As was to be expected, anti-Soviet forces in the US raised an obstreperous cry about the non-aggression pact. Though actually disappointed about the weakening of the anti-Soviet front, they were able to confuse some people with their repeated attempts to equate Nazi "totalitarianism" and Soviet "totalitarianism"—attempts that continued after the war. But many were able to pierce this veil of subterfuge. Harold Ickes, a key advisor and cabinet member in Roosevelt's administration revealed in his diary: "I find it difficult to blame Russia, Chamberlain alone is to blame. . . . Britain could have concluded a satisfactory treaty with Russia years ago. . . . Russia was ready. . . . (Britain) kept hoping she could embroil Russia and Germany with each other and thus escape scot-free herself." W.E.B. DuBois with his usual perspicacity agreed that the tactics of Britain and France helped make the non-aggression pact inevitable.

Now it was only a matter of time before Hitler's attack which finally came during the summer of 1941. But the peace policy of the Soviet Union did not remain dormant. This was especially true of the situation in the Balkans where repeated efforts were made to insure collective security. These efforts proved unavailing. The US, which had spurned collective security, found itself in a situation where it was inexorably drawn into an alliance with the Soviets—especially after December 7, 1941. Albert Einstein, who had seen first-hand the devastation, the benightedness, the racism of monopoly capital run rampant in Germany best expressed the view of US peace forces on Soviet foreign policy:

Soviet Russia has under the most difficult conditions strived to avoid warlike developments and is today one of the most powerful factors in the preventing of a new World War. Soviet foreign policy has been a clear and unequivocal policy of peace. With greater energy and consequence than any other great power, the Soviet Union has endeavored to create a system of international security.   □

Part Three
Women, National Minorities

11

ANGELA Y. DAVIS

Women's Promise for Freedom

The subjugation of women is one of the most persistent forms of oppression known to humankind. Although its contours and structures have varied from one historical epoch to another, it has remained a seemingly constant feature of human society. Some feminists in the capitalist world have concluded, in fact, that male supremacist attitudes and behavior emanate from inborn and inalterable traits in men. The dominant forces in capitalist countries certainly encourage such a superficial analysis, for it obscures the inextricable connection between the inferior status of women and the existence of social classes.

The link between class society and the oppression of women was dramatically confirmed in one of the monumental lessons of the October Revolution. For when the Russian working class demonstrated that class society could itself be expurgated from history, they also taught the world that male supremacy could be rooted out of the institutions of human society.

If we use the occasion of the 60th Anniversary of the October Revolution to review the enormous strides Soviet women have made in only six decades, we can glean from their experiences knowledge that will assist us to advance the cause of women throughout the world.

Despite immense technological progress—which ought to benefit women in the first place—working class women in the capitalist countries are largely excluded, even more so than their men, from the benefits of their societies. In the United States, not only are women still locked out of key areas of the economy; they can hardly claim equal wages for performing the same or

ANGELA Y. DAVIS is Co-Chairperson of the National Alliance Against Racist and Political Repression. Her *Autobiography* appeared in 1974.

comparable work as their working class brothers. Moreover, if equal opportunities were available, the lack of social services and job benefits, such as child care and maternity leaves, would deter women from taking advantage of them.

In the US, Black women and other women of oppressed nationalities bear the onus of institutionalized sexism. More than one-third of all Black women are single parents. Jobs, social services and special job benefits are therefore absolutely essential for survival. Yet, high unemployment rates, low wages, a degrading and racist welfare system, and forced sterilization of Black, Puerto Rican, Chicana and Native American women continue.

The socialist response, on the other hand, to women of all races and nationalities has been full employment and a constantly expanding network of social services and job benefits to facilitate women's participation in the economic and political life of their country. Moreover, in conjunction with these vast material improvements in the status of women, ideological campaigns against male supremacist attitudes—lingering in the minds of both men and women—are conducted on a continual basis.

Within a relatively brief historical period, the Soviet Union has leaped light years ahead of the most advanced capitalist countries. Engels said that the first precondition for the emancipation of women was the introduction of the entire female sex into public industry. This has been virtually achieved in the Soviet Union. In pre-revolutionary Russia, the women who worked for wages were confined primarily to household and farm work. According to the 1897 census, of the women who worked for a living, 55 per cent were domestic servants and 25 per cent were farm laborers. Only 13 per cent had jobs in industry. Today, women constitute 51 per cent of all industrial and office workers, which almost exactly reflects their proportion in the population at large.

This feat was not accomplished simply by proclaiming that women had the right to equal jobs and equal pay. A complex system of special provisions had to be created in order to bring women's duties as mothers and their economic role into harmony. The full integration of women into the economy presupposed, in the first place, a vast network of creches and child care centers and special measures guaranteeing expectant mothers and women with infant children equal rights on the job. Today, expectant mothers enjoy fully paid maternity leaves consisting of fifty-six days prior to delivery and fifty-six days afterwards. When they return to work, they have the right to nurse their infants during working hours, the minimum time allotted for this being thirty minutes every three hours.

When Lenin reflected upon the conditions for women's emancipation, there was one point about which he was adamant: women had to be released from household drudgery, for *petty housework* crushes, strangles, stultifies and degrades (the woman), chains her to the kitchen and the nursery, and she wastes her labor on barbarously unproductive and crushing drudgery. The real *emancipation of women*, real communism, will begin only where and when an all-out struggle begins (led by the proletariat wielding the state power) against this petty housekeeping, or rather when its *wholesale transformation* into a large-scale socialist economy begins. (*Collected Works*, Vol. 29, p. 429.)

The example of a factory in Moldavia demonstrates the determination to reduce the burden of housework on women. At this enterprise, which employs more than 5,000 women, women workers have at their service a hairdresser, a dress-making shop, a dry cleaner, a shoe repair shop, a food shop, a canteen, an out-patient polyclinic and a recently built balneological center. The administration and the trade union organization help women workers to combine their work with household duties.

Since the Revolution, in fact, the actual time spent on housework has been reduced by 20 per cent. Moreover, campaigns are continually conducted to persuade husbands to share equally in the performance of household tasks. At the same time, Soviet women and men alike understand that the equal distribution of housework is by no means the ultimate solution, which as Lenin pointed out, lies in the industrialization and socialization of the most onerous aspects of housework.

Pending the automation of housework, however, it is essential that men share in the household tasks that have been relegated, for so long, to women. In a recent Soviet sociological survey, it was discovered that half of all husbands play an equal role in caring for their children. From one-third to more than one-half join their wives in the cooking, dishwashing and everyday housekeeping. In some Central Asian republics, newly married men and young fathers participate in conferences during which they compete in demonstrating their ability to perform household tasks such as cooking and cleaning.

Creating the foundation for the emancipation of women in Central Asia in general demanded herculean efforts. In those areas previously under Moslem influence, the woman's place in society was hardly more significant than that of an animal—or, at best, a slave. If any single achievement establishes the absolute superiority of socialism with respect to the liberation of women, then it is the prodigious transformations in the condition of women in Central Asia.

Some decades ago, a visitor to Central Asia described what had been a very common scene in Uzbekistan. First, she said, you might have seen an Uzbek man

dressed in his bright-colored long mantle, unfastened and thrown open and glittering gaily in the sunshine. (He) rides on a wretched little mule . . . that is almost crushed beneath its load.

Some ten paces behind this man walks a human figure, funereally wrapped round from head to foot, whose age and sex cannot be determined. The face is covered with a thick, black net of horsehair; the body with a shapeless garment, thrown over the head and falling to the ground, and only the feet are visible. On the head, in rhythm with the steps, a bundle sways gently, and beneath the somber coverings, which cover even the hands, a second stirs in the arms: a living bundle.

What is the meaning of this group, with its strange contrast? Not so easy to guess: a married couple going on a visit. The husband rides on the donkey, but the wife walks at a respectful distance behind him. On her head she carries the flat loaves intended as a present, and in her arms—her baby. (Fannina W. Halle, *Women in the Soviet East,* p. 65.)

The unmitigated inferiority reflected in this everyday scene was all-pervasive in such areas as the present-day republics of Uzbekistan, Tadzhikstan, Turkmenia, Kazakhstan and Kirghizia. Perpetually under the control of a man, women were considered biological appendages to their fathers and husbands. In Uzbekistan, the garments worn by women—the long robes and the coarse, unsanitary horsehair veil—were indicative of the segregated life they led, for after they reached a certain age, no man, outside their husbands, was allowed to look upon their faces.

A proverb often repeated during those days conveys the tragic predicament of women in Central Asia: "There is only one God in this world, but man is a second for woman." Indeed, men's power over their women was so absolute that husbands who suspected their wives of adultery could kill them with impunity. The husbands, after all, had purchased their wives in the same way that they would purchase a cow.

The pre-revolutionary isolation of women in Central Asia did not, however, prevent them from playing an essential role in agriculture: In the words of Fannina W. Halle, "They reap and grind the corn, gather the cotton flowers, milk the cows, tend all the other animals, shear the sheep, clean the wool, and tan the leather. They cook and even make the family's shoes, mind the children, prepare the felt for the nomad tents, weave textiles and carpets . . ." While women's work was far more burdensome than men's, it was the men who controlled the products of women's labor.

That women were virtually slaves of men is not, of course, to say that in Central Asia men themselves were free. Given the prevailing feudal system or the nomadic existence led by some peoples, combined with the deleterious impact of Russian colonialism, the lot of most men was hardly enviable. Yet the situation of women was far worse. They were literally slaves of slaves.

Poverty, disease, illiteracy, cultural oppression—these were the problems of everyday life and were reinforced by the national subjugation of the peoples of Central Asia. In Uzbekistan, for example, only four per cent of the people could read and write prior to the revolution. Women, however, were four hundred times as illiterate as men, only one out of a thousand women having had access to any form of education. It was clear to Lenin and the leaders of the Russian

Revolution that national liberation in Central Asia depended, to a great degree, on a concerted battle for women's emancipation. The solution of the woman question was integrally related to the solution of the national question.

The enormous difficulties presented by the task of emancipating women can never be overestimated. Today, visitors to Uzbekistan or Tadzhikstan or any of the Central Asian Republics can see women active and playing leadership rules in every aspect of society: women industrial workers, women trade union leaders, women professors, etc. But six decades ago, in Uzbekistan, one could not even encounter a woman who was not shielded from public view by the *chachvan* and the *paranja*, the long robes and the thick, black horsehair veil. Sixty years ago it would have been a bizarre and outrageous dream to predict that a woman from Uzbekistan—Yadgar Nasriddinova—would one day preside over the Council of Nationalities of the Supreme Soviet, a leader, thus, of fifteen republics.

During the early days, there were few Moslem women activists. Russian women Communists had to provide the backbone for the struggle for women's emancipation in Central Asia. In fact, for the Russian women to have access to Central Asian women, they, too, had to don the veil. In Uzbekistan, Russian women wore the *chachvan* and the *paranja* in order to initiate the arduous process of persuading Moslem women to break out of their centuries-old isolation.

The Communist Party of the Soviet Union had no historical precedents in mapping out the movement for women's emancipation in Central Asia. Socialism had just broken onto the historical scene—and now, it was not only necessary to leap from feudalism to socialism in the former colonies; women had to be persuaded to repudiate centuries and centuries of tradition. Resistance was fierce and violent. Husbands murdered wives who cast away their veils. Activists literally risked their lives in organizing and agitating for women's liberation. During the most difficult period, over four hundred women activists were murdered in Central Asia.

At first, it was almost impossible to persuade women to attend mass meetings or even the schools established for the eradication of illiteracy. Gradually, however, by excluding men from gatherings involving women, it was possible to

induce the women of the East to overcome the timidity in which they had been brought up on for centuries. Only when they knew that they were safe from the eyes of strange men did they come in constantly growing numbers, uncovered their faces, and opened their hearts freely in the circle of fellow women about their sorrows and cares. (Halle, p. 242.)

Throughout Central Asia, women's clubs were established. Two of the salient issues in the beginning were wife bartering and marriage capture; the women's clubs played a major role in informing women about their new legal rights and in implementing the laws regarding marriage. Later, the clubs became learning centers; the imparting of basic reading and writing skills was indispensable to the furtherance of the liberation struggle. Finally, once the drive toward the elimination of illiteracy was underway, the emphasis shifted to teaching women the skills that would permit them to enter into industrial production.

If one thing was clear, it was that the liberation of women was an organic ingredient of the overall fight for the national and economic liberation of the peoples of Central Asia. The essential feature of this fight was the industrialization of the Central Asian republics and thus the creation of an industrial working class. The creation of the working class, as the conditions for socialism were being established, did more than anything else to hasten the emancipation of Central Asian women. The economic independence women workers achieved became a dramatic challenge to the old patterns of subordination within the family.

Women who worked in factories discovered new encouragement among their class sisters and brothers. Solidarity at the workplace was, for example, an indispensable incentive for the final, mass rejection of the veil. Women could also rely upon the support of their co-workers when they resisted tradition within their families. If a woman, for example, refused to accept a marriage arranged by her parents, she was often assisted in her challenge by the women on her job.

Today, women in the Central Asian republics constitute a large proportion of all industrial and office workers. They are 48 per cent of the work force in Kazakhstan and Kirghizia; 42 per cent in Uzbekistan; 40 per cent in Turkmenia and 39 per cent in Tajikistan. (In the USSR as a whole, of course, women are 51 per cent of the work force. The lag can be explained by the vestiges of the old traditions which still, understandably, exist.) The massive introduction of Central Asian women into social production did not occur automatically. Without the establishment of programs consciously designed to attract women to industry, it could not have been accomplished.

In the United States today, we are witnessing a concerted attack on affirmative action programs for people of color and women. The indispensable role played by similar programs in bringing masses of Central Asian women into production should act as a powerful incentive for forging a strong defense of affirmative action in the United States.

As industry itself developed in the Central Asian republics, minimum percentages were established, guaranteeing that women would fill a substantial number of the job positions available. Numerous training programs for women were also devised. For example, in the 1930s while textile factories were being built in Tadzhikstan and Uzbekistan, two hundred Tadzhik and Uzbek women received training in industrial cities like Moscow and Ivanovo.

The new role of women in social production had extensive repercussions throughout the society. For how could women assist in creating social wealth without also sharing in the political and cultural life of their republics? Parallel programs bringing designated numbers of women into Communist Party and government positions were therefore established and the long suppressed cultural yearnings of women in Central Asia were allowed, at last, to achieve fulfillment. In Uzbekistan today, "there are 88 female governors, mayors, county managers and heads of the Communist Party at those levels, 50 district attorneys and assistant district attorneys, 4.415 heads of labor unions. . . . They are 45 per cent of members of legislative bodies from the village up" (William Mandel, *Soviet Women*, p. 177-78). And throughout the Central Asian republics, women are acknowledged for their many outstanding cultural contributions. Not too many decades ago, actresses were murdered for showing their faces on stage. Today, women not only perform on stage, they are playwrights, novelists and poets.

Although women in Central Asia, like women throughout the Soviet Union, are still forging ahead on the road to liberation, the stunning achievements of only six decades are an eloquent confirmation of the potential socialism holds for the women of the world. The vision in these lines penned by a woman poet and political leader in Turkmenia about forty years ago has already moved from hope to reality:

> *O women! Tear the yashmak from your face!*
> *Submit no more in silence to disgrace!*
> *Lift up your voice: you will not speak alone!*
> *Millions now make their aspirations known:*
> *To work for peace and happiness of all,*
> *No longer abject, no more serfdom's thrall!*   □

12

GEORGE B. MURPHY, JR.

Peaceful Coexistence and The Struggle Against Racism

In the struggle waged by world peace forces, led by the Soviet Union, to rescue humanity from the growing threat of a nuclear holocaust that would destroy the human and material resources of our earth, the urgent need to stop the insane spiraling arms race and to make detente irreversible is mankind's number one imperative.

This fact is recognized by millions of working people throughout the world and peoples of all nationalities, races and creeds fighting for national liberation, independence, an end to racist oppression, and for democracy, equality, security and a better life.

Nothing defines more clearly the common sense role of detente in this perilous state of affairs than the astounding announcement by our government that it is giving serious consideration to the immediate production, stockpiling and deployment of a monstrous new "people-killer" weapon, the neutron bomb. With supreme racist arrogance our government declares, without shame, that the neutron bomb is a "clean" bomb because it does not destroy property, only people!

Thus US imperialism, in open defiance of the majority of the American people, the United Nations and world opinion, places its seal of approval on the concept of man's inhumanity to man as a natural, normal condition of life on our planet, in the name of monopoly capitalist greed.

The genocidal racist implication of the announcement becomes clearer when one remembers it was the US government that exploded the first atomic bomb over the Japanese people in Hiroshima. Our government introduced bacteriological warfare in the war of aggression against the Korean people. It was the US army that murdered, maimed and burned the heroic, freedom-loving people of Vietnam with napalm bombs in a futile effort to deprive them of the fruits of their victorious revolution.

GEORGE B. MURPHY, JR., long associated with the *Afro-American* newspapers, is Vice-Chairman of the Paul Robeson Friendship Society in Washington, D.C., and Editorial Consultant to *New World Review*.

In concert with the multinational corporations and the Pentagon, the US government is pouring billions of war-investment dollars into the African continent in a vain attempt to save racist apartheid, and fascist white minority government rule over the brave African peoples fighting for independence and self-determination in their own land in South Africa, Zimbabwe (Northern Rhodesia) and Namibia (South West Africa).

But, there is another, positive side of this coin. The tremendous economic power, enormous prestige and world influence exercised by the Soviet Union is by no means ignored by world imperialism whose center is in the United States, where inhuman racism based upon the capitalist-created myth of white supremacy has poisoned the atmosphere of social relations in every nook and cranny of our country for the past four hundred years.

In conjunction with its socialist allies the Soviet Union, where the capitalist roots of racism have been destroyed long ago, stands first and foremost among the world forces working for detente, in its untiring efforts to promote mutual respect, equal and beneficial relations among states based upon the Leninist principle of peaceful coexistence between nations and states with different social and economic systems.

Guided by the principles of internationalism proclaimed by Lenin in his historic appeal for unity between working people of the world and all oppressed peoples, the Soviet Union fulfills its international obligations in giving unstinting all-round economic, military, moral and cultural support to the peoples of Africa, Asia and Latin America fighting for freedom and independence against imperialism's racist aggression.

In August 1971, I was able to realize a long-held dream to visit the Soviet Union (other trips have followed). I organized an eleven-member delegation, mostly Blacks. We all had similar motivations. We wanted to learn about the life of the peoples of the world's first socialist state where the working class is in power and the nightmare of genocidal racism, unemployment, repression of minorities no longer exists; where life is secure, there are jobs for everyone and assured care from the cradle to the grave.

We visited two national republics—Uzbekistan and Tadzhikistan—whose people had endured slavery under the tsars. It was a great delight for us to see darker peoples, who had known only slavery but leaped over the brutality, arrogance and exploitation of man by man under capitalism and moved into socialism. This, to us, was the meaning of Soviet power because these peoples were able to make that leap with the loving interest and concern of Soviet power.

We saw that women in these republics, who for centuries had been semi-slaves to men, in addition to being slaves of the shahs, the emirs and the landowners, were walking with unveiled faces, beautiful faces! They were equal to men in their work, occupied positions of influence in the government, in medicine, power development, heavy industry, construction; in short, in the building of a new society. We also learned a lot from watching people, seeing with our own eyes how workers conduct themselves in a socialist country where they are in full control of their lives. It made us understand that working people can control a government they elect themselves, can build a new nation and a new society when they are the owners of the means of production.

One of the high spots of our trip was an illuminating conference with a group of Soviet specialists in African affairs at the Africa Institute in Moscow. The Institute is a member of the world-renowned USSR Academy of Sciences. It is also a collective member of the Soviet Association for Friendship with Peoples of Africa, a division of the USSR's All-Union Association for Friendship and Cultural Relations with Foreign Countries. It does a great deal to make Africa well known to the Soviet people through books, exhibits, numerous exchange projects, celebrations of "Africa Day," etc.

This conference gave us a vivid demonstration of the approach Soviet scientists take to their work. These Soviet scientists, in striking contrast with our scientists in the West, in their attitude to the study of African countries and their problems, are completely free of the racist, pseudoscientific concepts which make it possible for Western social scientists to serve the interests of American imperialism. True to the humanist principles of the Soviet peoples, they are convinced that all oppressed peoples have the right to independently determine their own destiny.

Most of our group were familiar with a book written twenty years ago by the distinguished Black American historian, John Hope Franklin. He gave a vivid description of how US capitalism, during our country's period of slavery, employed American scientists and historians to manufacture, out of thin air, a steady stream of pseudo-scientific racist concepts to justify keeping our people in bondage in order to conceal the fact of enormous profits derived from the unpaid labor of Black slaves.

In an article that appeared in the April 1957 issue of the *Journal of Negro History*, official publication of the Association for the Study of Afro-American Life and History, Dr. Franklin noted that a century ago one of the South's most distinguished scientists wrote a lengthy treatise on dreptomania, a malady that gave Negroes a compulsion to run away. It appears that whenever Negroes disappeared from the plantation it was not that they were unhappy or dissatisfied, but because they were afflicted with this dread disease that compelled them to run away! The scientist insisted that this was a historical fact, running back into the history of Negroes for centuries. This, and many similar unsupported and fantastic claims became a part of the written history of the Negroes of the United States.

Dr. Franklin had written: "The effect of this kind of written history has not only been far-reaching, but deadly. It has provided the historical justification for the whole complex of mischievous and pernicious laws designed to create and maintain an unbridgeable gulf between Negroes and whites."

As my mind focuses again on the picture of those friendly scientists working in Moscow's Africa Institute, their outgoing warmth, their eagerness to give honest answers to our questions, a new fact emerges. It becomes clearer than ever that, in the context of the struggle for world peace, there is an organic unity that links the struggle to make detente irreversible, to the struggle against capitalist-created racism. The two struggles fertilize and thus strengthen each other.

Detente is the peace weapon that the Soviet people place in the hands of the national liberation forces on the African continent, enabling the African freedom fighters to conduct winning struggles leading to eventual victory, instead of nuclear annihilation.

Our government fully recognizes the powerful, life-preserving logic of detente, even as it continues to employ the communications media to unleash a steady barrage of anti-Soviet, anti-communist propaganda, to conceal from the American people the truth about detente in relation to the Soviet Union's undeviating efforts to relax tensions and to solve international problems through peaceful negotiations.

The US-inspired anti-Soviet propaganda barrage is also aimed at trying to make the world forget that the Soviet Union, playing the leading role among the victorious Allied Powers, lost over twenty million citizens and one-third of its industrial resources in World War II to save humanity from Hitler fascism and its genocidal, white supremacy, master race theories.

Nevertheless, despite all disclaimers, the inescapable reality operating in world affairs is that there can be no final solution to the problems of world peace without the full and equal participation of the Soviet Union.

This year marks the 60th anniversary of the birth of the Soviet Union. It is also the year when the Soviet people will ratify their new constitution. Discussions have been going on in every type of peoples' organization, in every city, town and village Soviet in all Republics of the USSR, as the Soviet people make ready to pronounce their final judgment on this historic document.

Two articles of the Constitution spell out the guarantees of equal rights of all Soviet citizens without regard to nationality, race or sex. Article 34 declares: "Citizens of the USSR shall be equal before the law, irrespective of origin, social and property status, nationality or race, sex, education, language, attitude to religion, type or character of occupation, domicile, or other particulars." Article 36 provides that: "Soviet citizens of different nationalities and races shall have equal rights. The exercise of these rights shall be ensured by the policy of all-round development and drawing together of all nations and nationalities of the USSR, education of citizens in the spirit of Soviet patriotism, and socialist internationalism, and the opportunity for using their mother tongue as well as the languages of the other peoples of the USSR.

"Any and all direct or indirect restriction of the rights of, or the establishment of direct or indirect privileges for, citizens on grounds of race or nationality, and likewise any advocacy of racial or national exclusiveness, hostility or contempt, shall be punishable by law."

Sixty years is but a minute according to the clock of human history. Yet, in this short span of time, the Soviet Union, overcoming unbelievable obstacles, has risen from the status of a poverty-stricken, illiterate, backward country to the position of a great world power occupying one-sixth of the earth.

The 60th birthday of the Soviet Union is also the 60th anniversary of the emergence of a new, historic world phenomenon, a united family of peoples of all races and nationalities, building a socialist society, as they march confidently into the future under the sturdy banners of detente and peaceful coexistence.

Each new victory against racism, wherever it may appear, is also a victory for peaceful coexistence. Each new advance of peaceful coexistence and detente advances the struggle against racism. They are inextricably woven, part of the same struggle. The solution of the nationalities question in the USSR, as it breaks through the wall of anti-Soviet lies, will open the eyes of more and more Americans, the working class in particular, to the roots of American racism. As we intensify the struggle to make detente irreversible, this will create more and more contacts between our people—and the people are invincible!

This is the birthday message that the Soviet people, through thought, word and deed, bring to the people's forces fighting for freedom, justice and peace. It is a message that tells them they are not alone, that the people's right to life, security and happiness is not an idle dream, but an attainable achievement open to all humanity.   □

13

ALEXANDER ZEVELEV

How the National Question
Was Solved in the USSR

Historically, prerevolutionary Russia had developed as a multinational state. Settled on her vast expanses were more than 100 nationalities, large and small, the combined population in 1917 being 163 million, of whom Russians were 43 per cent. The people differed, both in nationality and in the level of their social and political development.

By the beginning of the 20th century, Russia on the whole had reached a mid-capitalist level. On the one hand, she had a high degree of concentration of monopoly capital and industrial production, and on the other, she was an agrarian country with predominantly rural population and with remnants of serfdom in the economy and political system.

The Russian nation had reached a mid-capitalist level which, to a certain extent, was also true of the Ukraine and Poland, forming parts of Russia. The peoples of Transcaucasia were at the initial stage of capitalist development, while those of Central Asia stood at a pre-capitalist level. There were ethnic groups which completely preserved patriarchal-feudal relations. Others had tribal forms of organization typical of hunting and cattle-raising nomads, and in some places even retaining vestiges of slavery.

The non-Russians were also oppressed by exploiters from among their own people—local feudal lords, *kulaks* (rich peasants, exploiting others), and local businessmen who owned, themselves or with Russian factory owners, enterprises for processing raw materials, small power stations, mineral deposits, etc.

Political inequality was aggravated by economic and cultural inequality. Economically, most of the outlying national areas were turned into agrarian and raw material appendages to the metropolis, and areas of investment for Russian and foreign capital. Foreigners controlled coal-mining and metal-making in the Ukraine, oil production in Azerbaidzhan, ore-mining in Kazakhstan, and cotton-processing in Central Asia. The tsarist administration tried to settle as

ALEXANDER ZEVELEV is a correspondent for Novosti Press Agency. This material is a condensation of a pamphlet Mr. Zevelev prepared for the Novosti Press Agency Publishing House in 1977.

129

many Russian *kulaks* there as possible, to secure these areas for its great-power ventures. Industry was embryonic in most of the outlying areas, represented, as a rule, by cottage crafts and small primitive enterprises.

In 1914, only 8,137,200 pupils, one-fifth of all children and adolescents, attended schools throughout tsarist Russia. The country had 91 institutions of higher learning, but none in Byelorussia, Azerbaidzhan, Armenia, Uzbekistan, Kazakhstan, Turkmenia, Kirghizia, or Tadzhikistan.

Over 40 nationalities had no written language of their own. In Central Asia and Kazakhstan before the revolution 98 per cent of the local population were illiterate, while in Kirghizia literacy stood at a shocking 0.5 per cent. Women in Central Asia and Kazakhstan were universally illiterate.

To fortify its power, tsarism cultivated reactionary religious and nationalist prejudices, sowed enmity among nationalities, and organized pogroms. An analysis of the great-power, chauvinistic policy of tsarism and of the relations which had developed among the nations gave Lenin the ground for calling Russia "a prison of nations."

Before the proletariat emerged as an independent political force, Russians and non-Russians had on many occasions risen together against tsarism. Despite their chaotic character and lack of coordination those rebellions weakened serfdom and rallied the masses in the face of their common enemy.

Democratically-minded Russians had always sided with the oppressed. With the appearance of the Bolshevik Party, the national-liberation movements acquired a powerful ally and leader. The 1905 revolution stirred the oppressed nationalities to action against tsarism, local feudal overlords, landowners and capitalists.

T he Communist Party's revolutionary program on the nationalities question was an integral part of the ideological, tactical, organizational and theoretical principles on which Lenin had worked so hard and so fruitfully. He put in the forefront the necessity of full equality of all the nations, irrespective of the level of their development, as essential for the achievement of self-determination. Full equality also meant the inadmissibility of setting Europeans against Asians, white-skinned people against black-skinned people, and so on.

Lenin wrote in this connection: ". . . we, the party of the proletariat, must always and unconditionally *oppose any attempt* to influence national self-determination from without *by violence or injustice*." This thesis was based upon the following: Russia was a multinational state; some of its nationalities, particularly those inhabiting outlying areas, possessed distinguishing features relating to economy, mode of life, etc.; the outlying nations and nationalities were oppressed; and, lastly, there was a need to achieve a close unity of all the nationalities for organizing a struggle, on the broadest possible basis, against the oppressors, for a democratic republic and socialism.

Lenin connected this with ending mutual enmity and mistrust, and strengthening friendship among peoples.

As to the right to secession, Lenin and the Party explained that this did not mean that every nation would be unconditionally supported. In its attitude the Party would be guided above all by the interests of the class struggle and the victorious socialist revolution. Lenin stressed that the nationalities knew from experience the advantages of a large state and would not risk secession unless national oppression and friction made their existence in a common state intolerable.

The international unity of the working people of all nationalities is another major premise of Leninism. Wherever exploitation rules, working people have common interests resulting from their similar economic and political status. The working class is thus the most consistent opponent of national oppression.

Other propositions of the Party program included a ban on all national privileges or restrictions, the rejection of a single state language, full equality of all languages with schools conducting instruction in all local languages, and recognition of the existence of elements of democratic and socialist culture in every national culture.

In questions of state structure the Communist Party advocated broad regional autonomy for people who inhabited definite territory.

On the very first day of Soviet government the Second All-Russia Congress of Soviets in the Appeal *To the Workers, Soldiers and Peasants* announced that the government would guarantee all the nationalities inhabiting Russia the genuine right to self-determination.

The historic *Declaration of Rights of the Peoples of Russia*, proclaimed on November 2 (15),1917, listed the following principles:

1. Equality and sovereignty of all nationalities;

2. The right of nationalities to free self-determination, up to secession and formation of independent states;

3. Abolition of all national and national-religious privileges and restrictions;

4. Free development of national minorities and ethnic groups.

These provisions were also to be found in the Appeal *To All the Working Moslems of Russia and the East,* the *Manifesto to the Ukrainian People with an Ultimatum to the Ukrainian Rada*, and others.

In January 1918, the Third All-Russia Congress of Soviets endorsed the *Declaration of Rights of the Working and Exploited People* written by Lenin, which proclaimed that "the Russian Soviet Republic is established on the principle of a free union of free nations, as a federation of Soviet national republics."

The Constitution of the RSFSR (Russian Soviet Federative Socialist Republic), drafted under Lenin's guidance and adopted July 10, 1918, legalized freedom and equality of nations. It declared that any privileges and advantages of citizens because of race or nationality, as well as any oppression of national minorities, would not be tolerated.

Another signal event took place in December 1922 when the Union of Soviet Socialist Republics (USSR) was formed. Prior to this the Russian Soviet Federative Socialist Republic, the Transcaucasian Soviet Federative Republic (Georgia, Armenia and Azerbaidzhan), the Ukrainian and Byelorussian Soviet Socialist Republics existed independently.

In the years of intervention and Civil War these republics formed a close military and political alliance, which strengthened contacts between the peoples and was decisive in the victory of Soviet power. It also provided for joint efforts in major economic sectors which led to mobilization of all potentialities to repel the enemy.

The drive toward unification intensified after the victory over external and internal counterrevolution. The joining of all the Soviet socialist republics into a united state was necessary to facilitate pooling of material, financial and other resources for the speediest rehabilitation of the country and successful development of the socialist economy.

The republics were building socialism in a situation of hostile capitalist encirclement. The unification of the republics was not only necessary, but objectively logical. For all of them had a common goal—the building of socialism; the same political system, Soviet power; and the same socio-economic structure—public ownership of the basic means of production and socialist organization of economy.

Today the USSR comprises fifteen equal union republics: The RSFSR, and the Ukrainian, Byelorussian, Uzbek, Kazakh, Georgian, Azerbaidzhan, Lithuanian, Moldavian, Latvian, Kirghiz, Tadzhik, Armenian, Turkmen, and Estonian Soviet Socialist Republics. Each republic is multinational.

After the founding of the USSR, the Communist Party and the Soviet Government began to carry out their policy to enable economically backward peoples to bypass the capitalist stage and go directly to socialism. This problem was of great importance since a third of the nations of prerevolutionary Russia lived under the feudal system.

The decisive social force which was able to set the peoples on the path of building socialism was the alliance of the Russian working class with the peasant masses of the former colonial peoples. As Lenin said, "internationalism on the part of oppressors . . . must consist not only in the observance of the formal equality of nations but even in an inequality of the oppressor nation . . . that must make up for the inequality which obtains in actual practice."

Overcoming economic inequality meant carrying out a stupendous program to raise the outlying national areas to the level of the country's central regions, setting up industrial centers and development of large-scale industry, training workers from among the local population, reconstructing agriculture along socialist lines, establishing and strengthening national statehood, and developing culture, national in form and socialist in content.

Lenin emphasized the importance of establishing correct relations between the Russian people and the formerly oppressed peoples. In *The Question of Nationalities or "Autonomization,"* he said, "In one way or another . . . it is necessary to compensate the non-Russians for the lack of trust, for the suspicion and the insults to which the government of the 'dominant' nation subjected them in the past." He particularly emphasized that every consideration should be given to all the characteristics of a given nation, the specific features of its daily life, religion, and customs, and that each, even the most backward, working person should be helped to see the socialist tasks as his vital cause. He laid special emphasis on electrification and irrigation, considering the former as one of the decisive conditions of going over to socialism.

The First Five-Year Plan (1929-1933) gave special attention to raising the economy and cultural level of backward national areas and regions.

The 16th Party Congress (1930) pointed out that setting up the country's second coal and metal-producing center in the East was of vital importance for the industrialization of the USSR. The Congress also considered it essential to speed development of other industries relying on local raw material resources, in the Urals, Siberia, Kazakhstan and Central Asia.

The Second Five-Year Plan allocated nearly half of investments in new heavy industry for the eastern regions. Out of 15 cotton mills, ten mills were to be built in Central Asia, Siberia and Transcaucasia. Thus the production of cotton fabrics in Central Asia was to be increased by 1,500 per cent as against a 100 per cent increase for the whole country. The 17th Party Congress (1934) stressed the need for intensive development in education, health service, art and the press in the national republics and regions.

As a result of these policies, during the Soviet years industrial output in Kazakhstan has gone up 600 times, in Tadzhikistan more than 500 times, in Kirghizia more than 400 times, and in Turkmenia more than 130 times. In 1940, on the eve of their joining the USSR, Lithuania, Latvia and Estonia were not backward national regions. Yet, in 1972, for example, Latvia's industrial output increased 31 times compared with the 1940 level, Estonia's 32 times, and Lithuania's 37 times.

Speaking on the occasion of the 50th anniversary of the formation of the USSR, Leonid Brezhnev said that much more modest achievements in the capitalist world were often called "miracles." "But," he continued, "we Communists do not consider what has happened in Soviet Central Asia and

Soviet Kazakhstan as being in any way supernatural. You might say that it is a natural miracle, because it is natural under Soviet power, under socialism, in conditions of relations of friendship and brotherhood of nations that have been established in this country."

There are two trends operating in the nationalities question after the victory of socialism and in conditions of building communism.

The first is the rapid and all-round progress—economic, political and cultural—of each nation, strengthening of sovereignty, and expansion of rights of constituent and autonomous republics.

The second is that socialist nations are drawn closer together on the basis of working class internationalism. The two trends operate simultaneously without excluding each other. Progress of national languages and cultures of peoples who prior to the Revolution had no opportunities to consolidate nations has been unprecedented. Forty-eight nationalities developed a written language of their own in Soviet time.

Territorial integrity of the socialist nations has been considerably strengthened. As an example, the Turkmen shaped into a nationality as far back as the 13th-15th centuries. Yet, they could not grow into a nation until after the October Revolution, because of economic backwardness and their being disunited territorially. Some 350,000 resided in the Transcaspian region of the Turkestan territory administered by the governor-general, 200,000 in the Khiva Khanate, 165,000 in the Bukhara Emirate, and considerable numbers in Iran and Afghanistan.

Only after the revolution, upon the initiative and under the leadership of the Communist Party was national and state demarcation carried out in Soviet Central Asia in 1924. The Turkmen and Uzbek, and later the Tadzhik and Kirghiz Soviet Socialist Republics were established, and subsequently became constituent republics of the USSR. Thus under the auspices of the Soviet government the peoples of the Soviet Central Asian Republics acquired national statehood, an important requisite for the emergence of socialist nations.

The population of most of the Soviet nations has increased in recent years. The Central Asian nationalities and the Azerbaidzhanians grew by 50 per cent in the course of eleven years (four per cent a year, one of the highest rates in the world). As a result the percentage of Central Asian nationalities in the country's population has increased from six to eight per cent.

The flourishing of nations united in a single socialist state is the result not only of the potentialities inherent in any single national republic but of cooperation between all the national republics, which has led to the emergence of a single socialist national economy. This, in turn, encourages a rational utilization of all the country's natural riches.

The Uzbek socialist nation is a good example. In Uzbekistan the material and technical base of socialism was built by overcoming the inequality of the Uzbek people through help from all the Soviet peoples. In the prewar period (1928-1941) whole new industries—engineering, metal-making, cotton, silk, food, etc.—emerged. Industrial giants such as the Chirchik Electrochemical Plant, Tashkent Textile Mills, Kuvasai Cement Works were built. By 1940 gross output of Uzbekistan's large-scale industry increased 4.7 times as against 1913. In the prewar period the working class took shape as 708,100 people were employed in industry.

During the Second World War Uzbekistan was one of the USSR's main arsenals: nearly 100 large-scale industrial enterprises were transferred here from the occupied territories leading to a sharp increase in the number of skilled industrial workers. Power production increased from 482 million kwh in 1940 to 1.187 million kwh in 1945, oil extraction from 119,000 to 478,000 tons respectively, etc.

Uzbekistan's industrial growth continued after the war. Today Uzbekistan has a highly-developed industry and an advanced agriculture. Good progress is being made by the gas and chemical industries, diverse engineering, oil, coal mining, metal-making, electrical engineering, light, food and the building industries. There are more than a thousand big industrial enterprises and over 100 branches of industry with up-to-date technical facilities. Now, Uzbekistan manufactures tractors, excavators, compressors, pumps, electric vacuum equipment, cables, spinning machines and roving frames. It supplies all of the country's cotton-growing republics with cotton-picking machines and equipment for cotton-cleaning plants.

During the Soviet years Uzbekistan, like the other Soviet republics, has made considerable progress in agriculture. Uzbek peasants who had been oppressed for ages began to till their own land, and took the road of collectivization which enabled them to develop their small backward holdings into large-scale up-to-date socialist enterprises. The republic's former 750,000 small peasant households have merged into 1,400 collective farms and over 300 state farms specializing in cotton, fruit, vine, grain and vegetable growing and animal husbandry.

The level of agriculture has gone up sharply, chemicals and comprehensive mechanization are widespread, and irrigation has been conducted on a gigantic scale. Former arid wastelands like the Hungry Steppe are now blossoming areas known for their abundant crop yields.

Socialist reorganization in agriculture has ensured regular bumper crops. In 1928 the republic reached the prerevolutionary level of cotton production—533,000 tons of raw cotton—a high figure for those years. Between 1945-1970 Uzbekistan produced 20,670,000 tons of cotton, and its yearly yields now top five million tons.

A genuine socialist revolution has been carried out in the sphere of culture. The number of students per 10,000 of the population in Uzbekistan is nearly double that of France, nearly three times that of Great Britain.

The drawing together of Soviet nations that began after the October Revolution was conducted by stages. The first involved gradual elimination of mistrust between peoples and development of mutual cooperation. The second was the elimination of exploiter classes. The building of socialism and the achievement of factual equality between nations have ushered in the third stage.

The drawing together of nations inside each republic is the result of the multinational character of all Union republics. The work force of each plant, factory, state or collective farm, the student body of educational institutions, and the staff at research institutions, are multinational.

Internationalization is making particular headway in big industrial centers. Tashkent's population includes 106 nations; that of Kiev, 89; and Dushanbe, 80. People of diverse nationalities inhabit the new cities of Siberia, the North, the Far East, and other regions. Even the most out-of-the-way rural areas are becoming multinational. This has been promoted by industrialization of agriculture, its growing mechanization and electrification, and the development of agricultural labor into a variety of industrial work.

The drawing together of nations has greatly increased the number of mixed marriages. In the USSR at least 100 such marriages per 1,000 couples are concluded and in big cities the figure goes up to 200 and even 300.

Mutual cultural influence and enrichment are an important means of drawing nations closer together to one another. One factor in this process is the translation of Soviet, Russian classical and foreign literature into the national languages. Days of national literatures and arts and film festivals which enable each republic to show its cultural achievements in the other republics do much to promote fraternal relations among peoples and increase their cultural influence upon each other. The reciprocal influence and enrichment of Soviet peoples' cultures led to the emergence of a single communist international culture, the embodiment of the best of national cultures and world culture.

As regards the role of the Russian language, a common language is required not only by the multinational character of the country. The USSR's single economic and social system and constant economic and cultural cooperation of the closest kind make a single language indispensable for effective economic and cultural progress.

The USSR Population Census of 1970 showed that 141.8 million people or 58.7 per cent of the Soviet population (Russians constitute 129 million) named Russian as their native language. Sociological data show that 90-95 per cent of the Soviet population know sufficient Russian to communicate in this language. A total of 41.9 million non-Russians give Russian as the second language which they speak fluently. This bilingualism is typical.

Non-Russian people study Russian along strictly voluntary lines. In the Union republics the bulk of the national population (over 90 per cent) gave their national language as their mother tongue. This fully refutes the allegations that a "forcible assimilation" and "Russification" is under way.

There are no economic or social grounds in the USSR for chauvinism or nationalism. This does not do away automatically with all manifestations of nationalism. Unfortunately, one still comes across cases of national arrogance among individuals who lack political knowledge. There are also cases when national interests are put above those of the whole state. Nationalist leftovers may also crop up when there is lack of a tactful attitude to the peoples' national life and national peculiarities.

Whatever the forms of these vestiges of nationalism they run counter to the true interests of all Soviet peoples. That is why the Communist Party always opposes all manifestations of nationalism.

During the years of building socialism there has emerged a new historical entity—the Soviet people. The concept of "Soviet people" embraces all the nations and nationalities of the USSR; as a single family of friendly nations they have been working hand in hand to build an advanced socialist society. The multinational Soviet people comprises over 130 nationalities and ethnic groups, a fact showing that at the present stage of development the new historical community of nations does not replace diverse nations and nationalities populating the USSR but promotes their further progress.

The Soviet of Nationalities (one of the Chambers of the USSR Supreme Soviet), which comprises 750 deputies, gives 66 seats to peoples comprising less than one per cent of the country's population. This is a truly democratic way of dealing with the nationalities question.

All the Soviet people, regardless of their nationality or the language they speak, are proud of the inspiring work carried on by millions of Soviet people who have built a new and truly just and free society and formed an unbreakable fraternal alliance of many peoples. They take pride in the feat performed by millions of heroes—the sons and daughters of these peoples—who gave up their lives in the struggle for these attainments. They are proud of the great results achieved by the peoples' unhindered effort, their scientific achievements and the flourishing of culture in a multitude of national forms, and of the entire way of life of the Soviet people who have opened up new horizons before mankind and given it new moral values and ideals. For it has absorbed all of the best that has been produced by the courageous effort and creative genius of the millions of Soviet people. □

Part Four
Economy, Politics, Society

14

JOHN PITTMAN

Socialist Democracy in the USSR

The year 1977 is rich in events embodying concrete manifestations of the developing process of socialist democracy in the Soviet Union. Such events in this 60th year of Soviet power bring into focus all the main components of the USSR's political system—the working people headed by the working class and its industrial front-rankers, their vanguard party, their state and public (mass) organizations.

Underlying every political system is an economic basis. The political system of the USSR functions on an economic basis of socialist (public) ownership of the means of production. These include state property, the property of collective farms and cooperatives, and the property of public (mass) organizations. The system of public ownership guarantees the equality of all citizens in relation to the means of production as co-owners, and is the material foundation of socialist democracy. On this foundation the political system operates through the ever-growing *participation of* and *control by* the working people.

The leading force of this on-going, all-encompassing democratic process is the multi-national, multi-racial working class. Working people of capitalist countries may well regard with envy the many tokens of Soviet society's esteem for its working class—statues and paintings of workers everywhere; parks, streets and institutions named for workers; government, party and public organizations headed by workers; the country's highest honors and awards

JOHN PITTMAN grew up in the Black ghetto of Atlanta, Georgia, was educated at Morehouse College in Atlanta and the University of California in Berkeley, and has been a journalist all his life, mainly for the Black and working-class press. He was accredited to the founding meeting of the United Nations and many sessions of its General Assembly. Formerly co-editor of the *Daily World*, he is now a member of the editorial staff of *World Marxist Review* and living in Czechoslovakia.

bestowed on workers. And all for good and sound reasons! From the beginnings of the revolutionary upsurge leading to the capture of state power, from the formation of the first Soviet government headed by Lenin, and the first acts of the new government—the decrees on peace, land, workers' control, nationalization of the banks, and the "Declaration of the Rights of the Working and Exploited People"—to the events of this year, working class hegemony has prevailed in the struggle to build socialism. So also has the profound democratic content of this hegemony.

One democratic measure of the new workers' state inaugurated a new epoch in the development of human society. The expropriation of the country's wealth by the producers and its transference to the whole of society was itself a democratic act of a transcendent magnitude never before achieved. By establishing this cornerstone of the material foundations of equality, the working class simultaneously ended the ages-old process of humans exploiting humans, and made labor the only source of livelihood. By asserting the human need to work it proclaimed work to be a paramount human right. Freedom from exploitation and freedom from unemployment are indeed the preconditions for all human freedoms, since deprivation of employment and security from impoverishment is a denial of the freedom to live, without which all other freedoms cannot be realized.

The capture of state power by the working class, which launched the transitional stage from capitalism to socialism, was also a supreme form of democracy. It was a practical rather than a verbal referendum and involved the conscious participation of the broadest masses. Moreover, the tasks of constructing socialist foundations at that stage, far from reducing the necessity for mass participation, could not have been accomplished without its constant enlargement.

As the political leader, organizer and educator of the working masses, the CPSU's role in the development of socialist democracy is a third, and decisive, factor. How is this role realized?

First of all, it is realized through ideological work, through dissemination among the people of the democratic, humanistic teachings of Marxism-Leninism. These teachings assert that the working masses, the majority of the people, are the real creators of history. And this emphasis underscores the class essence of democracy and humanism. The party furthers the trend to greater democracy also through political and organizational leadership and guidance. These involve determining political policy on all domestic and foreign questions and proposing measures to implement it. Organizational leadership involves direction of all state and mass organizations through the day-to-day activity of Communists working in them, through helping to select and train their leading personnel and control their performance.

Owing to the party's great authority, the steady improvement of democracy entails strict observance of the delineation of party, state and mass organization functions, and corrections of party assumption of administrative functions and tutelage of mass organizations whenever they occur. Corrections of past mistakes and deviations from this norm, such as emerged during the latter years of Stalin's leadership, have strengthened guarantees against the party's exercise of state power and replacement of other organizations, while enhancing its political, organizing and educating role.

Besides the delineation of functions in the fundamental law of the USSR, the CPSU itself has a built-in system of guarantees for promoting the trend toward ever-increasing democracy. This is the system of inner-party democracy. Its supreme principle is collectivism, since a party of voluntary members can function only through collectivism in policy-making and implementation. First place in the practical realization of this principle belongs to democratic centralism. This enables the party, through centralized leadership, to act as a united, disciplined force for influencing social processes, and, through the broadest involvement of party members in the formation and execution of party policy, to choose, instruct, direct the party's leading bodies and officers and control their activity. Democratic centralism implies the equality of all party members without exception in regard to the rights of criticism and making proposals for policy and action, the electivity of all officers and leading bodies on all levels, and the subordination of individual members or a minority to the will of the majority.

Democracy and collectivity are also promoted by the regularity and frequency of meetings, by the obligatory reports of party leaders to their organizations and to higher party bodies, and by the practice of criticism and self-criticism. This important corrective practice is aimed at eliminating shortcomings and errors and preventing their recurrence. Its exercise reinforces the equality of party members and the process of control and verification of the implementation of party policies.

The party's numerical strength and composition are important assets for the realization of democratic goals. CPSU membership (15,694,000 on the eve of the 25th Congress) is equivalent to one Communist for every 16 inhabitants among all sections of the population (41.6 per cent workers—six million, nearly 20 per cent technicians, 13.9 per cent collective farmers, 24 per cent workers in science, education, public health, management, literature, the arts and military spheres), with an organizational network grounded in 390,000 primary branches (150,000 in material production).

Of course, the definitive criterion of how the party improves democracy is the people's response to its initiatives and proposals. The traditions established by the first generation of Soviet workers are carried on in the movement for socialist emulation in the societies of rationalizers and innovators, and in front-ranking production brigades. This year's events give indications of what has become a way of life in the Soviet Union. November 7 is targeted by 16,000 of the country's collectives of working people for fulfillment of the first two-year goals of the Tenth Five-Year Plan. In April the Central Committee of the Young Communist League announced progress of the campaign of millions of young workers to fulfill two years' plans for the November 7 jubilee.

The scope and depth of popular enthusiasm for the party's initiatives and recommendations is striking, when compared to the situation in the capitalist countries. What party representing corporate monopolies and the super-rich formulates its policies through discussion and the active participation of all its members, proposes a program complete with ways and means of ensuring its implementation, regularly elects its officer and leading bodies, and controls their performance through the members' exercise of the rights of criticism and recall?

The CPSU's indisputable superiority in these democratic party functions disproves the claim that only a multi-party system, a plurality of parties, complies with the criteria of democracy. The evidence is overwhelming that a plurality of parties is no guarantee of democracy. Nor does socialism require a one-party system, as is evident in the number of socialist countries with more than one party. Soviet history shows that circumstances surrounding the formation of a party system determine whether party pluralism or a single party will prevail. The CPSU's Bolshevik predecessor emerged as the sole party committed to socialism after the Mensheviks and Socialist-Revolutionaries deserted to the forces of foreign intervention and counterrevolution.

Continuous improvement of the state apparatus is essential for the development of socialist democracy because of the state's role and powers under socialism. It is both a political and economic organization. More importantly, the socialist state is not a special organism standing above and outside society as under capitalism, but an integral part of the masses and society and its main embodiment and generator of democracy.

State power in socialist democracies is used to defend and consolidate the system of public ownership of the means of production. The crucial question regarding democracy and freedom is also applicable to the state: for whom, for what class?

The evolution from the temporary, transitional stage of the dictatorship of the proletariat to the *state of the whole people* implies democratic changes in both the coercive and the developing, organizing coordinating functions of state power. With the abolition of the exploiting, oppressing classes, the coercive function is increasingly assumed by the people themselves (volunteer public order squads, comrades courts, various forms of public control bodies). The state's coercive apparatus becomes gradually reduced to the punishment and prevention of serious crimes and offenses.

Likewise in relation to the state's organizing and developing function, its management of the economy and administration of social development, the increasing role of the public and mass organizations leads society toward public self-administration. Specific in Soviet society at this stage of its development is the simultaneous increase of this function of the state and the growth of the administrative, organizing functions of the public organizations, a preparatory stage for communist public self-administration.

Contrasting trends of the democratic process in capitalist and socialist states are sharply delineated in the contracting social base of state-monopoly capital's political system compared to the expanding social base of states of socialist democracy. A number of characteristic features of the state system of the USSR helps to explain the cause of these contrasting developments.

Structurally, the system of Soviets enhances development of the democratic process.* Its salient features are the combination of legislative and executive powers, the electivity of all its members without exception, their obligation to fulfill mandates of their constituents within a specified time, the obligatory accountability to their constituents, and their constituents' control of their performance. There is no separation of powers by means of which a legislative branch may escape responsibility for the implementation of its legislation or the executive may evade accountability to the electorate and act behind the people's back and against the will and interests of all to serve the interests of a few.

Mandatory duties of a Soviet deputy on all levels include the initiation, control of implementation, and accounting to constituents of proposals to fulfill explicitly stated requirements of his or her electors. Dereliction or malfeasance in the performance of these duties may evoke instant recall by a mere majority vote. (More than 4,000 deputies have been recalled in the past 10 years, including 11 of the USSR Supreme Soviet and about 100 of the Supreme Soviets of Union and Autonomous Republics. Control over a deputy's performance is exercised through obligatory accountability and by special organs of control formed by Soviets on all levels, combining state control with public control by the working people. Moreover, these features are uniform for all Soviets and are grounded in the USSR's fundamental law and in the laws of each of its territorial subdivisions.

Furthermore, instead of distributing powers between a "lower" and "upper" chamber, with the "upper" chamber empowered to decide major ques-

---

* For a recent eyewitness account of the functioning of Soviets on all levels, of which this writer was a co-author, see *World Marxist Review*, No. 5 (May), 1977.

tions and to override decisions of the "lower" chamber, the two houses of the USSR Supreme Soviet are distinguished according to whether they serve all people without regard to national differences, or whether they serve specific national interests of the different peoples of the USSR. This principle stipulates equal rights of the two chambers, which the electoral system guarantees.

The requirement that a deputy of the Soviet of the Union represent 300,000 inhabitants is a numerical guarantee of equality. The election of deputies to the Soviet of Nationalities, based on fixed quotas of 32 from each Union Republic, 11 from each Autonomous Republic, five from each Autonomous Region, and one from each National Area, ensures that numerical differences among nations and nationalities do not prevent the realization of their actual political equality. This enables nationalities of only a few thousands to have their own deputies. It is noteworthy that this structural organization of the highest organ of state power exemplifies and implements the CPSU's policies for realizing the practical as well as the legal equality of the different nations and nationalities among the USSR's population.

Democratic centralism, explained above with reference to the Party, applies in the functioning of state bodies as well.

The USSR's electoral system also makes clear fundamental differences between capitalist and socialist democracy which explain why popular enthusiasm and support of capitalist state systems is declining in contrast to its expansion in countries of socialist democracy. The elections on June 19 this year to 50,602 local Soviets in 2,229,785 electoral districts of the USSR provide up-to-date evidence of the people's participation in and control of elections throughout all its stages, including the registration of voters, the nomination of candidates, the counting of ballots and the announcement of winners.

Election commissions manage and control the entire process. These numbered 2,254,869 comprising 9,228,397 representatives of mass organizations of the working people. Of these, 61.6 per cent were workers and collective farmers, 47.6 per cent were women, 26.6 per cent were under 30 years of age, and 64.3 per cent were non-party people. Each commission was assisted by volunteers, thereby involving more millions of working people in the electoral process. The same mass organizations then proceeded to nominate a single candidate to represent the constituency of their members.

The nominating process involves, first, majority approval of a single candidate at a general meeting of not less than half of the workforce where the candidate works; second, the candidate's campaign after nomination at meetings, in the press and by television and radio; and third, approval of the candidate by an absolute majority of the voters at the election. Thus, the candidate who emerges successfully during the first nominating stage generally receives the endorsement of the entire electorate. Of the 166,200,403 voters registered by the election commissions, 166,169,714 or 99.98 per cent actually voted last June 19.

As a result of this process as many as 2,229,641 deputies were elected to two-year terms (two and one-half years under the new Constitution) in local Soviets. Of those elected, workers accounted for 42.3 per cent, collective farmers 26.1 per cent, women 49 per cent, young people under 30 years of age 32.4 per cent, Communists 43.2 per cent and non-party people 56.8 per cent. New elections were ordered in 144 election districts where candidates did not receive an absolute majority of the voters, where violations of the election procedure occurred, or where candidates were not ready to begin their work.

An important feature of this process is the unpaid work of everyone involved, all receiving only their usual wages or salaries at their places of employment. This practice obtains also for deputies, who receive only the remuneration paid at their places of employment. Even in the USSR Supreme Soviet, only the president and secretary of the Presidium and the chairpersons of the two chambers receive compensation for full-time employment. Politics in the USSR is neither a source of income or enrichment nor a springboard for future highly lucrative posts as corporation or bank executives.

Another important feature is the continuous renewal of the composition of Soviets. More than 44 per cent of the deputies elected on June 19 had not been elected to previous Soviets. This reflects the gradual fulfillment of Lenin's prediction that under socialism all will govern in turn and will soon become accustomed to no one governing—the path to communist public self-administration and the withering away of the state. (*Selected Works*, Vol. 2, page 373.)

Soviets form executive and administrative organs, organs of people's control, and elect standing commissions. The commissions enlist the assistance of volunteers and specialists for the collection and interpretation of data which provides the factual basis for drafting legislation. All administrative, executive and other organs are accountable to the Soviets, including the Councils of Ministers and their subordinate bodies formed by the Supreme Soviets of the USSR and the Union Republics.

This brief survey should bring into focus certain distinctive features of the electoral process in the USSR that demonstrate the deepening and broadening of democracy. To these should be added a number of the principal general features of the operation of the USSR's system of state power. The most noteworthy include:

1. Participation in the formulation and execution of policy by the people's mass organizations.

2. The electivity of all state bodies and officials. The election of all members

of Soviets on all levels involves nearly 100 per cent participation of the registered voters (a striking contrast to the marked decline of qualified voters' participation in elections in capitalist democracies) on the basis of universal, equal (one citizen 18 years and over—one vote), and direct suffrage by secret ballot, irrespective of race, nationality, sex, religious belief, social origin, property status or past activities.

3. Submission of all important matters of state for discussion and approval (by referendum) of the whole people.

4. The practice of achieving unanimity on all questions through discussion and debate before approval or disapproval is ratified by a final vote.

5. Predominance in all state bodies of working people of all nations and nationalities.

6. Mass-scale voluntary (unpaid) assistance to state bodies on all levels by individuals and organizations of activists, estimated to number more than 30 million.

An objective comparison based on the existence of all or any of these features will make evident the fraudulent and anti-popular essence of capitalist democracy.

The increasing role of mass non-party organizations in the formulation and execution of policy reflects the growing influence of the public and of public opinion. In the USSR "the public" is not an arbitrarily designated force separated from the working people as in capitalist states; it is the working people. Their influence is expressed in numerous ways, such as in elections and referenda, in various meetings of enterprises, institutions and collectives, and in the form of proposals, complaints, criticisms and opinions from individuals and collectives to government agencies and to the information media. Every issue of every one of the 8,000 newspapers in the USSR carries letters from the public. *Pravda*, the CPSU central committee's organ, receives more than 1,000 letters a day. And obviously the submission of all major legislative questions for public discussion implements the policy-making role of public opinion.

Mass organizations, however, are the main channels for the expression of the public's will and opinion. Of these, the most important are the All-Union Central Council of Trade Unions,* with its 113.5 million members (40 per cent are women) including 5.5 million collective farmers, organized in 700,000 locals of 25 industrial unions; the Young Communist League (Komsomol) with 35 million members, who helped draft more than 250 government decrees in 1963-73 to improve young people's conditions of work, study and recreation;

---

*For a detailed recent report on the Soviet trade unions, see the article by George Morris in *New World Review*, No. 3 (May-June), 1977.

the public control bodies with a membership of approximately nine million working people who supervise the implementation of policy; the All-Union Congress of Collective Farmers uniting 15 million farmers in developing self-administration of collective farms and raising agricultural output; the 130,700 standing production conferences in the plants, factories and mills, uniting millions of working people in the management of production; the many associations of professional workers and people engaged in artistic production.

The CPSU's policy is one of extending and deepening the influence of these organizations of the public. The drafters of the new Constitution ensured their right to participate in deciding political, social and cultural problems and their right to introduce legislation. Further assistance is extended to them by the CPSU in the selection, training and education of their leaders.

Mass organizations are led, administered and run by their members. All officers and leading bodies are elected. The organizations perform important state functions, and this role predetermines their future role in a communist society. They are important channels through which the state redistributes the national income, two-thirds of it budgeted for meeting the needs of the people and itself a major criterion of genuine democracy. They are a school of self-administration, successors to the role of the state. The continuous improvement and development of their role is both a result and a precondition of progress in constructing the material and technical base of communism and the evolution of socialist social relations into communist ones.

The definitive criterion of democracy is, of course, whether it conduces to the development of freedom for the individual and the all-round development of the human personality. It is wrong to counterpose the interests of individuals to those of society. Individuals are not isolated from society. Individual rights and freedom express relations of individuals to society. Accordingly, they bear the stamp of the social system, have a class content. Freedom under capitalist democracy is freedom to accumulate private property in the means of production with which to subjugate and exploit the working people. Freedom under socialist democracy is freedom from such subjugation and exploitation through co-ownership of the means of production and the universality of labor as the only source of a livelihood.

In a socialist society, which is committed to the realization of full social equality, it is clearly anti-social for the individual to claim and attempt to secure special freedoms or privileges which are obtainable only at the expense of other members of society or of society as a whole, not to speak of individualistic behavior that harms the development of socialism. Recognition of and submission to the will and interests of the collective, the democratic principle of majority rule, is the condition of the freedom of the individual.

What clearly differentiates socialist democracy from capitalist democracy is its guarantee of the exercise and enjoyment of individual freedoms. What is decisive is not the promise of human freedoms but the guarantee of the means and conditions for exercising and enjoying them. Socialist democracy promises only such freedoms as its economic, social and ideological development enables it to guarantee.

These are the principles embodied in the rights and duties of Soviet citizens, as defined and elaborated in the fundamental law of the USSR. They are an integral part of the USSR's political system, a Soviet "bill of rights" crowning the progress of socialist democracy during the past 60 years towards the realization of communist self-administration.   □

15

JOHN J. ABT

The New Soviet Constitution

The draft of a new Constitution of the USSR was approved by the Presidium of the Supreme Soviet in May of this year and presented to the people for nationwide discussion and proposed amendments before its submission to the Supreme Soviet for final action in October.

Publication of the draft invites comparison with its predecessors of 1918, 1924 and 1936. Each of the four Constitutions marks a new stage in the progress of the first land of socialism.

The earliest was adopted nine months after the Revolution when the young state, ravaged by four years of imperialist war and beleaguered by the armies of fourteen foreign powers and of counterrevolutionary White Guard generals, retained control only of Central Russia, while the Ukraine, the Cauasus, Central Asia, Siberia and other former Russian territories were under enemy occupation. The Constitution for what was then called the Russian Soviet Federal Socialist Republic declared as its goal "the abolition of the exploitation of men by men" and the establishment of a socialist society. It then proceeded to codify the measures already taken toward realization of this noble objective.

It nationalized the land, the banks and foreign trade and provided for "a first step" in nationalizing the means of industrial production and transportation. It guaranteed national self-determination in a land which under the tsars had been a prison of nations, "Leaving to the workers and peasants of every people; to decide . . . whether or not they desire to participate, and on what basis, in the Federal Government." It abolished racial and national discrimination, gave equal rights to women, and "sets itself the task of furnishing full and free education" to a population then 75 per cent illiterate.

It established a dictatorship of the proletariat, disenfranchising the propertied classes, giving industrial workers approximately three times the representation of peasants in the central government, and depriving all individuals and groups "of rights which could be utilized by them to the detriment of the Socialist Revolution." It fixed the voting age at 18 and set up a structure of government

JOHN J. ABT is a noted constitutional lawyer. He is counsel for the Communist Party, U.S.A., and defended many victims of the Smith and McCarran Acts.

vesting "all the central and local power" in the Soviets of Workers, Soldiers and Peasant Deputies. These were delegate bodies which, at the local level, were elected by meetings of voters at their work places, such as factories, army units and rural villages. Higher bodies, including the central government, were elected by the delegates to the next lower bodies. All delegates were subject to recall.

By 1922, after four years of devastating civil war and foreign intervention, the Revolution was victorious throughout the country as it exists today, except for the Baltic States which federated in 1939 and the territory acquired following World War II. As the enemy was driven out, Soviet Republics were established in the liberated areas. Initially, they entered into a loose federation with the RSFSR but soon found a closer union necessary. This was decided on at a Congress of the constituent republics in 1922 and formalized in 1924 by adoption of the Constitution of the Union of Soviet Socialist Republics. Its primary innovation was the creation of a federal structure which provided for a strong central government while guaranteeing each constitutent republic the fullest local and cultural autonomy and equal participation in the central government. This was secured by providing for the establishment for each of six Union Republics of a government elected by its citizens and a bicameral Central Executive Committee of the Union in which one chamber was elected on the basis of population while the other gave equal representation to each Union Republic, with the proviso that all action required the concurrence of both chambers.

If the 1924 Constitution marked the victory of the Revolution, its successor, adopted 12 years later, marked the victory of socialism. In little more than a decade, the face of the nation had been transformed. Agriculture was all but completely socialized by the system of collective and state farms. All industry was publicly owned, and output increased seven times. Socially owned wealth had risen from 48 per cent to 95.8 per cent of the country's fixed capital. Unemployment had been done away with by 1931, and illiteracy substantially eradicated.

The 1936 Constitution expressed the essence of this transformation by declaring the USSR to be "a socialist state of workers and peasants" in which capitalist exploitation of man by man had been replaced by the socialist principle, "From each according to his ability, to each according to his work."

The enormous progress made in industrializing the country and socializing agriculture made it possible for the state to provide its people, and for the 1936 Constitution to guarantee them, the most basic of all human rights—the right to work, to rest, to security in old age and disability, to free medical care, and to free education at every level.

The 1936 Constitution likewise reflected the victory of socialism by democratizing the electoral system. There being no exploiters to disenfranchise, the vote was given to all citizens at the age of 18, with eligibility for public office at 23, excepting only those legally certified as insane. The disproportion between urban and rural representation in the soviets was eliminated. Direct election by secret ballot at all levels of office was provided for. Territorial election districts, each with the same number of inhabitants, replaced the former work-place districts. The Central Executive Committee was replaced by a bicameral Supreme Soviet of the USSR composed of a Soviet of the Union and a Soviet of Nationalities.

In the 40 years since the 1936 Constitution proclaimed the victory of socialism, the Soviet Union has developed into a mature socialist society. Recovering from the incalculable losses of World War II, it has increased the overall volume of industrial production 29 times until it stands at 85 per cent of the US level and has surpassed the latter in steel, coal, oil and other key indicators. In the same period, socialized agriculture has increased output 3.2 times. Per capita real income doubles every 15 years and is more than five times higher than in 1936. Accompanying the betterment of the material conditions of the people has been a change in their social relations. Soviet society has become increasingly homogeneous as the differences in educational level and mode of life between town and country and between manual and intellectual workers have narrowed. Similarly, the equality of the nations comprising the Soviet Union which the 1936 Constitution guaranteed as a matter of law has now become equality in fact as affirmative action by the central government has raised the economic and cultural level of the formerly underdeveloped republics of Central Asia and elsewhere to a parity with what had been industrially advanced areas of the country.

As a result of these profound changes, the Soviet state is no longer characterized as a dictatorship of the proletariat but has developed into a form described as a state of the whole people.

The change in the international position of the Soviet Union has been no less far-reaching. No longer isolated by capitalist encirclement, it has become a member of a powerful socialist community. At the same time, dozens of new states in Asia and Africa have thrown off the colonial yoke and taken an anti-imperialist course of development with the aid and support of the socialist community of nations. As a result, the world balance of forces has been altered to the point where the prevention of world war has become a realistic possibility.

The draft of the new Constitution builds on the foundation laid by its predecessors, taking into account the tremendous advances of the last 40 years in the life of the country and in the international arena Like them, it is at once a programmatic document which sets forth the principles and goals applicable to the present stage of Soviet society and a codification of the nation's major social advances and political structure.

The draft's preamble characterizes the Soviet Union as a "developed socialist society" having "mature social relations" in which the state, after fulfilling the tasks of the dictatorship of the proletariat, "has become a state of the whole people" where "the law of life is the concern of all for the welfare of each and the concern of each for the welfare of all." Unlike any of its forerunners, the preamble then sets its sights on the transition to communism, the highest stage of socialist society. It states:

> The supreme purpose of the Soviet state is to build a classless communist society. The principle tasks of the state are: to build the material and technical basis of communism, to perfect socialist social relations, to mould the citizen of communist society, to raise the living standard and cultural level of the working people, to ensure the country's security, to help strengthen peace and to promote international cooperation.

In his report on the draft to the Central Committee of the Communist Party, General Secretary Brezhnev who chaired the commission that prepared it, capsulized its new features by stating that, "the main trend of the new elements contained in the draft is towards broadening and deepening socialist democracy." This trend manifests itself on two levels: in the expansion of the basic guarantees of economic and cultural rights of the people embodied in the 1936 Constitution, and in the increasing involvement of the people in the economic management and political administration of the country.

The 1936 Constitution's guarantee of the right to work has been expanded to include the right of people to choose their profession, trade or occupation "in accord with their vocation, abilities, training, education, and with account of the needs of society." Closely associated with this right is the draft's guarantee of the right to free education at all levels, including free textbooks and the provision of scholarships, grants and other benefits to students. Universal ten-year education is made compulsory (up from eight years in the 1936 Constitution), and the "extensive development of vocational, secondary specialized and higher education" is ensured.

The article on the right to rest and leisure provides for a general 41 hour work week with shorter hours for onerous occupations, including mining, chemical and textile, and reduced hours of night work, annual paid vacations, weekly days of rest, and "extension of the network of cultural, educational and health-building institutions, and development of sports, physical education and tourism on a mass scale."

The former right to free medical service has been materially extended to guarantee the "right to health protection" which includes "broad preventive measures and measures of enviromental improvement; special care for the health of the rising generation," and "development and improvement of safety techniques and sanitation in production."

The right to maintenance in old age, sickness or disability without cost to the worker has been extended to include collective farmers and to cover partial disability and "disability or loss of breadwinner." Currently, legislation provides for pensions ranging from 50 to 75 per cent of earnings at age 60 for men and 55 for women, reduced to 50 and 45 for certain hazardous occupations. Sick benefits are at the rate of 60 per cent of wages for up to five years of service, 80 per cent from five to eight, and 100 per cent after eight.

The draft adds a new and important right—the right to housing at low rent. This guarantee has been made possible by the massive construction program which rehoused the 25 million people left homeless by World War II and went on from there until a solution of the housing problem is now in sight. In the period from 1971 to 1975, some 56 million people had their housing improved, and homebuilding is currently at the rate of 6,000 apartments a day, five times the growth rate of the population. Today, 90 per cent of the people enjoy a separate apartment for each family at rents, stabilized at the 1928 level, of not more than four per cent of average family income, utilities included. Next goal is an apartment with a room for each member of the family and beyond that, with an additional room for the family as a whole.

The draft guarantees equal rights for women, including equal opportunities for education, employment, remuneration and promotion. Unlike the proposed Equal Rights Amendment to the US Constitution which lacks any safeguards, the draft ensures "special measures for the protection, material and moral support of mother and child, including paid leaves and other benefits to mothers and expectant mothers, and state aid to unmarried mothers." An additional article, not in the 1936 Constitution, provides for family aid by means of "an extensive network of child care institutions," extending and improving community services and public catering, and by allowances to families with many children.

As in the 1936 Constitution, all Soviet citizens are guaranteed equal rights, irrespective of nationality or race. And restriction of these rights and "any advocacy of racial or national exclusiveness, hostility or contempt" is punishable. Incitement of hostility or hatred on religious grounds is likewise prohibited.

No capitalist state has ever provided its whole people with these, the most fundamental of all human rights, let alone guaranteed them in its constitution. Capitalism, by its very nature, is incapable of doing so. It is an achievment which only socialist society can make possible. In such a society, these rights carry with them correlative duties on the part of the citizen which are enumerated in the draft. Among them are observance of Soviet law and the rules of socialist behavior, conscientious labor in one's "chosen socially useful occupation," the safeguarding of socialist property, respect for the national dignity and the rights of others, the protection of nature, the development of friendship with the peoples of other countries, defense of the motherland and service in its armed forces.

The draft contains guarantees of the freedoms of speech, press and assembly and the right of privacy when these are exercised "in conformity with the interests of the working people and for the purpose of strengthening socialism." The quoted qualification is the Soviet equivalent of the "clear and present danger" limitation on the exercise of First Amendment rights in the United States under which the advocacy of ideas may be restrained or punished if found to threaten the national security or the public peace. The difference is that the limitation is explicitly stated in the Soviet Constitution while, in this country, it has been supplied by a Supreme Court "interpretation" of the unconditional wording of the Amendment.

One may disagree with the extent of Soviet restraints on freedom of expression as excessive and lacking justification in any actual or threatened injury to the fabric of socialist society. But criticism must be tempered by the knowledge that from the moment of its birth, the Soviet Union has been the target of a conspiracy by the capitalist powers to overthrow, dismember or strangle it by every available means, including war, quarantine, "containment," "massive retaliation," "positions of strength," subversion, and discriminatory trade practices, and that these policies have by no means been abandoned today.*

"Our goal," Lenin wrote in 1918, "is the unpaid fulfillment of government duties by every worker. . . . Only in this change is the guarantee of the final transition to socialism." The draft constitution confirms and codifies the measures taken for the attainment of this goal.

The composition of the Supreme Soviet of the USSR is modified to provide that the Soviet of Nationalities shall be elected by the voters of the constituent republics on the basis of 32 for each of the 15 Union Republics, 11 for each of the 20 Autonomous Republics, five for each of the eight Autonomous Regions and one for each Autonomous Area established by the Supreme Soviet of the Union Republic of which it is a part. The Soviet of the Union will have the same number of deputies as the Soviet of Nationalities, elected by districts containing equal populations. The two chambers have equal rights, and all legislation requires the concurring votes of both.

---

*An appraisal of the state of human rights in the United States is beyond the purview of this article. It should be noted, however, that the most "liberal" Supreme Court decisions in the area of the First Amendment have upheld the freedom of the Klan and the Nazi Party to incite race hatred, while the Court has sanctioned the abridgment of First Amendment rights by such anti-communist laws as the Smith, McCarran and Taft-Hartley Acts and by witch-hunting congressional committees on the pretext that communists present a "clear and present danger" to the national security.

The draft reduces the age for eligibility to office at all levels, including the highest, from 23 to 18 (the present voting age). It lengthens the terms of deputies to the Supreme Soviets of the USSR and constitutent republics from four to five years and to other Soviets from two to two and one-half years. It provides that all deputies shall continue to work at their trades or professions but shall be released for the performance of their public duties and paid their average earnings for the time spent in doing so.

The right to nominate candidates for election election as deputies may be exercised by public organizations such as the Communist Party, the trade unions, cooperatives and cultural organizations, as well as by collective farms and other collectives. Nominations are made at public meetings of the voters whom the draft guarantees "free and all-sided discussion of the political, professional and personal qualities of the candidates" before nominations are made. Deputies are subject to recall by their electors who have exercised that right in some 4,000 cases over the past ten years.

A total of 2,200,000 deputies serve in Soviets from the city district or village level to the Supreme Soviet of the USSR. They represent more than 100 different nationalities. Workers or collective farmers make up 68 per cent, nearly one-half are women, and one-third are young people. Two-thirds are not members of the Communist Party.

Their duties are not confined to the sittings of the Soviets for the enactment of legislation. For unlike our Congress, state legislatures and city councils, they exercise executive as well as legislative power. In the words of the draft, they "resolve matters related to state, economic, social and cultural development, organize the execution of [their] decisions, and exercise control over the work of state organs, enterprises, institutions and organizations." In performing these functions, they serve on a wide variety of departments, boards and commissions covering every aspect of political and economic affairs within the jurisdiction of the particular Soviet. They are assisted in this work by 30 million volunteer "activists" so that one out of every eight Soviet citizens participates in administering the affairs of government.

Additionally, the draft provides for the formation of "organs of people's control." It is their function to "exercise control over the fulfillment of state plans and assignments, combat violations of state discipline, manifestations of parochialism, narrow departmental attitudes, mismanagement, wastefulness, red tape and bureaucracy, and help to improve the work of the state apparatus." Nine million people are already serving on these bodies.

Popular participation in government affairs is further ensured by four other provisions of the draft. First, every citizen is given the right to submit proposals to governmental bodies for improving their work and to criticize their shortcomings. Officials are obliged to examine these proposals and criticisms, reply to them "and take due action." Second, the draft requires that the "most impor-

tant matters of state'' shall be submitted to a referendum vote of the people.
Third, the draft provides that the right to initiate legislation shall be enjoyed not
only by the Soviets and their deputies but by ''mass public organizations [such
as the trade unions] represented by their all-Union organs.'' Finally, it is made
the duty of all deputies to report to their constituents on their own work and that
of the Soviets of which they are members. In 1976, report-back meetings of the
local Soviets were attended by 130 million voters, the great majority of the
voting population.

The draft includes a unique chapter on peace. It provides that ''war propaganda shall be prohibited by law,'' and states:

> The foreign policy of the U.S.S.R. shall be aimed at ensuring favorable international
> conditions for the building of communism in the U.S.S.R., at strengthening the posi-
> tions of world socialism, supporting the struggles of people for national liberation and
> social progress, preventing wars of aggression and consistently implementing the
> principle of peaceful coexistence of states with different social systems.

The basis of the relations of the USSR with other states is defined by adopting
the text of the Final Act of the Helsinki Conference:

> Observance of the principle of the mutual renunciation of the use or threat of force,
> and of the principles of sovereign equality, inviolability of frontiers, territorial integrity
> of states, peaceful settlement of disputes, non-interference in internal affairs, respect for
> human rights and basic freedoms, equality and the right of peoples to decide their own
> destiny, cooperation between states, scrupulous fulfilment of commitments arising from
> universally recognized principles and norms of international law, and the international
> treaties signed by the USSR.

This brief comparative survey of the four Soviet constitutions affords a
perspective on the arduous but triumphant road which the Soviet people have
travelled in the space of 60 short years, one-third of them disrupted by war and
postwar recovery. The achievements of those years establish the immense
superiority of a planned socialist society over capitalist exploitation and anarchy. They carry with them the assurance that, given the peace for which the
USSR has worked unceasingly since its birth, the Soviet people will march
steadily forward to realization of the goal inscribed in their new constitution—a
classless communist society.

The new constitution was adopted at a session of the Supreme Soviet of the
USSR on October 7, 1977. Adoption followed four months of unprecedented nationwide discussion that involved over 140 million people, 1.5
million meetings and what President Brezhnev, in his report to the session,
described as ''an unending flow of letters from Soviet people.'' The discussion

resulted in the submission to the Constitution Commission of some 400,000 proposals for amendments to the draft. After examining them all, the Commission recommended amendments to 110 of the 173 articles of the draft and the inclusion of one additional article:

> [T]he discussion of the Draft Constitution has largely gone well beyond the framework of an analysis of the text itself. It has developed into a frank and truly popular conversation on the key aspects of our life which are of a stirring concern to all Soviet people. Collectives of working people and individual citizens have made just and—not infrequently—sharp critical remarks on various aspects of the activity of state organs and social organizations, proposing measures for improving the work and eliminating the existing shortcomings . . .
>
> Millions upon millions of working people in town and country have supported the new Constitution by word and by deed. They compared every line of the Draft with their own practical work and with the work of their labor collectives. They made increased socialist pledges, amended production plans, discovered new reserves for enhancing production efficiency and improving work performance and met their new Constitution with great labor exploits. In short, our people have again shown themselves to be full masters of the socialist homeland.

☐

16

DAVID LAIBMAN

The Soviet Economy After Six Decades

Sixty years ago the Soviet economy was born, with the Bolsheviks' Decree on Land, ending the timeless oppression of the Russian peasantry. The years of "War Communism," 1918-22, saw Soviet power as an embattled fortress, compelled to use brute administrative force and rationing to beat back the famine and dislocation that necessarily accompanied World War and wars of intervention. Later, Lenin's inspired New Economic Policy—widely misunderstood as a "retreat" from socialist construction—was in reality a step toward the first Control Figures of 1925-26, and the first Five-Year Plan (FYP), announced in 1929. The NEP abolished wartime restrictions and allowed small commodity producers to operate, in effect, giving reality to the land reform promulgated by the Revolution. It also produced the first shoots of a socialist planning system, organized under the Council of People's Commissars, and provided the framework in which the rudiments of planning procedure—especially the method of planning by material and financial balances—were worked out.

Of course, the Soviet *socialist* economy is not 60 years of age. The first FYP, covering the years 1930-34, initiated the growth of a significant Soviet industrial sector, the core of the necessary rapid growth of productive forces and the ultimate source of growth of all other sectors. By the mid-1930s, one can speak of socialist production relations being secured in industry; and of the achievement of a specific form of socialist relations in the countryside, the organization of peasants into collective farms. The precious physical resources, organizational experience, and human skills, built up at enormous cost in a land where 75 per cent of the people had been illiterate and where the initially backward and stunted productive base had been largely destroyed in war, were committed in the sacred struggle to rid the world of Hitler fascism. This struggle cost the USSR over 20,000,000 lives and devastation of all that had been so dearly created. Add to all this the years of diplomatic isolation and economic boycott and encirclement, and subsequently the Cold War with its wasteful arms race. It

DAVID LAIBMAN is Assistant Professor of Economics at Brooklyn College (CUNY), and Assistant Editor of *New World Review*.

is fair to say, then, that *socialist* economic development has had barely three, not six, decades in which to prove itself.

Against this background, the record of Soviet economic growth takes on its full meaning. In comparison with 1913, the last prewar year before the Revolution, Soviet national income had increased 17.7 times by 1970, against a population increase of 73.5 per cent. Thus national income per capita went up more than ten-fold. Using the results of the 9th FYP and the targets of the 10th (1976-80), national income will stand at 28.6 times its 1913 level by 1980. Agricultural production had more than tripled by 1970, and will have more than quadrupled by 1980. Gross industrial output, key to modern economic growth, was more than 101 times as big in 1970 as in 1913; by 1980 that index will rise to 197! A rough estimate of living standards can be gained from data on food consumption per capita, 1970 in per cent of 1913: Meat (including poultry), 165.5; milk and milk products, 199.4; eggs, 329; fish, 230; vegetables, 207.5; grain and grain products, 74.5.

Soviet industrial production is now 85-90 per cent of US industrial production, and will clearly exceed the US 1975 level by 1980. (Comparison with the US 1980 level is not possible, because output levels in capitalist economies are simply not predictable.) The USSR now leads the world in the output of oil, pig iron, steel, cement, mineral fertilizers, tractors, cotton and woolen fabrics, leather footwear, sugar, milk and butter, and is closing the gap in many other industries, Soviet growth rates, while somewhat lower than in the past for reasons which merit full discussion elsewhere, maintain their significant lead over all capitalist countries. Taking average annual rates of growth for 1971-75 (USSR) and 1971-74 (the capitalist countries), only Japan exceeded the USSR's figure for national income of 5.6 per cent; no capitalist country came close to Soviet industrial growth of 7.4 per cent, capital investments of 6.9 per cent, and industrial labor productivity of 6.0 per cent; and only Britain exceeded the Soviet growth rate of agricultural output of 2.5 per cent. The USSR has one of the highest percentages of the population enrolled in educational institutions, the lowest student/teacher ratios, by far the most doctors and hospital beds per 10,000 population, and so on. The singular magnitude of the Soviet achievement can simply no longer be denied.

Still, it must be explained. What does a socialist economy *do* to create a record of progress like the one summarized above? The answer to this question goes to the heart of the essential difference between capitalism and socialism as forms of social-economic organization.

1. *Planning: the metabolism of an intentional society.* The last labor exchanges in the USSR were closed in 1930, for want of customers. Thus,

unemployment—except for a statistically negligible number of "frictionally" unemployed, those in transit between jobs—does not exist. The administration of an enterprise is prohibited by law (see articles 17, 18 and 91 of the Fundamental Labor Legislation of the USSR) from dismissing a worker from his/her job, without securing consent of the enterprise's trade union committee *in advance,* and then only for specific reasons stipulated. Transfer to another job can only take place with the worker's consent, and with no reduction in wages. Thus the phenomenon known in capitalist countries as *firing* does not exist. Finally, medical care and higher education are free of charge to the recipient, financed out of the general state budget as part of the social consumption fund. Adequate housing at minimal rent is provided by law to all Soviet citizens, a right now embodied in the new Constitution. Thus, there is no *aggravated insecurity* due to loss of dwelling, crippling medical expenses (especially in old age), or bearing the costs of educating one's children.

These remarkable and uncontested facts of Soviet life are usually cited simply to *describe* the quality of life in the USSR—and in that respect one wishes they were fully known to some 200 million Americans. I cite them here for an additional, and deeper, reason. Unemployment and insecurity are not only necessary results of capitalist functioning, in which all things come about as by-products of the unplanned drive for profits on the part of private capitals. They are the very heart of capitalism's coercive principle, in which workers are driven by a fear whose object appears not as the pre-eminence of a propertied ruling class but rather as the impersonal working of economic laws, of "markets." And conversely, the fundamental absence of unemployment and insecurity in the Soviet Union testify to the absence of this coercion, and suggests that the driving force in Soviet life is quite different.

The absence of an insecure quality in the lives of people, often noticed by travelers to the USSR, is directly due to the role of *planning* in Soviet society. Planning is comprehensive, reaching to all levels of organization. It counteracts and replaces spontaneity and chaos, brings social processes under conscious, intentional control, through a massive and constantly functioning democracy.

How does economic planning work? Here are the bare bones of the process, greatly simplified. In July, the State Planning Board of the USSR (Gosplan) issues control figures for the plan that will become operative the following year, after being passed into law by the Supreme Soviet. The Gosplan control figures are broken down by ministries, and by the planning boards of the Union Republics. When the figures reach the enterprises, enterprise personnel—here, as we will see, the trade unions play a major role—draft a detailed enterprise plan. A period of negotiation, in which the enterprises make counterproposals and the higher bodies revise their aggregate targets to re-establish consistency, lasts through September, when the ministries "lock in" the nine or ten general indicators under their jurisdiction—sales volume, total profit, rate of profit, total wage bill, basic output assortment, etc.—for each of the 50,000 enterprises in the economy. Within this framework the enterprise then adopts its own detailed plan, and breaks that plan down into department and team plans. The enterprise is accountable only for the officially approved indicators, although it registers its own detailed plan with the appropriate higher bodies, so that all other enterprises and interested parties can have access to it. The annual enterprise plan must also be reconciled with the targets of the five-year plan, which have already been broken down to the level of the work team and even the individual workers.

Millions of workers participate in this process, and thereby come to see how their own plan of work fits in with the larger plans, from the team to the brigade to the enterprise and ministry to the economy as a whole. Similarly, one is part of a conscious effort to move in a direction known beforehand; for example, the five-year targets for raising wages and pensions step by step, according to the various categories of labor and regions of the country, are known and indeed were widely discussed before they were adopted.

The distribution of tasks and income is planned. There are, of course, tradeoffs, and different interests arise; these must be reconciled through the planning process. But the process itself is political and principled. There is no elemental bargaining, no ''poker-playing.'' The plans which result must be effective and consistent, for there is no other means whereby economic activities are coordinated. So when Soviet social theorists speak of the ''law of planned, proportional development'' in a socialist society, they are not merely issuing propaganda blasts, as is so often assumed. They are referring to a very real objective characteristic of socialism.

Planning, of course, has come a long way since those early five-year plans. Today, more and more attention is given to the long-term ''perspective'' plans, such as the current one elaborated for 1976-1990. These must come to grips with changing demographic patterns, project major technological shifts, and much else of which H. G. Wells would be proud. The use of mathematical models in planning and electronic data processing and transmission make possible far more interaction among the several levels of planning; a more effective use of that ultimate scarce resource, time; more flexibility at lower levels; and increasingly reliance on methods for choosing optimal (or near-optimal) plans, as opposed to satisfactory (consistent) ones. Much work is being done on improving the structure of prices, and on criteria for investment choice, formation of bonuses, evaluation of labor, whether scientific, production or managerial. The effort in the 10th FYP is to incorporate the 25th CPSU Congress slogan, ''Efficiency and Quality,'' into planning, make it operational.

2. *Participation: the other side of the coin.* The organized activity of millions of workers replaces the spontaneous market process that fills in the details under capitalism. And here the evidence is massive, and non-ignorable.

Among mass organizations in the USSR, the trade unions stand out as the major vehicle for popular working-class participation in plan formation, execution and control. The unions now have 113.5 million members. There are 25 industrial (vertical) trade unions in the country, with about 700,000 primary organizations (locals), and 2.5 million "groups," or smaller organizational units. Trade-union participation in management is guaranteed by law; unions have "statutory status," including the right to initiate legislation. Article 16 of the new Constitution states: "Collectives of working people and public organizations shall participate in the management of enterprises and associations, in deciding matters concerning the organization of labor and everyday life, and the use of funds allocated for the development of production as well as for social and cultural requirements and material incentives."

The trade unions direct the work of the 131,000 standing production conferences, whose 5.5 million members hear reports and make recommendations to management, some two million of which are incorporated in collective agreements every year. Of course, as signatory to the collective agreement, which includes the full production and social plan of the enterprise, the trade union has indirect control over the main outlines of management activity. It also exercises control, in the interests of the workers, through safety inspection commissions, labor protection teams, people's control posts (with nine million workers active in them), societies of innovators and inventors, activists in the labor disputes commissions (half of whose members must be rank-and-file workers), etc.

The trade unions have *direct* control over a vast and increasingly important area of activity—the planning and administering of the social consumption funds, which will reach 115 billion rubles by 1980, and the budget for state social insurance, 29.8 billion rubles in 1977. ("Social consumption funds" cover education, medical care, pensions, housing, disability and training, child care, sanatoria, homes for the elderly, etc. Payments and benefits received from them average 35 per cent of a worker's money wage.) The trade unions operate 2,150 night sanatoria; more than a thousand health centers and holiday resorts; more than 950 tourist institutions; 22,000 clubs, 23,000 libraries, extensive sports facilities, cultural facilities, Young Pioneer camps for children, etc. All of these facilities rest on the participation of millions of trade-union activists.

The 10th FYP took shape through a process in which some 92 million workers met, discussed, and formulated more than one million proposals. In the 9th FYP period, the production conferences, through their elected memberships and in large shop-floor meetings, made nearly seven million proposals for improving economic activity. While individual workers undoubtedly range from loners to compulsive activists, one can hardly doubt that the great majority of working people become involved at one level or another. Indeed, to the extent that is *not* the case, the plans have a purely formal character, and therefore function poorly. Socialist organization is its own spur to its own improvement. But improvement does not come about automatically, and to indicate how seriously Soviet planners take this matter, one may refer to the 1971 Central Committee resolution "On Improving the Economic Education of the Working People." In the Ukraine alone, some 7.7 million people participated in economic education programs under this resolution, to increase their grasp of planning principles and techniques. The historical and practical character of socialist democracy comes through in one Soviet commentator's remark that "to further improve the activity of the democratic institutions of socialist production, it is important to raise the general educational level and the scientific-technical training of the working people." And conversely: in a society where the negative incentive of the irresponsible power of capital is systematically absent, rising educational levels must become operative in broadening and deepening of the institutions of socialist democracy.

3. *Consumption and production: a true "revised sequence."* Economist John Kenneth Galbraith, in *The New Industrial State*, observed that the giant corporations in the United States were managing and manipulating consumer demand in their own interests, rather than responding to consumer demand. Assuming it had indeed been otherwise in the past, Galbraith called this reversal of direction a "revised sequence."

The term actually can be adopted to describe an important watershed in the advance of a socialist economy, in which the labor activity of all working people is increasingly brought forward without external compulsion. Consumption has always been possible because of production, and only to the extent that goods have been produced; in this sense production determines consumption. There is, however, a basic change at work which is revising the sequence: given that working people in a socialist society cannot be driven by fear of poverty, fear of the unknown, fear of being cut adrift by irresponsible forces out of their control, further gains in productivity and output depend on growing self-motivation of workers, and this is linked to the entire quality of life—the level and quality of consumption, as it affects and is affected by the creativity and social relatedness of the labor process. High levels of consumption are increasingly central to the overcoming of alienation and growth of socialist consciousness, which in turn are the key to the qualitative overhaul of the functioning of socialist collectives—and this is basic to continued growth of production, in a period when the sources of simple extensive growth are disappearing.

The growth in living standards, then, is *"an important premise for the further growth of production and its efficiency,"* as Soviet Premier A. N.

Kosygin put it at the 25th CPSU Congress. Thus the "law of increasing satisfaction of material and cultural requirements," like the "law of planned, proportional development" mentioned earlier, is indeed a "law," necessary to the functioning and growth of an advanced socialist economy. It is especially important in that it shows the intimate connection between the reward of labor—material incentives—and the process leading to transformation of labor into life's prime need.

Underlying the gradual transformation in the quality of living standards is the material basis of consumption. Data on food consumption was given above. The picture in durable goods is similar, and striking when compared to the stagnation or deterioration evident in most capitalist countries. In the decade 1960-1970, TV sets in place per unit of population increased by 550 per cent; cameras, 63 per cent; motorcycles, 110 per cent, vacuum cleaners, 287 per cent; sewing machines, 50 per cent; refrigerators, 710 per cent; washing machines, 969 per cent. The scale of housing construction remains vast, unequaled anywhere in the world; in the 10th FYP period, one in every five Soviet citizens will change to new or improved housing. Real per capita income is planned to increase by 21 per cent; allocations out of the social consumption funds by 30 per cent; and services to the population by almost 50 per cent. The number of children in schools and day-care centers is planned to rise by 43.8 per cent, revealing a commitment to virtually eliminate existing shortages in this area. The plan provides for significant increases in the number and range of educational opportunities, especially for the adult population, and including an increase in secondary vocational-technical schools of 81.4 per cent.

Worthy of mention is the vast network of "People's Universities," facilities for continuing adult education and enrichment, and the Znanie (knowledge) Society, which organizes lectures and courses in natural and social science at factories, workers' clubs, etc.

All in all, the planned rise in standards of living illustrates the socialist "revised sequence": rising consumption is the key to advancing production. The quality of consumption includes successfully meeting specific demands, and flexibly adapting to changes in demand. Soviet planners are working on the shortcomings in practice in this area. The important point is that, unlike Galbraith's new industrial state, the Soviet economy contains no social force interested in manipulating or managing consumer demand for private profit. There are no "planners' preferences," as distinct from "consumers' preferences"; the dynamic of socialist development ensures that planners can "prefer" only to do what they must do—be good planners.

4. *Stratification: its gradual disappearance.* The capitalist past bequeathed to the Soviet Union, as to all countries building socialism, a bouquet of social strata. There are two main classes: the working class and the collective-farm

peasantry. Within the working class, broadly defined as all who work in state enterprises, there are production workers, office and clerical workers, scientific/research personnel and managerial/administrative personnel. Associated with the differences in money incomes resulting from the existence and correct use of material incentives are differences in levels of living.

Just as these differences are based on existing conditions in early socialist construction, so their objective basis gradually weakens, as technological development evens up the conditions of labor for the several categories of workers, and as socialist consciousness evolves accordingly.

Beginning with the distribution of income, the most noteworthy thing is the persistent and uninterrupted tendency toward equalization. By 1968, average money earnings had risen to about 156 per cent of their 1955 level; for minimum earnings, at the lower end of the scale, the corresponding increase was 255-286 per cent. In addition to earnings, the growth of the social consumption funds, rising as a proportion to total income and rising more rapidly than money wages (30 per cent and 17 per cent, respectively, in 1976-80), strengthens the tendency toward equalization of living standards. Raising the relatively lower income levels of collective farmers is an object of policy, and collective farm incomes are to rise by 26 per cent in 1976-80. Collective farmers, since the late 1960s, have had pensions, access to social insurance funds and other benefits accruing to workers, and their social position is drawing steadily closer to that of workers on state farms.

The most rapidly growing part of the working class is the scientific intelligentsia, whose numbers have increased ten-fold since before the war. At the same time, the educational level of production workers and technicians is constantly rising, both absolutely and in relation to that of the scientific-engineering personnel. Thus, at one plant the proportion of workers with a complete secondary and higher education approached 30 per cent in 1970. As educational opportunities expand, the category of *highly qualified worker*, with professional skills and a professional cultural and technical level, emerges; still a minority, this group is a microcosm of the working class in advanced socialism, which demonstrates an ability to disseminate higher education among the entire working population and merge it with production. By contrast, capitalist societies, maintaining the traditional separation between workers and intellectuals, produce a stratum of "overqualified unemployed."

Other data indicate that the foundations for a genuine merging of strata are being laid. One Soviet writer reports that "one in every three marriages is contracted between people belonging to different classes and social groups"; in other words marriages between professionals and factory workers, between production and managerial staff, are increasingly common. The home does not become a vehicle for imposing a stratified conception of society in the minds of children. Soviet cities are homogeneous; there are no managerial neighborhoods vs. "working class districts," no equivalents of Grosse Point, Michigan or inner-city ghettoes. School attendance is strictly on a neighborhood basis (with the exception of the special "physics-mathematics" schools for children who show special talent in these areas), and school funding, quality and curriculum are uniform throughout the country. Education is, of course, a powerful force for equalizing the conditions and opportunities of life. A single factual comparison will make clear that this force is operating effectively. Between the census years 1959 and 1970, the proportion of the population with a higher or (complete or incomplete) secondary education rose by 34 per cent. During the same period, the number of *working people* with this level of education increased by about 75 per cent. Taking into account the increase in the labor force, this amounts to an increase of 60-65 per cent in the proportion of the *working people* with at least incomplete secondary education. Higher levels of education are appearing more rapidly among production workers, and especially among those doing primarily physical labor.

Soviet researchers are careful, however, to avoid the conclusion that the merging process is complete, and that distinctions among classes and strata in Soviet society are now purely formal. They stress that the consolidation of the classless character of socialism is a long process, which cannot be artificially accelerated ahead of its material basis in the rising level and character of production, and its socio-political basis in the construction of socialist production relations.

An important part of socialist economic organization, of course, is the nature and role of the administrative and managerial stratum, numbering some 1.5 million people in 1970. It is here, naturally, that the professional critics of Soviet reality—from the likes of Djilas on the right to the Maoists and "capitalist restorationists" on the "left"—look for a new Soviet "ruling class" or "privileged bureaucracy." All available facts belie these claims. Data from numerous studies show that the leading personnel of industrial enterprises overwhelmingly come from families of workers and peasants, and started their working careers as production workers or farmers. The percentages for which this is true—typically 75-90 per cent—are comparable to those for the leading cadre in the Party and state organizations, and there is no tendency for these percentages to fall over time. For this reason and all those relating to residence, education and income levels given above, the notion that a hereditary privileged stratum exists or is forming is—to be charitable—an illusion.

There is also massive evidence against the claim that office-holding in the USSR is used by office-holders to exercise and consolidate arbitrary personal power—although there are abuses remaining to be eliminated, and weasknesses to be corrected. Space is lacking to cite examples of recall of enterprise managers, and other forms of disciplining management on the initiative of local trade union or public bodies. Less widely known is the rise of *collective management bodies* in the production associations (consolidations of small enterprises into a single, larger production unit) and industrial associations (middle-level management bodies, of which there are now some 3,000), where management councils, or collegiums, are constituted on a representative basis from the lower units. As a Soviet researcher writes: "Practice has confirmed that under today's conditions, even if the professional level of the production board is sufficiently high, the successful fulfillment of organizational-managerial tasks at the level of associations is no longer possible without increasing the number of participants in collective decision-making and without recruiting representatives of the working people."

This point can even be formulated as another *law* of advanced socialist economy, akin to planned, proportional development and satisfaction of material/cultural requirements: the progressive drawing together of strata, and unification of managerial and production work as an aspect of the drawing together of mental and manual labor. The objectivity of this law can be seen by stating its negative: the *impossibility* of the managerial function consolidating itself into a form of class power. Capitalist class power, as we have seen, is based on a specific form of social organization, which is inseparable from all of its elements, especially the nature of labor-power and capital as commodities whose values are formed in markets. In a society where the managerial stratum exercises the *power of capital*, the deformation of that function—"bureaucracy"—plays an essential role, indeed an indispensable one. In a society where the managerial stratum exercises the power of the working class and allied strata, and where the power of capital is absent, "bureaucratic" deformations are a drag on the production process, i.e., are positively *dis*functional. So it is not accidental that the CPSU 25th Congress raised to a new level the demands on enterprise managers, and the mandate to enterprise collectives, mass organizations and trade unions to increase their control and participation.

So we stand, at a distance of sixty years, and view the remarkable human achievement that is the Soviet economy. We also know that socialism at age 60—unlike a single human being—represents a social formation that is in its infancy, and that the stage of advanced socialism now reached poses new possibilities, and with them new problems; for the social progress of our unique species is a never-ending ascent along a road which becomes wider as it rises. To have pointed the way forward to an economy of equality, security and creativity in the service of the noblest of social ends is surely a sufficient accomplishment for Soviet socialism's first sixty years. ☐

17

LEM HARRIS

The Quality of Life on Soviet Farms

S oviet agriculture has attained a high level of production. As the first country to develop its farm operations on a socialist basis, there were many who wondered how farmers, who are supposed to be the world's greatest individualists, would react to changing over to collective operations. There is no longer any question; collective agriculture has been operating successfully in eight socialist countries. They have all met the food requirements of their peoples, and shortages, not to mention famine, no longer occur. Of great interest is the change in the quality of life which has accompanied the collectivization of farming.

Some idea of the achievement of Soviet agriculture can be gained by noting the production levels that have been reached:

Soviet *wheat* output has surpassed US levels every year since 1965. 1975 was a year of most unfavorable weather, but even that crop was slightly greater. In 1976 the USSR bounced back with a wheat crop more than double US production. 1977 is about the same as 1976.

Soviet *meat* output has been far behind the US level but has been slowly edging forward. In 1975, it was 76 per cent of the US level.

Milk production in the USSR has also increased. In 1965 it was 29 per cent more than in the US, and in 1975, 73 per cent more. Poultry is far behind the US level. In 1965 it was 14 per cent and in 1975 23 per cent. The fish catch was double and is now triple the American.

What have these production achievements meant in terms of diet of the Soviet people? Basically, increased per capita consumption of food and also important improvement in the quality of the average diet. Two items, grain products and potatoes, are being consumed in smaller quantities per capita. But, since 1950, meat including poultry has doubled; so have milk and milk products; eggs have tripled; fish more than doubled; vegetables and legumes are up 49 per cent; fruits and berries (excluding wine-making) more than tripled. This reflects improved dietary standards for all the people.

LEM HARRIS, specialist in agriculture economics, writes frequently for *New World Review* on developments in Soviet agriculture.

It should be noted that the decrease in consumption of grain products as food is accompanied by a large increase in the use of grain for livestock feed. At present, around 40 per cent of the whole grain crop is used for feed. It was to guarantee sufficient supplies for this purpose that sizeable imports of grain were arranged in recent years.

The socialization of agriculture opened the door for another important objective. Many millions of former peasants moved to the industrial centers to meet the expanding employment needs of growing industries. In 1958 there were 25 million collective farm workers; in 1975 there were only 15 million. Yet during that time, gross farm output increased more than one-third.

The above summation of the stage of production attained by Soviet agriculture invites a backward glance at the revolutionary changes that socialism has brought to the countryside. It will be recalled that in 1917, when Soviet power was established, two thirds of the land, and the best land at that, was owned by the landlords, nobility and clergy. Eighty-two per cent of the Russian population was peasantry, much of it landless and forced to work for a miserable living for the landlords and richer peasants.

One of the first decrees of the Soviet Government was the Decree on Land, providing for dispossession of all the large landholders and immediate distribution of the bulk of it to the peasantry—thus satisfying their centuries-old land hunger. The decree assured the support of the mass of the peasantry for the new regime but created a problem of feeding the cities. For the first time, peasants could retain enough of their own grain to properly meet their own needs. But a great part of the thousands of tons formerly requisitioned by the landowners and sold to the cities stayed in the villages. Years of civil war against counter-revolutionary armies which invaded the young Soviet State, plus serious drought in the valley of the Volga, created a desperate food shortage in the cities and in some farm regions. For the first decade of Soviet Russia, food was in short supply. The situation demanded revolutionary measures.

In 1928, the two basic forms of socialist farming were launched in a big nationwide campaign. The first was the collectivization of individual peasant farming. The whole Communist Party membership in rural areas and many thousands of comrades from industry were mobilized to campaign in the villages to convince peasants to put their land, cattle and implements into newly forming cooperative farms. Vital to the success of the collectives or kolkhozes was the supplying of thousands of tractors and necessary tractor drawn implements to assure deep plowing and timely seeding, cultivating and harvesting of large fields which replaced myriads of former peasant plots. The Soviet government had forseen this need and was ready with factories turning out thousands of tractors and implements. In 1930 the first Soviet combined harvesters and reapers (combines) appeared on the fields of the new collectives, causing quite a stir.

Model rules of organization were drawn up by the government and adopted by the kolkhozes. They provided that the land of the collective would be theirs in perpetuity; that the members should control the whole farm operation including the financing and distribution of the proceeds of the harvest. An amendment to the original rules provides that all collective farm members must receive regular wages each month and not have to wait as formerly for a distribution of the proceeds of the harvest. Of course, additional payments and bonuses are added after the total income from the year's crop becomes known. In other respects, the Model Rules remain virtually unchanged. To this day the director of the kolkhoz and the management of all its affairs are subject to the approval of the general membership meeting.

The second socialist measure was the organization of numerous rather large state-operated farms, or sovkhozes. Often specializing in certain crops, these state farms serve multiple purposes: experimental and demonstration methods, the use of the very largest tractors on huge areas to determine the efficiency of large scale operations, and of course the production of massive crops for the needs of the industrial sector.

Workers on the state farms are paid wages, receive social insurance on the same basis as industrial workers, get bonuses for good results, but do not share in the harvest. As in industrial enterprises, management is appointed by the organs of government, but must have the approval of the trade union of farm employees. A director of a state farm could not remain at his post if the members of the trade union voted his removal.

From the very start of collectivization, small individual plots averaging about an acre (or more in certain areas) were assigned to every farm family so that vegetables, fruit and berries, eggs and milk could be produced. Most of the products of these plots are consumed by the households which own them, but there is always a surplus which is sold on the open market. There is a tendency on the more advanced collective farms for members to dispense with their garden plots because they receive ample vegetables, fruit, eggs and milk as additions to their earned wages.

T oday, sixty years after the Bolshevik Revolution and about fifty years since the collectivization of farming and the introduction of improved agronomical methods, emphasis is now more and more on the quality of life in the countryside. The announced goal is to bring to the village all the amenities and cultural advantages of the city. Extending electric power to the rural communities was a first step. At first the state constructed large power generating plants with transmission lines extending to distant villages. The earliest such plant was the Dnieper Hydroelectric Station, generating power from the first big dam on that river.

It happened that in 1930 I visited a village receiving power from that dam. On entering the village I heard strains of Franz Liszt's Clock Symphony wafting thru the village from a loud speaker hooked to the only radio receiver in the village. I learned that a problem with the newly installed electric lights had arisen. Gradually the light bulbs had become dimmer and dimmer. People wondered if the enormous power dam on the Dnieper was failing. An electrical engineer was summoned and quickly found the cause. The trouble was peasant ingenuity. First one and then others twisted wire around a brick, hooked it to the line and were pleased to have a home made electric heater, of course using immense wattage. The homestyle heaters were banned and the town lights brightened. The great power dam was relieved of all responsibility.

Soon groups of collective farms were jointly constructing small generating units and supplying their own power. Telephone lines followed. Then came improved housing—sometimes city-type apartment houses but more recently the trend is to two-family and individual family homes. But whether in an apartment or individual home, a plot is always available for each family's fruit trees, cabbage, cucumber patch and whatever.

A great deal has been accomplished in the villages in carrying out the basic communist principle of bridging the gap between town and countryside and between manual and mental labor. Incomes of collective farm members more and more nearly approach those of city dwellers.

The whole life of the village has been completely transformed. Where in the past the church was the only social center and the main festivities were organized around religious holidays, there are a whole number of social institutions which never existed before the Revolution. Large collective farms, or several smaller ones together, have kindergartens, schools, libraries, movie theaters, hospitals, clinics, sports grounds, palaces of culture. As in the factories, farm workers have the opportunity to take up various amateur cultural or other activities with the help of professionals. Many rural youth return to the farm after vocational or higher education to work professionally in these institutions, or to do technical or scientific work on the farm.

The government has helped the villages greatly in massive irrigation and land improvement projects. Recent years have seen great progress in intensification, specialization and industrialization of agriculture. In many areas interfarm cooperative industrial enterprises have been established where food processing or other light industries connected with agriculture are being undertaken.

To really get the flavor of the new quality of life on the farm, let collective farmers speak for themselves. Recently a correspondent for the Soviet news agency Novosti visited a number of collectives in the Orlov region and wrote up the reactions of the people he interviewed:

"Excluding the two years I served in the army, all the 27 years of my life I have lived at our collective farm in Ilyinsky village. That is where I graduated from our school, that is where I drive our tractor . . .

"Did you notice that I'm always saying 'our' collective farm, 'our' school, 'our' tractor? It has occurred to me that I am using the words 'our' and 'ours' more and more often.

"Certainly, the word 'mine' also occupies a definite place I say 'my' home, 'my' children. There are other things that I designate as 'mine.' They are my library (about a hundred book titles), my hobby (song-birds), and my motorcycle.

"The collective farm is a wealthy enterprise. It does a great deal to develop production and improve the life of the farmers. For instance, we have built a whole street of excellent houses with all the amenities for the members of the farm. We have a beautiful House of Culture, and a ten-year secondary school. All that is our common property. That is why we come out indignantly against those (it is a pity but we still have them) who are capable of utilizing collective farm property in their own interests."

Andrei and Maria Kozhin are the parents of 12 children.

Andrei: "You ask about our children. Dimitri is the eldest. He is 21 and has a secondary education. After serving in the army he took a job in Orel, our regional center. He works in a steel mill there. He is going to be married soon.

"Our second son, Vanya, is working as a joiner in Belgorod after finishing eight classes. After he serves in the army, he says he will return to work at the collective farm. He loves the land.

"The rest are in school or preschool."

Maria: "During the difficult early postwar years, we went through a great deal before we attained our present easy circumstances. For instance this house we are living in. It was not all that easy to build. The collective farm helped us a lot.

"If you are interested in what adds up to make our family budget, I can tell you that Andrei brings in 170 rubles every month. The elder sons contribute their share. As mother with many children, I receive a state allowance of 48 rubles and the collective farm pays me an additional 45 rubles. In the summer months when the older girls have no classes, we work the best and make an additional 300 rubles or more. The cash income of our family, excluding the older sons, came to 4,600 rubles in 1976.

"Moreover, we get potatoes, vegetables, fruits, berries, and honey from our plot of land. We keep a cow and hens and fatten two to three young pigs every year. Last year we got a bonus of 240 kilograms of sugar from the collective farm.

"Of course other families in our collective farm that have not so many children and more working people are better off materially than we are. But on the other hand, you can't imagine how much we enjoy our little 'home-grown collective farm community'! That is something you cannot measure in rubles and kopeks, can you?

"As for leisure and entertainment, we have television in the house, we buy books, we have a whole library now, we go to the cinema and to the shows staged by our collective farm theater."

Andrei: "Maria and I have no regrets about raising such a big family. The children are no burden. We know that the state will help us raise them and make them useful citizens, whose work will be of benefit to society."

Vasily Klyukovsky is Chairman of the Karl Marx Collective Farm. "A demobilized tankman, I returned to my native Borkovo in 1947, and joined the others in raising the village from ruins. I did my best to make it better and more beautiful than it was before the war.

"We have achieved definite success in the past few years and our work has been highly assessed by the state. The most important thing is to move forward. But that is something we can not do without peace. I am not only a collective farm chairman but a Communist, a supporter of the policy of my Party and my government."

Leonid Kruzhkov, machine operator on the Zarya Collective Farm: "A machine operator is an important figure on a collective farm. A lot depends on him. What is more, he makes no less than a fitter or turner in town. My average income is 170 rubles per month. My family and I are well off for that is quite sufficient, though my wife does not work—she stays home with the baby. We get more from our orchard and kitchen garden than we can eat, so we sell the surplus to the village consumer cooperative.

"I am living now in my father's house, so we pay no rent. My wife, Tamara, and I have definitely decided we are going to build a house of our own. The collective farm will help us with building materials and manpower.

"I have other interests like reading. Besides the papers *Selskaya Zhizn* (Country Life) and *Orlovskaya Pravda*, I also subscribe to the magazines *Teknika Molodyozhni* (Young Technicians) and *Smena* (Change), a socio-political and literary monthly.

"My overalls are issued by the collective farm, just like factories issue them to their workers. In short there is practically no difference between me, a collective farm machine operator and an industrial worker in town.

"I work out of doors under the open sky and I love it. I am a co-owner of all the collective farm property. After all it is a cooperative enterprise, isn't it? My income depends on how the farm grows and how its harvests and income increase.

"So am I a farmer or industrial worker?"   □

18

ERWIN MARQUIT

Theory and Practice of Soviet Natural Science

The launching of Sputnik I or the landing of the lunar vehicle or the space probe on Venus would surely rank as the most outstanding Soviet achievement in the 60 years since the October Revolution. The Soviet space experiments clearly showed how the social forces released by the October Revolution were able in only 60 years to transform a huge country known for its backwardness, poverty, and illiteracy into a modern, dynamically developing society. The joint Soyuz-Apollo flight also symbolized the recognition by major US government leaders that the time had come to abandon the illusion of attaining technological superiority over the Soviet Union in space and to consider the alternative of international scientific and technological cooperation in this field.

Soviet progress in the development of controlled thermonuclear reactions has given rise to the hope of developing actual thermonuclear reactors in the 1980s. The newly developed Tokamak-10 "kindled" a temperature of six million degrees, which was sufficient to sustain briefly a controlled thermonuclear reaction in the hot plasma. This work is also important for international cooperation and peace as the Soviet Union is sharing its progress with the United States, where the main efforts on controlled thermonuclear reactions are also based on the Soviet tokamaks. By the end of the century, it is not unlikely that the radiation-free thermonuclear processes will replace nuclear fission for new electric power stations. Apart from the tokamaks, the Soviet Union is also leading in the application of superpowerful lasers and electron beams as alternate means of "igniting" thermonuclear reactions.

The Soviet Union has also built the largest experimental magnetohydrodynamic power station in the world. By means of magnetohydrodynamics, thermal energy is transformed directly into electric energy, thus making unnecessary the use of turbine-driven generators which convert only a small fraction of the thermal into electric energy. The United States and the

ERWIN MARQUIT is Professor of Physics at the University of Minnesota. He has written widely on philosophical problems in the natural sciences.

Soviet Union are cooperating on this research and part of the equipment was built by US scientists.

The Soviet space program, the thermonuclear research and other energy research programs require more than just groups of outstanding scientists as is usually the case in most experiments. These programs are of such a magnitude that they involve entire areas of Soviet technology and science. It will therefore be worthwhile reviewing how scientific research, which formerly was left to a tiny group of individuals from the privileged classes of tsarist Russia, could be turned into a nationwide effort.

Democratization of Soviet Science

The October Revolution opened the path that has already led the Soviet people from illiteracy to universal secondary education. The Soviet Union was the first country in the world to make scientific careers possible for children of workers and peasants. All tuition was abolished. The state introduced an extensive system of financial support to meet the students' daily needs. (Surveys I have conducted in my own classes, which are attended by science and engineering majors at the University of Minnesota, show that about two-thirds of the students have to work to support themselves, wholly or in part.) For a large number of formerly oppressed nationalities, democratization of science in the Soviet Union meant policies of affirmative action in education and science consciously designed to eliminate the consequences of centuries of national oppression. Written languages were created for peoples who did not have them. Democratization also meant the opening of scientific careers to women, so that today the Soviet Union has more women engineers than the United States has engineers altogether.

Soviet progress during the past sixty years has not only essentially reduced the lag in research technology relative to the most developed capitalist countries, but has even allowed Soviet science to pass the United States in many areas. The most important area in which the Soviet Union has still to catch up, and it is now making rapid progress in this direction, is in the general availability of high-speed electronics for computing and experimental research. Although these microelectronic components are available, they are in short supply in face of the demand for them by Soviet researchers.

Due to tremendous progress in developing the technological basis for scientific research, the Soviet Union can maintain a program of theoretical and experimental research which embraces many more researchers than the United States. Most of the leading Soviet scientific journals are now translated into English from cover to cover by various US agencies and scientific institutions.

The Soviet state was the first in the world to assume responsibility for coordinating and financing scientific resources, including the planning of research and the education and training of scientific personnel. In doing so, the

Soviet government had to ensure that funds for science were properly divided between the applied fields, which were vital to the national economy, and the so-called pure research fields, that is, research in areas that were not likely to produce immediate material benefits, but would add to the general store of scientific knowledge on which the applied sciences feed.

The Soviet government designated the Academy of Sciences of the USSR as the main vehicle for the coordination and administration of research. There is an important difference between the way the Academy functions and the way the state administers the scientific establishment in capitalist countries. Although the activities of the Academy of Sciences are closely coordinated with the needs of the national economy, the Academy functions with relative autonomy. For example, the president of the Academy is elected by the members of the Academy by secret ballot and is not imposed upon the scientific community by the state, as is the scientific adviser of the president of the United States. In general, the Soviet scientist and academic researcher today enjoys greater freedom of choice of topic and method of research than his/her counterpart in the United States, despite any instances of abuse that may be cited from the past.

Interestingly enough, it has been the widespread acceptance of the dialectical materialist outlook with its principle of universal interconnection of things that has led to the recognition of the necessity of approaching problems from the broadest possible perspectives and therefore with the greatest possible tolerance. In his book, *Science and Philosophy in the Soviet Union*, the non-Marxist US science historian, Loren R. Graham, writes:

> In terms of universality and degree of development, the dialectical materialist explanation of nature has no competitors among modern systems of thought. Indeed, one would have to jump centuries, to the Aristotelian scheme of a natural order or to Cartesian mechanical philosophy, to find a system based on nature that could rival dialectical materialism in the refinement and the wholeness of its fabric. . . . Soviet scientists as a group have, in fact, faced more openly the implications of their philosophic assumptions than have scientists in those countries—such as the United States and Great Britain—where the fashion is to maintain that philosophy has nothing to do with science.

In the United States it is only at the risk of one's career that a natural scientist dares to step out of the bounds of a government-sponsored research program, where the methodology of research is all laid out and approved in advance by political appointees. Full employment in the Soviet Union, which exists for scientists, as for all Soviet citizens, is a crucial factor, along with stable research budgets, in providing guarantees of academic freedom. Under conditions of full employment and stable funding, a researcher need not fear loss of job for striking out in uncharted directions. In the US Einstein used to warn young scientists who asked to work under him at Princeton University that they would be endangering their careers to do so, since despite his fame, Einstein's approach was unconventional and unfashionable and he was concerned that any one who had worked under him would have difficulties in finding a position in the highly competitive job market of US academia.

Major Achievements of Soviet Natural Science

Perhaps the first singularly outstanding research to be initiated after the Revolution was that of the biochemist Aleksandr I. Oparin, who in 1924 published an essay, "The Origin of Life." Oparin attempted to account for the natural formation of organic, but nonliving, compounds from which nonliving matter could evolve. He further developed his theory over the next 40 years, increasingly relying on the methods of dialectical materialism for its elaboration. Oparin considered living matter as a new level of matter, emerging from, but not identical to, nonliving matter, and therefore not reducible to chemistry.

In 1976, the noted evolutionist, Sidney W. Fox, incorporated key elements of Oparin's approach in projecting the formation of the first cell as "an act of sudden self-assembly" from organic molecules. "The theoretical meaning of the Oparin thesis that teaches us to look for the roots of phenomena in the earlier stages of evolution has been pervasive," he writes.

The first Soviet scientist to receive the Nobel prize after the October Revolution was the chemist Nikolay N. Semenov, who received it in 1956 for work on branched chain reactions—processes which take place during explosions. Semenov began this work in 1924, the same year Oparin published his first work on the origin of life. One cannot fail to note the similarity between chain reactions and the rapid formation of Oparin's calls. Both have the character of the rapid qualitative changes which play such an important role in materialist dialectics.

Perhaps the best-known Soviet physical scientist was Lev D. Landau, whose work spanned a number of areas of physics. His prinicipal contributions to physics were in the field of condensed matter (liquids and solids), in particular, his theory of superfluidity of helium. The term *superfluid* is applied to fluids without viscosity, that is, fluids that can easily flow through fine slits and capillaries which almost completely prevent the flow of all other fluids. Superfluidity was discovered by another Soviet physicist, Peter L. Kapitsa. Landau's theoretical approach also bore a certain similarity to Oparin's dialectical methodology. Unlike others who looked at the motion of liquid helium as motion associated with states of single atoms, Landau looked upon the whole liquid as a single state in motion, just as Oparin looked upon the entire cell as a single life process.

Landau's work on superfluidity was carried over into the related field of superconductivity, a state of matter in which electrical currents can flow without resistance or loss of energy. The technological importance of super-conductivity stems from electrical resistance: the thickness of a copper wire has to correspond to the current carried by it in order to prevent the build-up of heat. The use of superconductors could bring about tremendous economies in the cost of long-distance power transmission, electrical machinery, and public transportation. Unfortunately, superconductivity (and superfluidity) occurs only at very low temperatures, close to absolute zero, which makes practical application difficult. Landau's work provided the theoretical basis for studies on the development of materials which can become superconducting at higher temperatures. He was awarded the Nobel Prize in 1962.

Landau was seriously injured in an automobile accident and was in a coma for several months. The entire scientific world followed his progress as he emerged from the coma and slowly recovered. But he was never able to resume his work on its former scale. The most frequent question asked Soviet scientists at international conferences or by scientists visiting the Soviet Union from the time of the accident to his death in 1968 was "How is Landau?"

Soviet scientific leadership in the field of condensed matter continues to this day and is universally recognized. One of the topics of extreme current interest is the Soviet discovery of electron-hole droplets in semiconductors. These electron-hole droplets, or excitons as they are also called, are now the subject of intensive study.

The work on excitons involved several teams of physicists. Excitons were first predicted by V. L. Ginzburg, a leading world specialist on the theory of general relativity, who seems to feel at home in a wide variety of fields in physics. Ginzburg's recent book, available in English under the title *Key Problems of Physics and Astrophysics*, is on its way to becoming a best seller in the US physics community after an impressive review in the journal *Physics Today*. The book was written to guide potential graduate students in the choice of a career in physics.

It has been suggested that excitons may provide a means for obtaining superconductivity at higher temperature, since they simulate highly dense hydrogen. Soviet scientists have predicted that if hydrogen is sufficiently compressed, it will turn into metallic hydrogen, which can eventually become superconducting. They already claim to have observed an appreciable increase in the electrical conductivity of hydrogen under a pressure of three million atmospheres, which they attribute to their actually having created metallic hydrogen.

The optical aspects of the work with excitons is connected with another field in which Soviet work has been impressive, quantum generators—lasers and masers. Soviet scientists A. Prokhorov and N. Bosov were awarded a Nobel

Prize, which they shared with the US physicist C. H. Townes, for developing the first lasers and masers.

Another field of particular importance to Soviet science is high-energy physics, or, as it is sometimes called, elementary-particle physics. This field has played a special role in relations between the socialist and capitalist countries. During the worst years of the Cold War, high-energy physics was almost the only major scientific field in which contacts between scientists of the socialist and capitalist countries could be maintained, despite the general embargo placed by the United States on exchanges between US and Soviet scientific information. For example, in the 1950s, the US government would not allow US publishers to accept from socialist countries subscriptions to scientific journals that could be ordered by any resident of a nonsocialist country. Nevertheless, high-energy physicists would meet at international conferences and even take part in limited joint experiments on cosmic rays and share experimental materials from high-energy accelerators. Many of the initial steps towards detente found expression through the initiation of cooperation in this field. One reason for the high priority assigned by the USSR to research in high-energy physics, one of the most costly research fields, may well have been its role in opening the door to relations of cooperation and peace. Indeed, it is one of the first fields in which teams of scientists from the Soviet Union and other socialist countries worked together with teams from the United States and other capitalist countries, sharing both ideas and equipment. International conferences in high-energy physics are now held every two years with cities in the United States, Western Europe, and the Soviet Union being chosen in succession as the sites for the conferences.

Soviet scientists, in particular V. I. Veksler, originated important design principles for high-energy accelerators in the 1930s at a time when the Soviet Union did not have the technological capacity to undertake their construction. Recently, the late Academician Gersh Budker of the Institute of Nuclear Physics at Akademgorodok, the famous Science City near Novosibirsk in Eastern Siberia, astounded the scientific community when he announced that his institute would be "mass producing" small accelerators to produce electron-positron colliding beams for use in research in chemistry, biology and solid-state physics.

The Soviet accelerator at Serpukhov, which produces particles of energy of 76 billion electron-volts was, until recently, the most powerful accelerator in the world. Teams of foreign scientists from socialist and capitalist countries work with their Soviet colleagues on joint experiments. One of the principal techniques used for the identification of particles at high energies is the Cherenkov counter, a device based on discoveries by the Nobel-Prize winning Soviet scientists, Peter Cherenkov, Igor Tamm and Ilya Frank.

Another field in which the Soviet Union has won worldwide respect is that of chemical catalysts—the use of chemical substances of one kind to accelerate chemical reactions involving other substances. The Catalysis Institute of the USSR Academy of Sciences headed by Academician Georgi Boreskov receives a steady stream of visitors from all over the world. Catalysis is used in metal and oil refining and in the production of chemicals. Despite the long-known importance of catalysis, the science of catalysis has been largely based on trial-and-error methods. The Catalysis Institute, also located at Science City, has now laid out the theoretical foundations of forecasting catalytic action by means of mathematical simulation with the aid of computers.

There are many, many fields which we have not mentioned, including mathematics, geology, geophysics, metallurgy, astronomy, and astrophysics. Despite the exciting achievements in these areas, I would like to use the remaining space allocated for this review to discuss in broader terms the relationship between scientific research and economic and social development in the Soviet Union.

Science and Economic-Social Development

The most famous construction projects of the first five-year plans were the huge dams for the hydroelectric power stations. As Soviet industrial production continues to grow, the problem of ensuring adequate electric energy undergoes a qualitative change. New techniques of power production and distribution have to be developed. On the other hand, capitalist countries, too, have to worry about electric energy production as we all know so well today. Yet it is interesting to ask why the United States, with its still greater technological base, fell behind the Soviet Union in scientific research connected with new techniques of electric power generation and distribution. The first nuclear reactor was built in the United States, but the first atomic power station was built in the Soviet Union. The first thermonuclear device was triggered by the United States, but the Soviet Union leads the world in research on controlled thermonuclear reactions. Soviet scientists are building the first electric power transmission lines with voltage above one million volts. The highest voltage used in the United States is 765,000 volts. (It is more economical to transmit electricity at higher voltages, but it is more difficult technologically to design equipment to do the job.) No lines at higher voltages have yet been planned in the US.

The Soviet lead in energy research is clearly connected with the difference between the two social systems.

In the Soviet Union, the growth of any industry is carried out under the principle of planned and proportionate development of the economy. The growth rate of Soviet electric energy production is roughly the same as the growth rate of industrial production as a whole, now averaging 5-6 per cent a year, and therefore no energy crisis awaits the Soviet economy. Research allocations are made on the basis of the long-term needs of the economy. An article in the February 1977 issue of the journal *Spectrum*, published by the Institute of Electrical and Electronic Engineers in the United States, discusses research on ultra-high voltage for electric power transmission. In explaining the Soviet lead in this field, the article states that "the principal difference between Russia and the US is political. In the USSR, funding of R&D [research and development], energy resource exploitation, and power generation and transmission is government sponsored and controlled; in the US it is largely privately financed, with some small assistance or funding from the US government."

The advantage of a centrally planned economy is best illustrated precisely in the electric power industry. Soviet scientists have the task of solving the problem of creating one electrical grid for the entire Soviet Union, so that as the peak-load region travels with the sun across the country, the productive capacity in one region can be used to meet the needs of any other region. The socialist countries of Eastern and Central Europe are to be connected into this grid so that an area that extends over 12 time zones (literally, halfway around the surface of the Earth) can meet its energy needs with a minimum investment of resources. Accomplishment of this task is not simply a question of construction, but involves great numbers of scientists who have to break new ground in dealing with the production and transmission of electric power on an unprecedented scale, coordination of productive capacity with demands of peak loads, protection against blackouts and brownouts. Moreover, the safety and health of the populations served by the power grid must not be jeopardized.

There is a long history of the priority nature of electric energy production in the Soviet Union. The first economic plan prepared in the young Soviet republic was the report of the State Commission for the Electrification of Russia in 1920. Electrification was the key to ending the backwardness of Russia. Even today, the continued expansion of electric power is vital to the creation of a communist society in which all arduous and monotonous labor will be done by machine, so that human beings can employ their full talents in creative activity.

In the sixty years that have passed since the October Socialist Revolution, Lenin's projections for a dense network of electric power stations and powerful technical installations have become a reality. The continuing rapid pace of development made possible by a socialist planned economy places the Soviet Union in the first position in the world when it comes to new construction of all kinds. To sustain this growth, the Soviet Union employs a force of engineers three times as great as the United States. No other country has as many research workers of all kinds. The development of education and culture are an inseparable part of this growth of science and technology, so that the percentage of the Soviet population engaged in the creative arts is greater than any capitalist country. In these respects, the Soviet Union has set high standards for the future course of all society.   □

Part Five
Aspects of Soviet Life

19

MIKE DAVIDOW

The Right to the Most Human Life

I came to Moscow in March 1969 after witnessing and reporting on the ghetto outbursts. These rebellions of the "insulted and injured" had blazoned a message across the length and breadth of our country: *Life in our great cities can never be livable until it is livable for all—including the discriminated minorities.* I returned home on December 15, 1974 after a near-six-year stay in the USSR. It was a painful homecoming. Not only because the crisis of our cities had immeasurably deepened. Not only because the streets of my childhood and youth resembled bombed-out areas. What made it so painful was that it was all so unnecessary and irrational. I had just come from a land which had overcome the heritage of tsarism and had sustained losses in World War II we can't even imagine: 20 million dead, 25 million homeless, 1,700 towns and 70,000 villages destroyed. I saw how it had used its three decades of peace to build cities without crisis, cities of brotherhood.

On all sides I was urged to readapt myself. But six years of living in a truly human world had "spoiled" me. Never again will I be able to "adapt" myself to our inhuman way of life. Indeed, in the six years of my absence life had become much more irrational and inhuman. New York teetered on the brink of bankruptcy and other cities were in similar straits. Once again, as in the 1930s, Americans were walking the streets in search of non-existent jobs. In the ghettos a new depression was piled on one that had never ended. Only this time it brought an uninvited guest to sit at their hungry table—inflation.

MIKE DAVIDOW, well-known progressive and labor journalist, was for six years the Moscow correspondent of the *Daily World*. Among his books about the USSR: *Cities Without Crisis; Life Without Landlords;* and *People's Theater: From the Box Office to the Stage.*

Notwithstanding all the studies, our Bourbons in Washington, our state capitals and city halls had learned nothing from the ghetto rebellions. A few more Black faces appeared on television and window-dressed the banks and offices of big business, but this was little comfort to the 40-60 per cent of Black, Puerto Rican and Chicano youth who walked the streets. The President of the US told New York to "drop dead." New York responded by passing on this invitation to thousands of teachers, hospital, park and sanitation workers, particularly from minority groups, and placing itself in receivership to a consortium of bankers and financiers euphemistically called the Municipal Assistance Corporation (Big Mac).

The new occupant in the White House has busied himself with more "serious" matters than devastated ghettos—the "human rights" of a people who have discovered how to live a life without unemployment and inflation, without ghettos and racism, without landlords and doctor bills, without cities of crisis and fear and without the most deadly fear of all—fear of tomorrow. "Human Rights" and the neutron bomb—this is the cold war "normalcy" we are asked to adapt ourselves to.

The New York Blackout of July 13 demonstrated to the world that the ghettos would not accept this "normalcy." Tom Wicker, prominent *New York Times* columnist warned on July 13, 1977 that nothing as drastic as a blackout will be needed "to spark off the next ghetto rebellion." Citing the worsening of conditions in the center cities since the upsurges of the 1960s, Wicker cautioned: "Mr. Carter would do well to look into his economic priorities." He could have added, "and his human rights priorities." Clayton Riley, writer and teacher at Cornell University, writing in the same issue, put the crux of our problem in these words of rage and frustration: "But the larger point is that while we know how to describe and we know how to observe, how to argue and how to draw conclusions, we don't know, *three-quarters of the way through the 20th century, still don't know what to do*" (emphasis added). What makes this ignorance all the more tragic and incomprehensible is that the answer is there for the asking.

For 60 years there has existed a way of life that is far more rational and human than our crisis-ridden existence. Anti-Sovietism is above all, responsible for our "not knowing" what more than one-third of the world has come not only to know, but to experience. The fight against anti-Sovietism is not just a struggle against the slanders heaped upon the long-maligned Soviet people. It is a fight for our own right to know. We have a right to know whether there is another way of life, without rat-ridden ghettos, without "hot summers," without slumlords, without doctor bills, without unemployment and inflation, without cities in crisis, without cities of fear. *Is there a more human way of life?*

Today, six decades after a courageous people dared to blaze the uncharted trail to that new world, the answer more than ever is:

There is! The immortal John Reed saw it in the midst of the devastation, abysmal poverty and illiteracy of war-torn, backward Russia in the birthpangs of the Great October (as did our own Jessica Smith). Lincoln Steffens saw "the future and it works" in the land of the First Five-Year Plan. But, it was understandable why this vision was denied the mass of Americans. For many years, Soviet everyday life lagged considerably behind that of the "richest country of the world." The "richest country" never inherited its poverty, backwardness and illiteracy and a multitude of other social ills. The "richest country" in the world never suffered two devastating wars on its soil besides intervention and civil war.

But today the picture is quite different—this notwithstanding many still existing difficulties in the USSR. It is no secret that in the quantity, variety and quality of many consumer goods as well as services, the US is clearly ahead (though even here the gap is steadily being narrowed. But today—60 years and nine-and-a-half five year plans after the October Revolution—Soviet life in those aspects that are most meaningful to average Americans, especially workers and minority groups, is already far superior to life in the United States.

From its very inception, Soviet life was in essence superior because it introduced a new quality of life, *life without exploitation or exploiters.* Today that quality of life exists in a mature form in a country of advanced socialism. It is this new stage in the development of socialism that must be grasped if the superiority of Soviet life over ours is to be understood. Never have so many Americans questioned the *quality* of life in our free enterprise world. Never have they demanded a higher quality of life. This in itself is a new and significant development. *Quantity,* whether in gadgets or automobiles (always quite limited for millions of ordinary Americans, especially of minority groups) is no longer the sole or even the main yardstick.

In our six years in the Soviet Union, I applied the yardstick of quality to life in the two worlds. And I have done so in the three years since our return to the US. Let me briefly contrast the two worlds on some of the essential elements that make up the quality of life.

The security of one's home: In the Soviet Union, one of our greatest joys was what every American dreams of: life without landlords! It was expressed in our nominal rent, 18 rubles 32 kopeks a month (about $24). We returned to find that never was the American home more insecure and that the American Dream of a cottage in the suburbs had become a nightmare. Never were landlords more truly *lords of the land!* We began a frantic search for a landlord we could afford (only by cutting down on other necessities). And such are the powers of adjustment that we came to consider ourselves "fortunate" when we found a three-room apartment for *only* $232 a month! But our "good fortune" was short-lived. Our landlord sold the building to another "lord." and like the feudal serfs of old we were gripped by the fear of losing our "master." Our fears proved to be well-founded. The new "lord" did not even deign to present himself to us. We simply received a curt letter announcing our rent would be raised almost $100 a month. And so once again we began a desperate search for a landlord we could "afford." Never have so many Americans been so repeatedly engaged in such search. It has introduced a new instability into our increasingly unstable lives. Nowhere more so than in the ghettos where for $200-$300 a month tenants get slumlords, rats, roaches and deteriorating buildings in the midst of decay.

Article 44, Section 7 of the new Soviet Constitution guarantees *as a right* decent housing at low rent for every Soviet citizen. We would call it practically free rent since it is no more than four per cent of income. *No society before has ever dared to guarantee such a right.* Few countries faced the kind of a housing crisis the Soviet Union knew. Aside from the pitiful heritage bequeathed by tsarism and capitalism, the Nazi invasion left 25 million homeless. The Soviet Union still faces serious problems, especially in relation to providing housing for young families but today it can write that guarantee into its constitution because for many successive years it has built 11 million housing units a year.

The right to protection of one's health: Or consider medical care. Article 42, section 7 states that Soviet citizens have the right to protection of their health free of charge. For six years we came to accept free comprehensive medical care as "normal"! But we were brought down to our "free enterprise earth" with a rude jolt. On January 8, 1976 Gail and I suffered a near-fatal accident. A tenant in our building left her car running in the garage under our apartment. We were overcome by carbon monoxide. Fortunately, we were taken to the hospital in time but it was necessary for me to stay overnight in the coronary intensive care unit. We went home and tried to forget the nightmarish experience. But not so, our hospital! Shortly after I received a bill for $661! And it was itemized— $441 for room and board! Serious sickness is not only a health hazard, it is a financial disaster in our society.

Talking versus working democracy: In our society democracy is largely a battle of words. No country has so studied and publicly reported on its ills with so little results as ours. The rebellions in the Black ghettos of the 1960s resulted in token actions but numerous wordy studies. Yet, the situation in the ghettos is worse than ever as the outbursts of the July 13 blackout in New York made clear. I found the contrasting situation in the USSR particularly refreshing. I must confess that coming from a *talking* democracy it took time to get used to a *working democracy.* For me, the most significant thing about the inspiring new Soviet Constitution is that it *registers Soviet reality. It is a living demonstration of the unity between words and deeds.* The essence of Soviet democracy which is in such stark contrast with our own version is contained in the following simple statement in Article 102, Section 14: "Deputies shall exercise their power without discontinuing work in their trade or professions." What a world is contained in those simple words! One of the most thrilling sights in the Soviet Union to me was not the giant hydroelectric power stations but the little pin emblems in the lapels of the men and women construction workers denoting them as deputies to the Supreme Soviet. More than half of the Soviet Senators, Congressmen and Congresswomen are workers and farmers directly engaged in production. Most of the others are workers in science, arts and literature. There is not a *single* worker in our Senate and only six in Congress (who have long since ceased being workers) but there are 215 corporation lawyers and 81 bankers and businessmen in the House and 65 and 13 respectively in the Senate.

Article 102 not only states that a deputy shall remain on his or her job but that when engaged in governmental duties he or she shall be paid *only the average wage earned on the job* (aside from normal business expenses). But for our Congresspersons and Senators, politics is their business and a very lucrative one at that (aside from aiding their private affairs).

When I served as Moscow correspondent, I observed how my colleagues from the commercial press applied the standards of *talking democracy* to the Supreme Soviet. *Who talks more? That was what concerned them.* Well, by that yardstick our Senate and Congress win hands down. You have to go some to beat our representatives in that respect. After all, who can talk more than a Congress of corporation lawyers? But why don't they apply the real test most meaningful to the American as well as the Soviet people? Who *does more* for the people?

I met many Soviet deputies and watched the way they work. These non-professional politicians do their main work in committees and draw on their particular experience. Moreover they are accountable to their constituents, to whom they must regularly report, very often right in their work place.

Or consider the nationwide discussions on the new Constitution. Just try to imagine *The New York Times* opening its pages to its readers to a similar discussion, multiply it by thousands and you get some idea of how important pieces of legislation are adopted in the Soviet Union.

On July 27, 1967 a Presidential commission investigating the causes for the ghetto rebellions of the 1960s attributed them in large measure to the taunting contradiction between words and deeds. It declared: "The expectations aroused by the great judicial and legislative victories have led to frustration, hostility and cynicism in the face of the persistent gap between promise and fulfillment." And it warned: "Our nation is moving toward *two societies, one Black, one white—separate and unequal*" (emphasis added).

Prophesy is being fulfilled because even the palliatives provided in the wake of the ghetto rebellion are being discarded. Affirmative action is under sharp attack. Hardest hit in the economy wave are the ghettos where schools, hospitals, libraries are being closed, remedial and bilingual classes curtailed. The material for future and perhaps even more explosive outbursts is being piled high. It is therefore, nothing less than willful and self-defeating blindness for us to ignore the eminently successful experience of the Soviet Union in solving the problem of nations and nationalities. Few countries faced it in a more complex or more sharp form than did the land which was known under the tsars as the prison of nations, the country where 100 peoples now live in brotherhood and harmony.

Nothing is more thrilling or more instructive than the story of the leap made by once backward peoples, particularly in Central Asia and in the Far North and Far East, from illiteracy to Academy of Sciences, from nomadism to modern industries on the par with that of the most advanced countries in the world. And this was made possible because the very point rejected by our society and government—the need to *make up* for past oppression and backwardness inflicted on oppressed peoples—was the starting point of the approach by Soviet society and government to solving the national question. The more backward Republics were accorded a status of *special equality*. No one attacked this as granting them a privileged status. On the contrary, it was recognized by the Russian people that more equality for those penalized by history and tsarist oppression meant sacrifices by the Russian people who in a backward, war-torn country, still occupied a more advanced position. Few people in history accepted and carried out with greater honor such sacrifices.

Perhaps one of the most difficult adjustments we had to make on our return home was to adapt ourselves to *coexistence with fear*. One of the most pleasant aspects of Soviet life is that its cities are cities without fear. Not that crime has been totally wiped out. That is not the case—the elimination of crime is a complicated and a prolonged social process. But organized crime has been done away with and the streets and parks truly belong to the Soviet people. There is much talk today of "life style." Well, the massive and brutal character of crime in our country, especially in our cities, has indeed, changed the life style of millions of Americans. "Night life" for millions has ceased to exist. With the approach of darkness, they not only go and remain indoors but behind tightly locked doors. For large numbers of the elderly living in high crime areas, fear dominates the streets during daylight too. Shopping for them is a daily risk.

If I were to be asked: What about the quality of Soviet life that is particularly in stark contrast to ours, I would say: *the absence of fear!* The absence of fear in the streets, of fear of the loss of one's job, of fear of the high cost of illness, of fear of the high cost of education, of fear of racism and police brutality. In a word, the *absence of fear of today and tomorrow. And the absence of fear in the streets is only possible because the other fears have been eliminated.*

The Soviet militia (police) would be the first to tell you that the elimination of crime is hardly just a matter for the police. Soviet cities are cities without fear because they are cities without unemploymtn, without slums and slumlords, without ghettos, without drug pushers, without incessant glorification of violence, without pornography. The fight against crime is not only a fight against the economic ills which are its basic source. It is a fight against the moral decay eating away at the very fiber of our country. The struggle against moral decay is a fight for the very *spiritual health of our country*. Never have so many felt the inhumanness and soulessness of life in the USA today. Never have so many yearned for an alternative, a more human way of life. After all, isn't the history of humanity the story of the struggle for a truly *human way of life?* Isn't it time, 60 years after the great October Socialist Revolution, that we took a good objective look at the country which pioneered in creating a *new quality of life* that has eliminated the fears, tensions and decay, making life in the richest country in the world more and more unbearable for increasing numbcrs of Americans? Isn't it time for us to demand the Right to the Most Human Life? □

20

SARA HARRIS

A School in Moscow: As We Live It

I knew practically nothing about the Soviet school system when, four years ago, my seven-year-old American-Russian son, Andre, entered the first grade. Therefore, I was almost as excited as he was when, as is traditional in the Soviet Union, our whole family escorted him to school on September first. Little Dmitri carried his big brother's briefcase, but Andre wouldn't entrust anyone with the fresh asters he had for the teacher.

The children, overly scrubbed and starched, were already gathering by class in the football field behind the school when we got there. Their parents, many with cameras, were hurrying to get front-row standing-room on the rise surrounding the field. The principal opened the ceremony with some welcoming remarks to the children. These were followed by a representative of the parents' committee. Then the microphone was handed to a tall man in his late 30s who was introduced as a worker in the local furniture factory. In a slightly hesitating manner, he explained that his factory had "adopted" School No. 103. If there was any special handiwork that needed to be done, such as custom cabinets for the science labs or construction work for the "Mariners Club," his factory would help out. Then, to the applause of the upperclassmen, he announced that during the summer they had built four new ping-pong tables for the gym. (Our school is noted in the neighborhood for its ping-pong club.) The first-graders were then asked to step forward and the entire student body joined in welcoming them.

When the brief ceremony was over, the top student of the school was given the honor of ringing the first bell of the new school year. Then, class by class followed her past the rows of sentimental parents into the school building, with the tenth-graders chaperoning the first-graders at the head of the line.

It is no wonder that much is made of the first day of school, particularly for the first-graders. School is taken very seriously. It is, indeed, a lot of responsi-

SARA HARRIS, born and raised in the New York City area, is now married to Soviet journalist Alexander Kamenshikov, and lives in Moscow with her husband and two sons. She is pursuing the Candidate of Science degree in economics at Moscow University. Her article about student life at the University appeared in NWR, No. 4, 1969.

bility and hard work. The amount of information that Soviet children are exposed to in their ten years of schooling is proof of that. The required program includes, besides all the more common subjects, botany, zoology, anatomy, economic and physical geography of the world, mechanical drawing, astronomy, four years of chemistry, five years of physics (which covers the basics of nuclear physics), plus heavy emphasis on history, literature, a foreign language, etc.

But just listing the subjects gives you no idea of their depth. Let's glance at some of the textbooks: The fourth grade "reader" is a collection of short stories, poems and excerpts from some of the world's great authors: Tolstoy, Pushkin, Turgenyev, Hans Christian Andersen, to name a few.

Ancient History for the fifth grade has a substantial chapter on primitive man and each of the ancient cultures of Egypt, Mesopotamia, India and China, as well as an extensive study of the ancient Greek and Roman empires.

Botany, which is studied for three semesters of the fifth and sixth grades, has a detailed chapter on each segment of a plant: root, stalk, leaf, etc. What I remember studying in my high school biology classes (basic plant types, parts of a flower, pollination, etc.) are covered here in the introduction! The chapter on mushrooms is particularly enlightening. Now I know why the Soviets are so brave about eating the fungi they find in the woods. And the experiments that are suggested to do in your mother's kitchen! (What will happen when Andre takes chemistry?) No wonder some protective grandparents claim that childhood ends with the first grade.

The significant thing—at least for people who have been taught to think that there are students who can learn and those who can't—is that this program, which is basic in every school in the country, regardless of which republic or distant rural area it might be, is not meant for the "whiz-kids" but is geared to the most average schoolchild.* I remember the stares of amazement we got when an American teacher friend of mine asked some Soviet educators what they do for those students who haven't learned to read by the third or fourth grade. I am impressed by how much average children can produce when properly challenged and how excited they get by well-presented subjects. Andre was so inspired by the fifth grade atlases for history and geography a friend introduced him to, that he has since bought up all the atlases for both of those subjects through the tenth grade. His favorite pastime now is to ask me questions such as the import-export ratio of Australia, or when and where was the Second Punic War, and undoubtedly catch me on the answers. My high school education hardly puts me at an equal advantage.

---

*Nor are the "whiz-kids" ignored. There is a series of electives added to the program for those who wish further to deepen their knowledge, as well as a number of schools that specialize in a foreign language, mathematics or a science.

Another thing I have observed is that not once has a child in my hearing, including my own son, complained of boredom in school. There's just no time for that.

Andre, in the fourth grade now, has four lessons of 45 minutes each (the upperclassmen have five or six), with a ten minute break between each. After two lessons, the children have a "second breakfast" in the cafeteria which consists usually of a hot dish: cereal, eggs, franks or some such, a beverage and bread. By 12:15 Andre is through school for the day.

I know what you're thinking: "That doesn't give a mother much free time." Actually it's not that bad. Andre can have a full dinner in school after classes. (The food is always cooked fresh including the soup, nothing canned.) Since my husband has his big meal at work and Dmitri has his in nursery school, it has the additional advantage of allowing me not to cook dinner each day. (I'm one of those "I hate to cook" mothers.)

If I am working or just busy and want my child "off the street" (although homework is pretty good at doing that for a couple of hours each day), I can send him to the "extended day" program which is free except for the price of dinner (40 cents). A teacher is hired specifically to take the children from after school till 6 p.m. During this time they eat, play outdoors, do their homework with her supervision and also raise the roof, I am told. Sometimes the teacher takes them to a movie or they watch educational programs on TV. To a great extent, the success of this program depends on the individual teacher. There has been criticism in the Soviet press lately about extended day programs that are poorly organized and mirror the classroom atmosphere with not enough emphasis on games, sports and cultural activities. However, I am still going to send Andre to this program this year, not to keep him off the street, but to keep him *on* it. Knowing him, if he's left on his own he'll curl up with a book the minute he gets home and never see the daylight.

Actually the "street" isn't exactly as you probably imagine it. The new residential districts like ours are planned so that, as far as is possible, all major streets surround them on the far sides. Between the buildings you have only alleys and driveways which don't even have names. (This makes it quite a game to give someone directions to find your house among the 60-odd buildings in the district.) Surrounding every apartment building is a large park area which, for the most part, the residents landscape to suit themselves. So, there is plenty of room for active ten-year-olds. Except for traffic, the "street" doesn't present any other hazards that a mother would worry about. I would prefer that Andre be "on the street" than in the house when I am away.

I am discovering that school in this country is far more than a place of learning. This spring Andre became a "Young Pioneer." I have to smile when I see how solemnly he ties his red tie each morning before school. Being a "Pioneer" is both an honor and a responsibility. The last time I went to school I witnessed the following scene: Two first-graders were shoving each other with their briefcases in the hallway during a break. A girl, passing them and just a few grades older, but wearing a red tie, put down her briefcase, separated the two aggressors, sent them off to their respective classrooms, picked up her briefcase and matter-of-factly went about her business.

Let me tell you about the "subbotnik." Andre and his classmates had been wearing their red ties for all of two weeks. This was their first big project as "Young Pioneers." Their "link" of ten children decided to hold a "subbotnik"—a voluntary work project held usually on Saturday or *subbota*. This was an individual decision as the major "subbotnik" held throughout the country every spring was to be a week later. But, full of pioneer spirit, these children couldn't wait all of seven days to volunteer their services. (One little girl left her own birthday party long enough to attend!) Being early April, the group decided to clean up one of the yards around an apartment house. Parents supplied the children with rakes and they went to work on the old leaves, broken branches and papers that had been buried under five months of snow. They had a jolly time gathering the trash into a big pile and then started to burn it as they had seen the grownups do. At this point an old woman who had been observing this whole operation, lost her patience, "You darn kids have been here too long, trampling on everything, making noise and trouble . . ." and she chased them off the yard they had worked hard and so enthusiastically to clean.

The insult was deep. What could they do? "Let's write a complaint to our newspaper!" (Here, you must understand the character of the Soviet press. All newspapers, from *Pioneer Pravda*, a biweekly newspaper for school children, up to *Pravda* itself, the official paper of the Soviet Communist Party, serve the function of examining and pressuring to relieve complaints from readers. These can relate to any kind of problem, economic, social, moral, even very personal problems.) Carefully, so the parents wouldn't know, or so they thought, the Pioneers of Link No. 2, third grade class "a," School No. 103, of Moscow, sent a letter to the editors of *Pioneer Pravda*, a national newspaper, describing their "subbotnik" and its unhappy conclusion. Whether or not the children received a direct reply from *Pioneer Pravda* I haven't heard. But I am sure they have begun to recognize both their rights and social duties as "Young Pioneers."

As an American mother, I was particularly concerned about the question of conformity in the Soviet schools. I had heard a lot, from Western sources, about how one of the worst offenses is to be "different." Here was my poor son, condemned to non-conformity from birth by his American heritage. What would happen to him?

At one of the first parents' meetings he was indeed singled out, not for his international heritage, it is true, but for his universal languor. "Nothing fazes this boy," the teacher said, "Five minutes after the bell I see him wandering casually toward the school building. If a handgrenade were to explode next to him, I doubt that he would move any faster." Then she added, "But don't try to change him. With the hectic pace that life takes on these days, I envy him his calmness. Let him remain that way." I respect Lydia Nikoliovna. Never, in the three years of being Andre's primary school teacher, did she change that basic attitude toward him although there was many a time he tested her patience.

As far as I'm concerned, the best way to guard against conformity is to give all your young citizens an extensive, well-rounded education which will provide them with the tools necessary to think independently and to critically evaluate their daily experiences. This is, as far as I can tell, exactly what Andre's very average, neighborhood school is doing for him.

I guess, more important than my evaluation of Andre's school, is his own attitude toward it. I'm sure you will find this very hard to believe, but it actually happened. May 30 was the last day of classes for this school year. The teacher had warned that they would have three rather than the usual four lessons. As we had an appointment to make, I waited for Andre after school. But he didn't appear. My first reaction was, "He probably got his report card today and it's bad!" Finally, I went to school to look for him. It turned out that the teacher had dismissed the class after the third lesson but only a few pupils left. The rest decided to run the fourth lesson themselves. By schedule, it was to be a discussion of books they had read at home that week. So the children, often with considerable humor, started discussing books and stories. The class became so enthusiastic that finally the janitor had to chase them out of the classroom. And this, on the last day of school! □

21

DAVID B. KIMMELMAN, M.D.

Health Care in the USSR

I f someone in the USSR, anywhere in the USSR, suddenly feels ill, a relative, friend or passerby will dial "03" and a well-equipped ambulance with a physician will arrive within 10 or 15 minutes. In large cities like Moscow, it could be within five minutes. (The Moscow Central ambulance station has over 1,500 ambulances, and there are 25 sub-stations in outlying Moscow districts besides.) Emergency help for remote areas is provided by air, and where even helicopters can't go, as in Central Asia's highest mountains, physicians trained as mountain climbers are available.

According to the symptoms at the call, there might be a "special purpose" ambulance, with a *sub*-specialist, e.g., an orthopedist if a fracture is suspected; an obstetrician; or a specialist in reanimation in case of sudden death. In the USSR emergency medicine is a specialty just like others, and it has sub-specialties; ambulances, hospitals or clinics are specially equipped particularly for these sub-specialties.

Of course the medical care required is followed through to recovery, either as in- or out-patient care. There is no cost to the patient. If he or she is a worker, the workplace is notified if necessary to get a substitute. The worker is compensated for loss of pay, and the job is held until recovery.

Any pertinent medical information is put on the patient's health record, which, incidentally, will follow him wherever he goes. If the diagnosis indicates a work-related condition, the workplace doctors and epidemiologists are immediately alerted. Is there a hazard for other workers? How prevalent is the condition? What steps are needed to prevent new cases? The statistics are not only local, but eventually nation-wide—to determine trends, causes, and prevention.

If the job turns out dangerous for the health of that worker (i.e., allergy) the state is responsible for training for another, safer job, at no cost, and with

DAVID B. KIMMELMAN, M.D., practices ophthalmology in New York City. Following his working trip to Cuba in 1969, he was instrumental in founding the US-Cuba Health Exchange. Among other countries, he worked in Hanoi, North Vietnam, in 1973. He acknowledges with deep gratitude the help of Mrs. Vita Barsky, who shared valuable material prepared by the late Dr. Edward K. Barsky following their trip to the Soviet Union.

continued pay. These rights are guaranteed and enforced by the trade union.

It is difficult to compare all this with what would happen in the US to a person suddenly ill. Whom to call? An ambulance might take a very long time and it has no doctor. How much will it all cost? What about no show at the job? Will the boss hold the job if the condition is serious? Will a record of any health condition be held against the worker?

In the US, there is no national health service. It is the only major nation without one. Although such service is far superior in the socialist countries, those capitalist countries with a national health service have a marked improvement in delivery and availability of health care. In spite of our advanced technology, the US without a system of health care delivery is like a crippled giant, unable to fulfill its potential.

Of course a national health service will not be handed out. It must be fought for. To win such concessions from the monopolies requires struggle primarily by the working class in our country. The Soviet health system affords an outstanding example of what a working class state can do for its people, and is an inspiration for that struggle.

The Soviet health system is one of the marvels produced by mankind on this planet. The "mankind" is socialist, its workers owning the means of production, and perhaps that is why the good health of its people is considered of prime importance, regardless of their economic circumstances.

While we are decreasing hospital beds, the USSR is building hospitals and bed capacity. Our emergency services are getting scarcer, while in the USSR they are trying to break their own records for speed of response to calls. An extra day of hospitalization is called wasteful here; a safety measure there. Fumes at work go unheeded deliberately here; they are sought and eliminated there. With high productivity in US coal mines goes black lung, while in the USSR good health of the miner takes precedence over risky conditions.

In the USSR "Fundamentals of Health Legislation," the aims of health care are stated as follows: "To insure the harmonious physical and mental development of citizens, their health, high working ability, and many years of active life; to preserve health and reduce incidence of disease; to further reduce disablement and mortality; and to eradicate factors and conditions harmful to the health of its citizens."

The Draft of the new Constitution of the USSR guarantees the *right to health protection*. Article 42 states: "This right shall be ensured by free competent medical care rendered by state health institutions, development and improvement of safety techniques and sanitation in production, extension of the network of medical and health-building institutions; by broad preventive measures; and measures of environmental improvement; special care for the health of the rising generation; prohibition of child labor; furtherance of scientific research directed to preventing and reducing the incidence of disease; and to ensuring a long active life for citizens.''

Other guaranteed human rights relating directly or indirectly to health in the new Constitution are the right to rest and leisure, the right to work, the right to maintenance in old age, sickness and partial or complete disability, and the rights to housing, education, freedom of creative work, access to achievement of culture, etc. All specify how each right is ensured.

These human rights, absent in the US for all except the privileged, must be an important contribution to mental health, freedom from diseases of stress, humane, civilized attitudes to one another and to peoples of other nations. We need only to picture the universal existence of these rights in this country to imagine the effects on health. The Soviet constitution further guarantees complete equality regardless of race, sex, nationality or attitude toward religion, and makes ''advocacy of racial or national exclusiveness, hostility or contempt'' punishable by law. Think how racism, anti-semitism and media violence would be abated by such laws! Why is our media silent on these rights?

The basic principles of the Soviet health system are: 1) complete socialization, with full state responsibility; 2) accessible and free health services; 3) disease and injury prevention and prophylaxis; 4) democratic approach. This means widespread public participation and use of information to guarantee good health. Public health committees exist in all soviets, factories, schools, residential areas. The USSR Red Cross and Red Crescent societies play an active role in propagandizing for good health habits.

The presence of standing health committees in the Supreme Soviet, and all region, town and district soviets, also assures that the work of the Ministry of Health is scrutinized by people's representatives.

As can be imagined, the scope of the health system is enormous. It includes: 1) hospitals, general and special; out-patient clinics; dispensaries; children's polyclinics; women's centers; sanatoria; rest homes; preventive care and epidemiological stations. 2) Ministries of Health of the USSR and of the Union Republics; the Academy of Medical Sciences consisting of highly talented leaders in the field of health, and its 40 associated research institutes staffed by thousands of researchers. In addition, each Union Republic has its own research institutions. 3) Specialized secondary educational and advanced training schools. This includes nursing, pharmacy, laboratory work and many special technical subjects (X-ray, electronic medicine, etc.). 4) The Ministry of Medical Industry. Completely integrated into the general activities of the health system, it is responsible for the manufacture of drugs, bacterial and virus vaccines, antitoxins and other sera, and medical and surgical instruments and equipment. As can be imagined, this is an enormous industry, producing everything needed in the field of health. Its work is coordinated closely with research in the production of new drugs. Sophisticated electronic devices for reanimation, for diagnosis and treatment are manufactured in a planned way, without the inaccuracies of statements by competing manufacturers, which fool even highly trained M.D.s in our society. By the end of next year all the necessary instruments, equipment and chemopharmaceuticals will be produced to satisfy common needs.

In the training of physicians, present emphasis is on quality and increased specialization. Of 830,000 M.D.s at the end of 1975 (about one doctor for 307 people—the highest ratio in the world), 210,000 graduated from postgraduate medical schools between 1971 and 1975. The USSR is now producing new specialists directly from its 82 medical schools. At present more than one doctor out of every four in the world is a Soviet M.D.!

The Health Ministry also trains many medical and paramedical personnel from the developing countries at the USSR's expense.

When I was first in the Soviet Union, I was struck time and again, in conversations with Soviet doctors, by their intense interest in their work, how to perfect it, to diagnose and treat more effectively, to learn from colleagues. Interest remained constant and sincere. This may seem an ordinary observation; yet it would apply unevenly in the US.

I came to realize this attitude existed in every socialist country I visited, and not only among doctors, but also among paramedical personnel, and in fact all people in the field of health sciences. They are not worried about personal extraneous concerns like making a living and can concentrate on their tasks. Their attitudes reflect a striving for constant improvement in their work.

Nowhere is this more evident than in the field of occupational health and safety. The vast worker protection network, in a certain sense, typifies the entire Soviet health system.

Before describing the Soviet occupational health protection system, it would be worthwhile to examine our efforts and results in this field in the US. After many years of struggle Congress finally was pressured in 1970 into passing the Occupational Safety and Health Act (OSHA), which set certain standards. But the number of inspectors is miniscule compared to the needs; and the small fines amounting to wrist slaps only encourage violations. And now that our miners, steel and other workers in basic industry are demanding their rights to better protection, there is a movement among industrialists and their spokesmen in the media and Congress to nullify OSHA as "expensive," and "worsening instead of bettering." As usual, costs of safety lose out to profits. The protection of US workers demands much higher levels of struggle to succeed, as it surely will, especially as information already learned in other countries finally gets to our own workers. Why is it that liver cancer among vinyl chloride workers became public knowledge in the US in the 70s, but was known and reported, and safety standards set, in the 30s and 40s in the USSR and Western Europe as well? Black lung was "discovered" in the late 60s in the US, but was documented in Europe in the early 40s. Byssinosis from cotton dust was reported in the early 70s here as though the cause had just been discovered, yet this lung disease was reported in England in the early 50s. Obviously what is necessary is greater communication abroad, and in the first place to learn what worker protection can really mean when carried out in a workers' state.

The Soviet Ministry of Health shares responsibility for enforcing labor protection. It hires 20,000 safety and health inspectors, who have the power to impose penalties, close factories, and even jail plant managers or industrial ministry officials who do not comply with legal safety standards. Under the Ministry is the Institute of Industrial Hygiene and Occupational Diseases. It does the main research for safety standards and procedures, acceptable concentrations of various potentially dangerous substances; and coordinates its work with 15 other specialty institutes in various regions—for example, in Tashkent hazards associated with cotton and textile production; in Baku oil-related hazards. These institutes, especially the central one in Moscow, study the physiology of various kinds of labor in order to prevent incapacity resulting from the overuse of certain muscles and the underuse of others, as an example of the kind of research aimed at the future years of certain workers. They may develop special exercises. Special hazard areas are carefully studied and conclusions drawn as to what kinds of labor need special protection. Regular meetings make safety recommendations to the Ministry, from which standards are set.

The major information feedback from all over the country comes from the 4,500 "sanepid" stations (sanitary epidemiology service). These employ 120,000 people, and are responsible for environmental health, both research and practice. The sanepids, as of 1975, received ten per cent of the Health Ministry budget. They are involved in every medical problems in their districts, including infections, epidemic or potentially so; food, water and environmental pollution; occupational health. In addition, they check that health standards are met, coordinate annual physical examinations, and collect all health data for the Central Bureau of Statistics of the Health Ministry. Workers in hazardous occupations such as mining, chemicals, etc., as well as young workers, must have examinations every six months.

Sharing responsibility for labor protection with the Health Ministry is the All-Union Central Council of Trade Unions (AUCCTU), representing about 113 million workers in 25 unions. It employs an additional 5,500 full-time health and safety inspectors who share enforcement powers with the Health Ministry. The AUCCTU also carries out programs in particular fields, such as noise, ventilation, fumes, microwaves, mines, etc. Institutes under the Central

Council, financed entirely by the trade unions, test protective equipment and set standards of workplace safety. They employ scientists, hygienists, physicians and other experts. They coordinate the labor protection departments of each of the affiliated unions.

An example is the labor medicine program of the Metallurgical Workers Union on coke ovens in the steel industry, which are cancer causing and otherwise dangerous. They worked with the Health Ministry and the Steel Ministry and succeeded in greatly reducing hazards through development of the "dry quenching" process. Their methods are known but considered too extravagant here, although European and Japanese workers won the Soviet system of coke oven protection for their mills.

It is interesting to compare the "maximum safe airborne concentrations of substances," called TLVs (threshold limit values) in the US and the comparable figures in the USSR, called MAC (maximum allowable concentrations). TLVs do not protect workers with increased susceptibility, but are meant as an average safe value. On the other hand, MACs are set at a value which will protect every worker from any deviation from normal. Any exposure that might cause any change is forbidden. In fact, in the USSR MACs are only temporary because the optimum value is considered to be zero.

A few examples: TLVs (US) for ammonia, carbon monoxide and sulfur dioxide are, respectively, 35, 55, and 13 mg/cubic meter. The MACs (USSR) for the same are, 0.2, 3, and 0.5. These comparisons are not especially selected. They explain why work is so much safer in the USSR.

Even more important than the figures are the trends. In the USSR there is constant striving for better health and safety measures. In the US the striving is constantly to increase exploitation and profits at the expense or disregard of health unless forced by the workers' demands for better protection. Not that the USSR has solved every problem. Irregularities and violations still occur, and are publicly and vehemently exposed and denounced in the Soviet press. But they are acted upon, corrected, and all striving is in the interest of the people.

As mentioned earlier, the Soviet draft Constitution guarantees the right to rest and leisure. In April 1919, Lenin signed the decree on "Health Resort Areas of National Importance" in which property was to be set aside for medical treatment of the working population and their families. Today there are 14,000 institutions for holiday use, tourism, spa and sanatorium treatment, which can accommodate two million people at a time. In 1975, 45 million workers and their families had such vacations. Also, 10 million school children vacationed at trade-union administered Pioneer camps. But in the 1976-1980 five year period much new construction is taking place to expand quality and quantity. Holiday centers are being built in conjunction with large factories and enterprises, making for greater convenience especially in cases of needed health care. The costs of vacations are generally less than the equivalent of two weeks pay, a large amount of the vacation expense being borne by the trade union. Health care is closely associated with vacations, and made a part of them, and includes routine examinations, the use of various therapies and spas, diets, calisthenics and the special facilities of the particular region.

A few words about mother and child care. These are connected because the health of fetus and infant is dependent on the well-being of the mother. The USSR has a network of women's health care centers which guarantee availability of proper care. Soviet law frees pregnant women from night work after four months pregnancy; forbids overtime and business trips. Nursing mothers have time with pay for nursing in creches, and/or workday shortened by one hour. Paid maternity leave of 56 days before and 56 days after birth is the law. Mothers may also take unpaid leave until the baby is one year old; and return to the old job at full pay including any raises gained by the union in that time. A mother is given sick-leave at full pay if her child is ill for up to seven days. Beyond that, necessary care is given by the children's hospitals.

There are now 100,000 pediatricians in the USSR, and 500,000 hospital beds for children. Over 56 million children have annual physical exams.

Health research in the USSR is under the direction of the Academy of Medical Sciences, and carried out by the affiliated research institutes. Some 75 to 80 "problems" are set up for study by "problem committees" and submitted to the Academy presidium for approval. Programs are drafted and submitted to the Ministry of Health also for approval. Results of research are supplied countrywide.

Major achievements in recent years are in parasitic diseases; lung surgery; kidney transplants; cancer diagnostic methods and treatment; heart surgery and artificial heart construction; vascular and eye surgery. Technical electronic and ultrasonic instrument manufacture has opened new fields. There are now more than 800,000 Soviet cancer patients who have lived five years after treatment, and over 400,000 have lived ten years or more, because of early diagnosis and effective treatment. A Soviet researcher recently developed a device which, implanted beneath the skin, provides timed release of small insulin doses in response to the blood sugar level.

In the last decade or so, aside from the close cooperation that the USSR has had with the World Health Organization of the United Nations, there has developed a cooperative organization within the Council for Mutual Economic Assistance (CMEA). In manufacturing, for example, Bulgaria has developed electronic diagnostic equipment; Hungary radiological facilities; the German Democratic Republic optical equipment. These are tiny examples of the overall cooperation, which in many cases involves two or more countries in a particular project. In addition, the mass health check-up figures from all these countries are of important epidemiological value, but require a unified electronic computer system. This has now been built, and information is fed into it from all the socialist countries cooperating on a scale unheard of before. Aside from research done in individual countries there are now cooperative projects involving some 180 scientific programs. Regular conferences of the Health Ministers take place to exchange experiences and improve work.

In line with Soviet policy of assistance to developing nations, the USSR has trained many doctors and other health personnel from Asia, Africa, and Latin America. In addition, the USSR has built hospitals and other facilities in India, Ethiopia, Egypt, Yemen, Algeria, Iraq, Afghanistan, Burma, Nepal, Kenya, Somalia, Bangladesh, Cambodia, Pakistan, Nigeria and many other countries.

The USSR cooperates in research with some 56 countries as of 1975. Some of the most exciting and promising work in the field of heart disease, cancer, influenza and diabetes is taking place in conjunction with US doctors and health workers. The earliest agreement, signed in 1972, was that on cancer. Work so far has included exploration of ways to stimulate the body's immunological system to fight leukemia. In influenza studies, researchers have joined forces to find new virus strains and develop new vaccines. The tremendous work in the health field done by the USSR is after all for the benefit of all peoples, and it hurts all peoples when the beneficial discoveries and means of health care cannot be utilized because of suspicion and mistrust. Detente, in an atmosphere of cooperation and trust, will allow the people of the whole world to share in the health triumphs of the USSR on its 60th birthday.   □

22

ROBERT DAGLISH

The Making of a People's Culture

The October Revolution of 1917 made the creation of a culture in which all members of society would be involved and from which all would benefit a practical possibility. The idea was no less revolutionary than the events that engendered it. It set up a new focus of attraction in intellectual life. Liberal ideas once patted to and fro in drawing rooms acquired an unpredictable spin and rebound. Vast areas of human activity previously wrapped in shadow were heaved into the sunlight.

The development of Soviet culture in the early years owes much to Anatoly Lunacharsky, literary critic, playwright, translator and professional revolutionary who became Commissar for Education in 1918. He had seen the inside of many tsarist prisons and known long years in exile in the West. His experience, erudition and tireless ability as a writer and impromptu public speaker made him the ideal man to mold and apply Party policy in the arts and education. His articles and studies available to us (they fill eight volumes) provide a vivid picture of the times.

In 1925, for instance, he wrote a slim booklet called *Why We Are Preserving the Bolshoi Theater*. The purpose was not so much to mark the theater's centenary as to make sure that 1925 did not sound its death knell. Fifty years later, when the Bolshoi celebrated its 150th anniversary, it did so amid world acclaim. Not only had it been the Soviet Union's most successful ambassador of the arts, enormously enriching world ballet and opera. It had also been a delighter and educator of millions who, but for the revolution, might never have seen an opera or ballet in their lives. Its schools had trained thousands of dancers and singers and its influence had been carried far and wide across all the Soviet republics.

And yet, in 1925 its very existence was in question. Though he was a commissar, Lunacharsky was not writing from strength when he argued with those who said "send your big hurdy-gurdy to the devil; it's always playing the

ROBERT DAGLISH, a Briton long resident in Moscow, is a writer, critic, and translator, and also plays English and American parts in Soviet films. A profound observer of the Soviet cultural scene, Mr. Daglish is a regular correspondent of the *Anglo-Soviet Journal* in England; his writing appears frequently in NWR.

same tunes and costs too much.''

The main trouble, of course, was money. The very size and splendor of the theater symbolized the class for whom it had previously performed. But the young Soviet republic was desperately poor and vast projects in education cried out for priority. But with his usual thoroughness and candor Lunacharsky detailed the arguments. The Russian ballet was the only full-scale ballet company still extant in Europe. The orchestra, perhaps one of the best in the world, was far too good to disband. And anyhow the building would probably cost more to keep up empty than in operation. But then with characteristic elan he drew a picture inspired by his enthusiasm for the classical theater of ancient Greece (also state-owned, and with no entrance charges!) and the works of the early Wagner. Here was a model of what the Bolshoi could become in the future.

The theater did not take quite the course that he had expected, and it was some years before the talents of Prokofiev, Khachaturyan, Ulanova, Grigorovich, Plisetskaya, Shchedrin and many others made it the source of culture and enlightenment that it is today.

The decision to preserve the cultural heritage was based on Lenin's insistence that anyone who wanted to become a Communist should ''enrich his memory with all the treasurers created by mankind.'' Lenin had also predicted (as early as 1905) that the new literature would be a ''free literature because the idea of socialism and sympathy with the working people, and not greed or careerism, will bring ever new forces to its ranks.''

The old art was to be cherished and examined again and again for the insights and flashes of genius that bourgeois taste had habitually ignored, while the new art was to be actively encouraged. In 1919, after seeing a production of *Measure for Measure* at the Model Theater, Lunacharsky wrote in *Izvestia* that one of Shakespeare's most neglected plays was ''an analysis of so-called 'justice' no less profound than Dostoyevsky's *Crime and Punishment* or Tolstoy's *Resurrection*.''

It was Lunacharsky who invited Meyerhold to Moscow to play his part in developing the new people's theater. Already famous as an innovative director before the revolution, Meyerhold had recently been liberated by the Red Army from Whiteguard captivity in Novorossisk. The two men were on excellent terms, but even before the revolution they had often been at loggerheads over art. Now Meyerhold wanted to ''put a padlock on all those academic theaters; no more whining, no more psychology,'' and Lunacharsky was determined not to be led away by Meyerhold's enthusiasm for futurism and biomechanics. But he was fascinated by the vigor and originality of Meyerhold's productions and warmly applauded when he found that his futurism was becoming a ''revolutionary futurism,'' as in the production of Erdman's *The Mandate*, for instance. Tairov was another remarkable director who earned both criticism and encouragement from the Commissar for Education. But Lunacharsky was adamant in his opposition to Bulgakov's *The Turbins*, which except for the second act, he saw as a cosy little family drama attempting to justify the role of the officer class in the civil war. At the end of a devastating review, however, he found that "productions of such plays should be welcomed" because this one's very feebleness showed how hard pressed the petty bourgeois intellectual was when seeking anything he could possibly defend in his former attitudes. As it turned out, the play has scarcely ever been off the Soviet stage and was recently given an excellent production on television.

New theaters were springing up all over Moscow and Leningrad. Libraries were being opened. Private premises handed over to the public. The Moscow Art Theater acquired a new theater studio that afterwards became the famous Vakhtangov Theater. Lunacharsky, however, was constantly worried about the "purchasing power" of the new audiences. So whenever he spotted a good production he would urge the Theater Center, the commissariats or trade unions to make every effort to fill that theater with workers or Red Army men.

The revolution had not swept away all social ills overnight and the civil war and the march of the imperialist armies into Russia to crush the revolution in its cradle had made some of them considerably worse. Industry was at a standstill, the countryside had been ravaged, typhus was an ever-present danger, hordes of homeless children roamed the cities. In the fight against these potential disasters the artists and teachers found the inspiration and experience that helped them to build a truly popular culture. The educator Makarenko pioneered the task of rehabilitating the waifs and strays of the civil war. His book about this, describing the colony where hundreds of apparently hopeless cases were recovered for useful and sometimes brilliant service to the community (the Moscow symphony conductor Konstantin Ivanov, for instance), is well described in its title, *A Pedagogical Poem*.

But unemployment remained a problem that was not solved by the limited introduction of private enterprise under the new economic policy of the twenties. There were still labor exchanges and long queues outside them. The thing that banished the labor exchange forever was the Five-Year Plan. One of the targets of the first plan (1929-34) was to reduce the number of unemployed from 1,500,000 to 510,000. It was more than fulfilled. The queues of workless vanished almost overnight.

The gigantic new drive to build a socialist industry had to be financed, which meant food rationing and other sacrifices. And it called for a similar effort in the ideological field. It must have been rather like a doubling or trebling of the effort to consciously serve a cause made by many British and American authors during the war against Hitler. Mayakovsky, the futurist, turned all his marvelous word power, his lyricism and epic strength to the service of the revolution. His open espousal of the cause subtracted little from his poetry. In fact, it added a new breadth and poignancy, as in *150,000,000* and *Good*. Among the many remarkable works of this period were Gladkov's *Cement*, Nikolay Ostrovsky's *How the Steel was Tempered* and Marietta Shaginyan's *Hydrocentral*. They became best-sellers among a newly literate and eager reading public. The impact of industrialization on former country folk, the equality of women, their escape from their old inferior status as house-slaves and drudges, the complex relationships with old regime engineers and specialists from abroad (Katayev's *Forward, Time!*), the ethical problems of rivalry and competition among workers themselves were themes that had a vital importance for the readers of thos days and have not lost their interest today.

Marietta Shaginyan once told me how she acquired her first knowledge of industry. Eager to teach factory weaving methods to the women of Central Asia, she learned the trade herself by writing a book about it. A progressive intellectual of prerevolutionary years with strong religious leanings (she did not join the Communist Party until 1942) she wholeheartedly supported the cause of the revolution, writing novels, adventure stories and serious literary studies (Goethe, Nizami). In the sixties she combined these forms in her rediscovery of the Czech 18th century composer Myslivecik. She is still writing persuasively at the age of 89.

Throughout the thirties Sholokhov's two great novels became a *cause célèbre* of an entirely new kind in the literary world. Never before had so many workers and peasants written letters to an author. There had never been such a general feeling of involvement. Some of the letter-writers were naive, of course, imploring Sholokhov to turn his hero back on to the right path. Sholokhov had to face formidable criticism from such professional critics as Sergey Dynamov, who accused him of naturalism in description and romanticizing the old Cossack ways. At one point he was even suspected of counter-revolutionary activities.

Only a little later, in 1938, the young poet Alexander Tvardovsky made an impression with his *Land of Muravia* (the Russian peasant's Never-Never Land). Alexander was the son of a Smolensk blacksmith, who had turned to farming shortly before the revolution. In his autobiography he amusingly describes how he brought his verses to Moscow in the twenties only to be told by an editor that they would never have any success because they were far too comprehensible. He went home and tried to live up to the new demands but the pull of the life around him proved too strong and he began discussing its problems in verse. He became even more committed to the heroism and tragedy, the laughter and tears of real life when he was called up as a war correspondent in 1939. It was this experience and the Pushkin-like naturalness and flexibility in his verse that produced from the adventures of a character he had invented for a frontline newspaper, Vassily Tyorkin (the name implies "been through the mill"), one of the great poems of the war.

As Lunacharsky had hoped, the revolution was already beginning to produce its own generation of intellectuals, brought up in the spirit and ideals of the young socialist republic. Men and women were transforming themselves in the process of transforming their world. The trade unions play a new and important role in this process. Besides their many other functions they form the link between production and the higher forms of culture. This is a very direct, physical link, providing additional facilities where the workers can enjoy and practice the arts. The trade unions also provide the means whereby the working people, inspired by their contact with the arts, find new outlets for their creative abilities. The *subbotniks* of the early days (and today), the Stakhanovite production drives of the thirties, the present-day movement of rationalizers of production and the Work and Live in a Communist Way movement have all functioned largely through the trade unions. Such cultural centers as Railwaymen's House and the Metro Workers Palace of Culture and scores of similar centers in every city have properly equipped theaters and concert halls and also provide facilities where workers can try out their inventions and practice skills not directly connected with their job. Like the local Soviets the trade unions are a school of citizenship and it is an interesting fact that two-thirds of the members of the local trade union, elected to the Soviets by their fellow workers, are women. Though not part of culture in the narrow sense, these activities are a big factor in molding personality and are partly responsible for the "outgoingness" of Soviet people.

One of the most unjust charges brought against the new culture is that it is chauvinistic. In fact it is internationally minded. From the very start, in 1918, when Gorky set up the World Literature Publishing House, hundreds of intellectuals were drawn into the work of translating from all the world's major languages. Today over 150 million copies of books by American authors have been published in scores of languages of the peoples of the USSR and the current rate of translations from English into Russian is far higher than that of Soviet books into English. Admittedly, it is not easy to find copies in the bookshops because the work of Robert Frost, Updike, Faulkner, Thornton Wilder, Hemingway and dozens of others are snapped up as soon as they appear. But this is surely to be taken as evidence of the universal interest and official encouragement, for the editions are rarely less than 50,000.

But the revolution did more than open the floodgates of world literature and culture for the masses of the former tsarist empire. It initiated an entirely new policy towards the non-Russian peoples, especially those who had no written language, like the peoples of the Far North, the Chukchi and the Nentsi. Today these peoples have their own writers and artists. Yakutsk, capital of Yakutia, where winter temperatures average 40°C below zero, has theaters, cinemas and its own University.

Sixty years ago the notion of Uzbeks, Tatars, Russians, Georgians and Ukrainians living on equal and friendly terms was but a concept in the minds of progressive thinkers. It took a complete redistribution of wealth throughout the former Russian Empire and a deliberate policy of investment in the underdeveloped parts to lay the foundation of this friendship in the USSR. The wise policy of raising the economic level of the outlying regions to that of the metropolis involved sacrifices at the center. It was a policy that had to be carried out with tact, insight and attention to detail. In an article written in the thirties, Nadezhda Krupskaya, Lenin's widow, who contributed much to Soviet educational policy, warned that it was dangerous to keep telling the children of one nationality how backward other nationalities had been before the revolution, however true that might be. It might evoke a feeling of superiority in a child's mind and more emphasis should be placed on the glorious periods in their history.

The spread of education and particularly medical education was an important factor in this process. In Central Asia in 1917 only about 10 per cent of the people could read or write and in Uzbekistan literacy was as low as two per cent. Women, still housebound and veiled, were almost totally illiterate. The first university in Usbekistan was opened in Tashkent in 1922, the teachers and equipment being provided by the Russian Federation despite that republic's own needs. A similar pattern was followed in other Central Asian republics, Kazakh, Kirghiz, Tadzhik and Turkmen. In Uzbekistan today the ratio of students to population is higher than in either Britain or the USA. In Kazakhstan there are 22 doctors and 80 qualified medical staff per 10,000 of the population, which compares very favorably with Britain. These republics really are thriving. They have been able to tap vast new natural resources. Thanks to the elimination of serious epidemic diseases and universal medical care the population is growing fast, much faster than in Russia itself. It would have been a sad story for international friendship if unemployment had remained the problem it was in the twenties, but the planned economy and the ever more ambitious projects that lie ahead have eliminated any possibility of national enmity being stirred by a job shortage.

The far-sighted policy adopted at the outset, a policy that recognized every person's basic affection for his homeland and the need to provide conditions in which people of every nationality could live in and develop the country of their birth, has also burgeoned in the cultural field. A stream of original and increasingly thoughtful art now flows from the national republics to the Russian heartland, enriching and quickening the artistic circulation of the whole organism. A play by Chinghiz Aitmatov of Kirghizia is currently running in Moscow, and recently opened in London. No poetry almanac is complete without a contribution from Rasul Gamzatov of Daghestan. The young poet Olzhas Suleimenov with firm roots in his own Eastern soil and a mind that has obviously ranged over all Russian poetry and much of the West's has a catalytic effect much like that of the Russian Andrey Voznesensky. In a recent, admittedly much criticized, essay he showed that he has some highly original ideas about the influence of the Turkic languages on Russian.

As the *lingua franca*, Russian has played an important part in this intertraffic. It has never been imposed. Everyone has the right to be taught in his own language. But I have heard of situations in Byelorussia, for instance, where a young Byelorussian tractor-driver being interviewed by the local radio has replied in the Russian that comes more naturally to him while the interviewer, sticking conscientiously to regulations, asks his questions in Byelorussian. Such assimilation is bound to take place in some areas, but where the national language is vigorous and not so closely related to Russian, in Estonia or Georgia, for instance, translation into Russian is essential and enormously increases the audience and readership of writers from the smaller ethnic groups. Some of these, brought up in a two-language culture, acquire fluency in both. Fazil Iskander, for instance, an Abkhazian, writes in Russian and delights his readers with a humor that has a distinctly Caucasian flavor. In other fields too this reciprocal enrichment is becoming more and more evident, particularly the cinema, where Kirghiz, Georgian and Byelorussian films are often outstanding.

Soviet culture received a severe setback in the years of distrust and tension immediately preceding the second world war. As the icy shadows of fascism lengthened across Europe in the thirties, the anxiety of some critics to see success and perfection blossoming everywhere resulted in grave injustices being done to many innocent experimenters in the arts. It also produced the theory of the "conflictless" novel that did so much danger after the war. But these difficulties were overcome, though with much pain and soul-searching. In 1937, one year after his opera *Lady Macbeth of Mtsensk* had been sharply criticized in *Pravda*, Shostakovich produced his breathtaking Fifth Symphony, which has retained its place in world repertoire ever since. And he went on composing all through the war, reaching heroic heights in the Leningrad Symphony, looking back for an instant in the post-war Tenth and then plunging into the new period in collaboration with the poet Yevtushenko. He turned again to poetry, Lorca's, in his Fourteenth Symphony, which though he followed it with other works, soon proved to be his requiem. Music often says things in greater depth than any words and Shostakovich's work is perhaps the greatest single expression of the Soviet people's movement towards their goal—the intense, continual effort, the disappointed hopes, a gritty humor.

great tumescent moments of renewed hope and struggle and the final joy of overcoming, which is never final because there is always a new vista and a new problem ahead.

One of the new problems the people's culture faced in the sixties was, paradoxically, the technology of the postwar era. Television, which had seemed at first such a boon to the propagandist, was found also to have the effect of drawing people out of the orbit of social activity. The consumerism that was becoming increasingly possible as prosperity increased also tended to wean people away from the former, more austere social interests—the public lecture hall, the reading room, training for sports, and so on. As a survey conducted in 1972 showed, in some areas far more workers were watching sport on television than taking part in it. New life-styles were emerging and art had to adapt itself to meet current needs or risk being only half heard and half seen. A young generation that had known none of the rigors of the early years was eager for fresh approaches.

Yekaterina Furtseva, then Minister of Culture, urged the television studios to give more time to amateur dance groups and singers, to all sorts of contests and games. Television programs, plays and serials were devised that would be likely to stimulate more active participation in the arts and public life. Actors and musicians were called in for get-togethers on screen to discuss their work. All this had its effect. The ever popular guitar acquired a new status and in the hands of such exponents as the poet and novelist Bulat Okudzhava and the actor Vladimir Vysotsky, almost a new social role. Certainly they have hundreds of imitators among workers and students, who sing ballads of their own composition, from high passion and romantic longing to social satire. A parallel process took place in the theaters and cinema and productions with a distinctive theatrical or cinematic style aroused intense interest (Lyubimov's Taganka Theater and the films of Andrey Tarkovsky).

Amateur activities had always been encouraged and with more funds available they had an added boost in the sixties and seventies. All industrial and agricultural enterprises have a wide range of amateur cultural activities in which all workers can participate. So have the Pioneer Palaces for children. Now, more than 23 million people participate in amateur artistic activities of one sort or another, and amateur artists give more than two million concerts and performances a year.

Several new theaters have sprung up in Moscow, one of them a children's theater run almost entirely by children. The Children's Theater with professional actors and producers had been pioneered in 1918 with lasting success. But this is a new departure. The children not only act and produce, they look after the building, keep the accounts and sell the tickets. The interesting thing is the scope for participation that is given at an early age.

The musical schools, and those in other arts, where children get a serious musical or other artistic training as well as general education, also encourage early participation in the arts. Here one might say the tendency is towards professionalism. Of course, there always will be a gap between the professional and amateur in art, but in a people's culture the dividing line is not so fixed. On the one hand, there is not the same risk attached to trying to become a professional artist (fear of unemployment or missing the boat in another profession); on the other, there are bigger opportunities for training, both through the schools and in after-work activities at the People's Theaters and so on, which also have their professional teachers. Somewhere in between come the remarkable organizations for special groups, such as the Theater of the Deaf. Run by the Society for the Deaf, this theater has everything—a fine modern building with a full-size auditorium and a specially equipped stage, specialist teachers and producers, musicians, the deaf actors themselves and their speaking counterparts who stand in the wings and vocalize for them. All this is professional, of course, and the theater sells tickets to members of the public, who can enjoy an unusual evening in the company of the deaf members of the audience, watching *Prometheus Unbound* or even *The Three Musketeers*, for there are voices and music as well as gestures, lip-movements and dancing. And the object of it all is to bring an opportunity of full participation in social life for people with even this grave disability.

But none of these organizational factors would have had much effect if there had not been a middle and younger generation of writers and producers with something very important to say about the life around them. The postwar war literature was the first to take a new plunge into the psychological. This is the distinctive feature of Vassil Bykov, Yuri Bondarev and Grigori Baklanov, not to mention the later work (The Living and the Dead trilogy) of the veteran Konstantin Simonov, already famous for his wartime reporting and poetry. But it was also necessary to search human motives in the present, to uncover the hidden springs of loyalty and betrayal in apparently humdrum events, in acquiring a new flat, for instance, or defending a thesis. Viktor Rozov, the playwright and Granin the novelist, had pioneered this approach in the fifties. Yuri Trifonov, starting a little later, has revealed a Chekhovian ability to tear away the veils of human vanity and self-esteem and his knack of linking the revolutionary past with the present often has a chastening effect.

Perhaps the most typical and yet outstanding representative of the new culture was Vassily Shukshin, the young man from the Siberian backwoods, truck-driver, sailor and odd-job man, who became first an actor, then a writer of short-stories and finally the Soviet Union's most popular actor-director. His death from heart-failure while on location filming a Sholokhov novel was an event of national mourning. Shukshin knew as no one else the heart and soul of the rank-and-file Soviet workers in town and country, and especially those who moved between the city and the village. His love of oddball characters, his humor and his quick sense of protest at arrogance and indifference sparked immediate sympathy in the reader and his collected short stories will, I am sure, be read by many succeeding generations. His intense humanity has already been taken up by such young writers as Valentin Rasputin. One of their great concerns is the environment and all that this implies in human terms. And in this they seem to have the backing of the Communist Party, which realizes that a true love of nature and attention to every detail of human welfare cannot be instilled by legislation alone. Those who read Rasputin's *Farewell, Matyora*, the story of one tragic incident in the building of the Angara Dam, will notice a striking contrast between it and the early "production" novels but they will also feel a connecting thread if they remember the stages in the development of this truly popular culture.

In this survey, which touches upon only a few of the salient features and personalities of a crowded and constantly changing scene. I have attempted to show some of the problems that faced the young republic of workers and peasants and the astonishing achievements by which they have been solved. Sometimes the cost was great, but it has always seemed wrong to me, even at moments of startling revelations, to regard Soviet culture as something static, much less to pick on its failures and setbacks and hold them up as evidence that man is forever in the grip of original sin and can no more escape it than lift himself by his own bootlaces. Those who do so, however revealing they may sound at first, usually end up as quite ordinary reactionaries who would prefer to see the people back where they belonged in the days of Russian Orthodoxy, on their knees in front of an ikon. The Soviet people, however, will go on with their work of building a truly great popular culture that will continue to astonish the world, the more so because so many people in the West are kept in ignorance of what is really being achieved. For those who believe that the only true art must be pure and uncommitted I hope that what little I have been able to say here will perhaps have suggested how mistaken it would have been for artists to turn aside from the new life, and how infinitely more inspiring it was to step forward and grapple with its problems.   □

23

DANIEL ROSENBERG

The Revolution and Youth: A Heritage, a Challenge

The degree to which a society answers young people's special concerns is a gauge of that society's democratic content. Youth's rights, above all their rights to earn, learn, and live are a criterion for testing social progress. These rights are also basic human rights. In this regard much has been said in the past year about "human rights" in the Soviet Union and the socialist countries. The occasion of the 60th Anniversary is a good time to look at Soviet youth's rights, responsibilities and attitudes; considering the amount of material on Soviet "violations" of human rights written in our country such an examination is highly appropriate.

For youth everywhere the present and future revolve around the most important human right: the right to work. The significance for youth of this guaranteed right is striking. US youth's unemployment rate soars (reaching 86 per cent for Black youth and 74 per cent for white youth in New York City, aged 16-19), seriously endangering the hopes and ambitions of millions of young people. Job prospects and joblessness affect one's entire outlook, influence youth's approach in general and the development of the personality in particular.

Soviet society has full youth employment. Young people may begin work at 16 (15 in rare cases approved by the union), with a 24-hour week for the youngest workers (15-16) and a 36-hour week for 16-18 year olds. They are paid at the same rate as co-workers in the same category working a full day. Soviet law bars youth from night work, arduous labor, and dangerous working conditions.

Every Soviet enterprise and factory gives special on-the-job training, with pay, to young workers. The older workers assist them in mastering skills. Enterprises often have history museums; veterans or "mentors" acquaint newcomers with working class spirit. Young workers are welcomed, for

DANIEL ROSENBERG is a graduate student in history. He participated in American-Soviet youth meetings in 1974, 1975, and 1976, and recently served as representative of the Young Workers Liberation League to the Bureau of the World Federation of Democratic Youth in Budapest.

example, into the Promsoyuz Plan in Azerbaidzhan with an honorary "Labor Mandate" signed by the veteran workers.

Because free education guarantees the right to learn, Soviet youth are able to more *securely* outline the course of their futures. The Soviet schools and trade unions, assisted by the Young Communist League (Komsomol), provide youth with the raw material for a sense of direction, and of confidence.

Youth who prefer not to go on to higher education receive job counseling and placement in accordance with their interests. Graduates of higher institutions of learning are located in jobs in their specialties though not necessarily near their home-towns. Soviet society reserves the right to ask of young graduates that they devote their initial two years of work to meeting certain needs of the country. The free education and other social services of socialism are in a sense thereby "repaid," though no one is obligated to remain at that first job beyond two years.

Young people are acquainted with career opportunities while still in school. The continual growth of Moscow's Lenin Komsomol Auto Plant engenders a need for more workers. Here, as elsewhere, "open houses" are arranged for high school students. Alexander Andreikov, a Komsomol leader at this plant, asserted that the aim was to encourage young people to think about this field, along with all the others.

Although plants themselves recruit young workers, employment offices provide extensive lists of job openings in various trades in every Soviet community. The press and media also report job openings.

Youth in the Soviet Union often choose roads vastly divergent from those of their elders. No matter what their background, they have the opportunity to enter any field for which they have ability and in which jobs are available. Alisa Shistko, a young Ukrainian musician, told me that she was the first in her family to study music; her mother is a hotel clerk, her father an historian. Beginning at the children's Pioneer Palace in Rubezhnoye she studied free of charge, went on to a music school and then to the Kiev Conservatory (tuition free) where she became a conductor.

Bulat Minzhkilkiyev, a young opera singer from Kirghizia told me he had no musical education whatsoever until his naval command discovered his talents and urged him to attend the conservatory's special two-year introductory course. From there he went on to study in Tashkent and eventually in Italy—all at no cost to him.

A Soviet lawyer with whom I spoke not long ago stated that his parents were auto workers; a petrochemical engineer from Baku said his parents worked on a state farm.

Of course, career choices are not always smooth sailing, in the USSR as elsewhere. A young man I met in 1975 told me that throughout his boyhood and early youth in Moscow he had longed to write for a newspaper, to become a journalist. He studied in the field and got a job after graduation only to find that, to him, the job was not really as exciting as he'd imagined. He went back to school to the Institute for Foreign Languages and is now employed in a job he enjoys, as translator, interpreter and teacher.

The factories are centers of youth activity. Over 70 per cent of the work force at the Second Moscow Watch Production Plant which I visited recently, is under 30. The Komsomol branch takes the initiative in organizing clubs, cultural and sports activities, and other offerings particularly suited to young people. The plant has a yacht and a yacht club; also a chorus, a photo club, a stadium, and drama groups.

The young workers at the Kiev Textile Factory also have a yacht club. The same is true at the Kiev Institute for "Super-Hard Materials" (synthetic diamonds): workers take two week cruises down the Dnieper.

The profits from the Minsk Tractor Works go toward the building of new apartments, sports facilities, and the plant polyclinic's medical equipment.

Trade unions and union members work closely with young people in the community.They directly help in the funding of sports clubs (gymnastics, soccer and hockey in particular) and of cultural groups (young people's orchestra, dance companies, drama groups); trade union and Komsomol branches work together in arranging all sorts of recreational activities, including dances, hiking and camping expeditions, ski trips, picnics, tourist excursions etc.

Furthermore young people receive personal guidance in selecting fields of interest and careers through factory and office "patronage" over particular schools. An enterprise and its trade union "adopt" a local school and help out with supplies, equipment, and vocational training.

With the aid of the Komsomol and the trade unions, enterprises ensure the opportunity to study while on the job. The number of workers going to school is three to six times greater in the USSR than in the USA. Shorter work weeks, guaranteed paid (full) leaves at exam time, evening and correspondence courses, free child care, complete technical training and seminars on the basics of economics and production management enable the young worker to learn and grow on the job. The young worker always has plenty of interesting things to do, whether he or she is on the assembly line, in the classroom, or cruising on a yacht.

In the spirit of emulation young workers and farmers and their work teams seek to improve the methods and quality of production. The effort at making production more "rational" has given rise to a movement of "young rationalizers." These working youth, part of the All-Union Society of Inventors and Rationalizers, submit hundreds of thousands of proposals each year for better use of machinery, alteration of shifts and work team rotation, new cycles and processes of production, etc. The increase in productivity and quality is not done by "speed-up," but rather by improving methods of work. Of the 1,650,000 proposals by youth from 1971 to 1974, said then (1974) Komsomol head Yevgeny Tyazhelnikov, over 65 per cent were implemented, resulting in savings of over a billion rubles: funds that were then employed for other purposes, including youth's social and cultural needs at enterprises. The Exhibition of Economic Achievements in Moscow features a special exhibit of youth's scientific and technical "inventions."

Young people's interests are politically represented at every level of government. Concretely, youth under 30 constitute nearly 20 per cent of the deputies to the Supreme Soviet of the USSR and higher percentages of the lower Soviets. Kiev's local Soviets include 930 young deputies. The head of the local Soviet of a small town outside Kiev told me that 85 per cent of its deputies are under 30; 50 per cent of them are women. Komsomol members sit on the boards of top national bodies: the Ministries of Public Education, Culture, Higher and Specialized Education and the Committees for State TV and Radio, and for Physical Culture and Sport.

All Soviets have Youth Commissions; young deputies form the largest bloc of commission members. From the Chairwoman of the Executive Committee of the Kiev City Soviet I learned that its Youth Commission has 29 deputies: 12 youth (11 in the Komsomol), plus workers, professors and social scientists. The tasks of the Youth Commission, she said, are to improve youth's conditions of work and leisure; to improve student life; to build youth clubs and restaurants; and to organize cultural performances and sports competitions. The Commission meets with Soviet youth and organizations, often directly at a plant or school where a particular question has come up. Jobs Committees, which aid young people in determining and pursuing their careers, can be found within both local and higher Soviets. The Youth Commissions provide job counseling and help to locate young people in their first jobs.

There are 12,000 Youth Commissions in the Soviet Union. The Commission in one local Soviet in the RSFSR recently tackled the problem of a dwindling proportion of young workers in a textile mill. A government official's explanation that objective problems would inevitably reduce their proportion was found unacceptable by the Commission, which recommended the modernization of the plant, improvement in the cultural and athletic offerings for youth and the building of newer housing in the area. The resolution passed and young workers have begun to take jobs at the mill.

Therefore, at the 60th year of the October Revolution, the input of youth and the impact of youth concerns are felt in the political sense, in the governmental application of Soviet youth rights policy.

Soviet youth's response to challenge is nowhere better revealed than in its participation in the country's mammoth construction projects. The thousands of young workers flocking to the non-black earth regions of the USSR will transform "a huge territory in the heartland of the country," Tyazhelnikov said at the 17th Komsomol Congress (1974). Indeed, youth's mass contribution to the development of the Soviet countryside, to the "virgin lands," the non-black earth areas, to the Siberian hinterlands has affected rural areas in a basic way. The Komsomol reported that the developments "could not but influence the village youth, their general and professional orientation. The migration of young people from the countryside has decreased."

Among all the Komsomol's major construction "Priority Projects" there is none so dramatic as the building of the Baikal-Amur Railroad (BAM). This is *the* project of the decade. BAM will cover 2,000 miles, allowing exploitation of rich Siberian mineral deposits, for example copper ore in Udokan and coal in Chitkondinskoye and Apsatskoye. Towns are rising along the route (*towns of young workers*, where 25 is the average age), ultimately 60 towns in all, each with a projected population of 100,000. BAM means even newer and broader horizons for the Soviet East. The multinational Soviet youth's decisive contribution helps, through economic development, the formerly specially oppressed peoples of such regions as Yakutia.

BAM and the Trans-Siberian Railroad will lead to the Pacific. The Baikal-Amur Railroad passes through permafrost regions with temperatures as low as -60°C (-76°F), through areas of seismic activity ranging 7-8 on the Richter Scale. BAM crosses mountains in seven locations, some as high as five kilometers (three miles).

The Komsomol wages a special campaign for the construction of this railroad. I spoke with the Central Committee Secretary, Leonid Frylov, who coordinates the overall drive. He told me that since April 1974 (when a 600-person brigade commenced work) over 30,000 youth from every Soviet republic have been to the construction sites. Three-quarters are below the age of 28. There are Komsomol branches all along the track, for more than half the young people are members. Thirty-five per cent of the workers are women. As the track is laid, towns, with hospitals, apartments, clubs, kindergartens, day care centers, and schools are built.

The youth building Tynda, a new town, are presently constructing apartment houses, a palace of culture, a stadium, and a Pioneer Palace. The "priority project" workers on BAM also include young architects.

The Komsomol initiates seminars on BAM all over the USSR. Komsomol radio stations and mass media feature stories on BAM. Youth of other socialist countries also work on the project: there are now several hundred young Hungarian and Bulgarian workers there.

Vladimir Yanishevsky, a member of the Komsomol Central Committee who worked on BAM, notes that he and many of his co-workers now consider the Siberian construction site as home. "How did this happen?" he asks. "Probably because we began from nothing. We ourselves cut down the pines and built the houses we now live in.''

As they work, the youth of BAM grow and change in a basic way. Victor Lakomov, a deputy to the Russian Federation's Supreme Soviet and a veteran railroad worker, viewed the wave of young workers with a little skepticism at first; but after a time, he reports, ''these young people turned into adults before our eyes. I am convinced that there's no better school, no better preparation for life, than our construction project.''

Projects such as BAM help inspire in youth a sense of respect for work, collectivity, an appreciation of the many nationalities constituting the Soviet people and an understanding of their own worth.

The Komsomol plays an essentially educational role. It acts independently of, and fraternally with, the Communist Party, uniting youth of over 100 Soviet nationalities. With membership voluntary (65 per cent of the youth are in it) it now counts 36 million members ranging in age from 14 to 28. The Komsomol makes its most important contribution in the realm of labor, particularly in the mobilization of millions of young workers in the most challenging construction exploits, whose completion is vital to the nation. It is instrumental as well in the personal development and realization of the potential of each young participant.

The Young Communist League is active in the elaboration of youth's rights and responsibilities, working to enhance youth's role in production, education, art, sports and culture. The Komsomol seeks to improve the well-being of youth in the course of augmenting their overall contribution to Soviet development.

Branch meetings (branches range from ten members in rural areas to 42,000 members in Moscow) are at maximum two hours in length and special steps are taken to make them attractive.

Letters to the Komsomol are sorted, distributed to the responsible people and answered within ten days of their arrival. The First Secretary of the Moscow organization told me that after answering the letters, which often deal with particular situations and suggestions (*i.e.*, improving cultural and athletic offerings, organizing dances and other activities, better coordination of youth's relations with local unions and factories, better utilization of work time, etc.), Komsomol leaders write down on index cards the subject of the correspondence and the proposed solution. The cards are followed up later to check on the accountability of leadership to young people and their problems.

A top Komsomol secretary, often the head of the local organization, is assigned daily to the sole task of receiving visitors and resolving grievances and complaints. The Komsomol thus conducts a campaign for constant contact between leadership and membership and between Komsomol and non-Komsomol youth.

The Komsomol provides many outlets for youth's self-expression, creative writing, etc. Youth newspapers, magazines and publishing houses abound in every city. The Komsomol of the Ukraine sponsors 25 radio and 15 television stations providing broad possibilities for young people to gain experience in the broadcasting and cultural fields.

The Communist Party of the Soviet Union and the Komsomol helps young people gain a knowledge of history and struggle, an understanding of their multinational union of republics, an identification with the working people and an active sympathy for all struggling peoples.

In addition, as Leonid Brezhnev stated at the 25th CPSU Congress, "life itself keeps setting before the YCL growing demands. After all, it is in the YCL that young people are actively brought into conscious participation in communist construction. It is no easy task to foster such consciousness, especially considering the fact that one has to deal with young people whose character has yet to mature."

International solidarity is an important element in the thinking of Soviet youth. National and racial equality at home, in a union of 100 Soviet peoples, has given root to Soviet youth's respect and sympathy for the peoples of all countries.

The present generation of Soviet young people has grown up under peaceful skies. They are part of the Soviet Union's "peace offensive," part of the world peace movement. Only a generation removed from the struggle against Hitler fascism, Soviet youth understand the significance of the struggles for disarmament and detente. Virtually every young Soviet has signed the Stockholm Peace Appeal, and young workers, students, professionals, athletes and cultural artists have campaigned actively for it.

The Soviet Komsomol and Committee of Youth Organizations help mobilize Soviet youth's international activity. Countless mass rallies were conducted in support of the Vietnamese people, of Angela Davis, of the People's Republic of Angola. Young Soviet specialists working in progressive, developing countries make a tangible contribution to the anti-imperialist struggle.

Such a team of young specialists, which I saw in Brazzaville, People's Republic of Congo, constituted one of the largest delegations to the funeral of the late noted anti-imperialist martyr, President Marien Ngouabi.

A component of the world anti-imperialist youth movement, affiliated to the World Federation of Democratic Youth, the International Union of Students and other bodies, Soviet youth's solidarity activities now focus on Chile and Southern Africa. Soviet youth are involved in campaigns of material support, boycott and raising solidarity funds. Local branches of the Komsomol have telephoned to Santiago, Chile to demand of the Junta the whereabouts of the so-called "disappeared," including Jose Weibal of the Communist youth and Carlos Lorca of the Socialist youth.

The Komsomol in Moscow actively promotes international solidarity work, its First Secretary told me. It has helped to involve its 1,250,000 members in subbotniks (days of voluntary labor) raising money to assist the Chile anti-fascist movement; 150,000 Moscow YCL'ers sent birthday greetings to Luís Corvalán, General Secretary of the Chilean Communist Party last year. "For us," said the head of the Moscow YCL, "Chile in 1977 is like Spain in 1937."

The Komsomol has been instrumental in building a European youth movement crossing over a vast political spectrum in the interest of security and cooperation. An extraordinarily successful meeting of European youth from almost every single political trend was held in Warsaw, June 1976. The Soviet youth organizations take a tremendous part in winning new forces to this European youth movement. They have a flexibility and sincerity in working with political forces of diverse outlooks that has helped greatly to strengthen detente. With the principled, consistent support of the Soviet Komsomol, an even larger European youth meeting will be held in December 1977 on disarmament, with the participation of the Young Workers Liberation League of the USA.

Soviet youth in every city and republic have expressed their indignation at Jimmy Carter's provocative "human rights" campaign. A young Leningrad electrical worker told me that the workers in her plant know a great deal about the USA, see US films, exhibitions, read US journals in the plant library. At the Fifth US-Soviet Youth Forum in 1976, a young woman doctor from Kiev commented on the corruption of US elections, quoting from Mark Twain. A young researcher at the Institute for the Study of the USA and Canada recently acknowledged to a US youth delegation that there were indeed limits on Soviet "freedoms," namely the "freedoms" to propagandize in favor of war and in favor of racism, and her partner asked the visiting youth how the US government could crow about "human rights" while Ben Chavis and the Wilmington 10 were in prison and the ballot rights of the US Communist Party limited.

The Soviet youth, led by their Komsomol, play an important role in the annual International Day of Solidarity with Youth Fighting Racism in the USA, designated as April 4 (the anniversary of the murder of Martin Luther King, Jr.) by the World Federation of Democratic Youth. The Komsomol helped initiate the Federation's historic global activities in support of the struggle against youth unemployment in the developed capitalist countries, and has pledged to organize solidarity rallies throughout the Soviet Union.

Finally, in this jubilee year, Soviet youth are engaged in truly gargantuan preparations for the 11th World Festival of Youth and Students to be held next summer in Havana, Cuba.

With the October Revolution a generation of youth arose, distinct from all preceding generations of youth. They were *Soviet* youth: the young people who saw and helped build socialism *first*; who came to realize their hopes and ambitions in a way and to an *extent* previously unknown; who came into adulthood free from the burdens of class, national and racial oppression, in a land where affirmative action and equality are law and the rights of youth are as natural as human nature.

Today's Soviet young people are the third generation to live under socialism. Consequently, their tasks and activities differ from those of their predecessors; for as Lenin noted, while an earlier generation laid the foundation, the next generation built upon it "under new conditions, in a situation in which relations based on the exploitation of man by man no longer exist."

Now advanced socialism, a new stage, has been reached, and Soviet youth assume responsibilities commensurate with this development. Raised in the spirit of brotherhood and peace, honesty and equality, concern and collectivity, respect for work and for working people, Soviet youth reflect the ongoing dynamism of the Soviet Union at the 60th anniversary of the socialist revolution.   □

24

MIKE JAY

Sports in the USSR

The achievements of Soviet athletes have amazed the world ever since the USSR burst onto the Olympic scene in 1952 at Helsinki. That year the men and women athletes of the USSR finished second to the mighty United States squad in the unofficial team standings. The US team wound up with a total of 76 medals: 40 gold, 19 silver and 17 bronze. The Soviet athletes returned home with 71 medals: 22 gold, 30 silver and 19 bronze.

Few outside of the USSR expected the Soviet athletes to fare so well. In 1952 the Soviet people were still struggling to overcome the devastation caused by World War II, not to mention the economic backwardness inherited from tsarist Russia less than 35 years earlier.

But the Soviet performance in the 1952 Olympics was no fluke. In 1956 the USSR athletes improved their record at the Melbourne Olympics and they continued to increase their medals total at Rome in 1960 and Tokyo in 1964. At the 20th Olympic Games in Munich in 1972, the USSR athletes scored a convincing victory, bringing home 99 medals, including an unprecedented 50 gold. (The US was second with 94 medals, 33 of which were gold.)

In 1976 at Montreal the Soviet athletes were again triumphant, amassing a total of 125 medals: 47 gold, 43 silver and 35 bronze. The US was second in total medals with 94, but dropped to third in the number of gold medals with 34. The socialist German Democratic Republic, with a population of only 17 million, was second in gold medals with 40.

A similar picture exists with regard to the Winter Olympics. The USSR finished first at Innsbruck in 1976 with 27 medals (13 gold, six silver and seven bronze) and the US was third with 10 (three gold, three silver and four bronze).

During the 1950s and 60s the international successes of the Soviet athletes were often explained away in the West by cold war terminology: secret drugs, forced training, etc. Such explanations still persist (usually as excuses for defeat), but with increasingly less acceptance. More and more the athletes and sports fans in Western countries look with admiration and respect at the achievements of athletes from socialist countries.

MIKE JAY is the regular sports columnist for the *Daily World*.

The performances of Olga Korbut, Lyudmila Turischeva and other Soviet gymnasts at the 1972 Munich Olympics helped to popularize gymnastics in the United States as never before. As a result, many thousands of youngsters, especially girls, have since taken up the sport, North American ice-hockey players have learned much from their Soviet counterparts since the first Team Canada-USSR series in 1972, and hockey fans in North America have come to appreciate the Soviet hockey style, with its emphasis on fine skating and teamwork rather than on the bullying roughhouse play that too often characterizes professional hockey.

The international achievements of Soviet athletes are the end result of a system which has emphasized the primacy of mass participation since its inception in 1917. "In our country, physical culture means sport for the whole people," Soviet President Mikhail Kalinin wrote in 1938. "Millions participate in the physical culture movement. And it is obvious that talented athletes will sooner be found among those millions than among thousands, and that it is easier to find talented athletes among thousands than among hundreds."

In the Soviet Union, as in all socialist countries, physical culture and sport are seen as playing a major role in the harmonious development of a person. The right of citizens to engage in sports and recreation activities is guaranteed by law.

According to the 1976 USSR Yearbook, published by the Novosti Press Agency, "socialist society attaches great importance to physical education. It considers the bringing up of a physically fit and harmoniously developed young citizen one of its most important tasks." Physical education is compulsory in all kindergartens, schools, colleges and universities in the USSR.

The amateur sports movement embraces all those who join sports clubs and engage in different sports at their place of work or study—at factories, construction sites, offices, educational establishments, collective and state farms. (This is in addition to daily collective exercise breaks which take place at most workplaces.) Any wage or salary earner or any member of his/her family has the right to join the sports club of his organization. The entrance fee and the membership dues of any Soviet sports club are 30 kopeks a year (about 40 cents). Members do not have to pay for the use of equipment and facilities or for the services of coaches.

There are more than 217,000 such clubs and sports groups in the USSR. They are affiliated to different sports societies on the basis of their members' jobs and place of residence.

Each union republic has two sports societies—one for urban communities and one for the countryside. In addition there are seven all-Union, i.e. national, sports societies which have clubs all over the USSR. The two largest and most popular among these are "Spartak" and "Dynamo"—others are "Burevestnik" (for students), the Central Army Sports Club ("TsSKA") and the "Labor Reserves" (vocational school students). There are also the "Lokomotiv" (railway workers) and "Vodnik" (river transport workers) sports societies. Altogether the Soviet Union has 37 sports societies with a total membership of about 50 million, or roughly one fifth of the population.

A Committee for Physical Culture and Sports under the USSR Council of Ministers is responsible for the general management of sports activities in the country and the coordination of work of the sports societies and the various federations for particular sports. It is the stated aim of all Soviet sports clubs to include as many people as possible in sports and recreation activities, regardless of age. Thus the emphasis on physical culture, a lifetime approach to fitness and health, in addition to sport, which implies polished technique and regular competitions and is mainly the activity of the young.

The lifetime approach is promoted through the "Ready for Labor and Defense" (GTO) program, which originated some 40 years ago. (Today it is sometimes referred to as "Prepared for Work and Defense," PWD—an attempt to simplify the English translation—but most English-speaking observers still call it GTO.) This program is designed for people of all ages, ranging from schoolchildren to those over 60. It is accordingly divided into five stages, with appropriate exercises for each stage. Those who successfully meet the GTO qualifications receive badges.

In Soviet society there are no private individuals or organizations who make a profit from sports. Soviet athletes are not paid for taking part in sports events. Each athlete has his own profession or trade which provides him with means of a livelihood. There are no professional sports in the USSR; rather, sport is a pastime or hobby.

However, during training periods and competitions Soviet athletes continue to draw their regular salaries or stipends. Their fares to and from competitions inside the USSR and abroad are also paid for.

Sixty-six different sports are taken up in the USSR, not including many traditional types of national sports. These latter also remain popular. Many Russians, for example, still enjoy *gorodki*, a game in which a long stick is hurled at a square containing wooden pegs, the aim being to knock, successively, various configurations of pegs out of the square, the *lapta*, a game similar to rounders or baseball. Georgian athletes go in for *chidaoba*, a type of wrestling, *lelo*, which resembles soccer and rugby, and several equestrian sports. National forms of wrestling and equestrian sports are also highly developed in Kazakhstan, Kirghizia, Uzbekistan and Armenia. The Yakuts hold lasso throwing contests, the Buryats are known for their archery ability, and the Nentsi hold reindeer races. A Federation of National Sports conducts competitions in 26 such sports.

The most popular sports in the USSR today, however, can be found among the 66 which are pursued nationwide. More than six million people take part in track and field events, 5.5 million participate in organized volleyball, 4.5 million practice skiing and four million play soccer. Fast gaining in popularity in recent years, particularly among families, is "tourism," which in the USSR embraces such activities as hiking, backpacking, camping, etc.

Other sports which have gained a following include karting, auto racing, flying, parachuting etc.

There are no "elite" sports in the Soviet Union. Sports such as yachting, skiing and equestrian events, which are expensive to take up in the capitalist countries, are open to all, at nominal expense. The contrast is evident at international competitions, especially in the equestrian events, where it is not uncommon for the sons and daughters of Soviet workers to test their skills against members of the royal families of Western Europe and England.

Some of the popular sports, such as modern (or rhythmic) gymnastics and "sambo" wrestling (a kind of judo which combines techniques used in various national forms) originated in the USSR and have achieved international recognition.

There is a unified system of sports classification in the USSR, covering 50 sports. Special ratings based on achievement levels have been introduced in most sports: Third, Second and First rating (both for youth and adults), Candidate Master of Sports of the USSR, Master of Sports of the USSR and Master of Sports of the USSR, International Class.

Requirements for getting a rating are high, and they are constantly being upgraded as better results are achieved. For example, to receive the Master of Sports rating in the 100-meter sprint a male athlete has to run it in 10.3 seconds. For the International Class rating he has to run it in 10 seconds flat, which is the European record.

Soviet athletes who win titles as Olympic, World and European Champions are awarded the honorary title of Merited Master of Sports of the USSR. Today there are some 2,000 Merited Masters of Sports in the USSR.

Coaches and physical education instructors are trained at 23 state institutes of physical culture, at 84 physical education departments of teachers' training colleges, at 25 specialized secondary schools and ten schools for coaches.

Research work in the field of sports is carried on at the institutes of physical culture and numerous research and medical establishments in Moscow, Leningrad, Kiev, Tbilisi and other cities. They study sociological, medical, biological, psychological, organizational and other problems pertaining to the development of the mass physical education movement and competitive sports. In Kiev, for example, research is being carried out on the medical and biological problems connected with physical culture. The findings of such research will benefit not only the relatively few gifted athletes, but the population as a whole.

Soviet scientists are members of the International Council of Sport and Physical Education and of the International Federation of Sportive Medicine. Soviet doctors are widely credited with playing a pioneering role in the field of sports medicine, which is just coming into its own as a specialty in Western countries such as the US.

Each year the amount of money allocated for sports and physical culture, including construction of facilities, increases. Funds are provided from the state budget, trade union funds, deductions from the profits of enterprises and organizations and profits from gate receipts of athletic events, which are not subject to taxation. New facilities are constantly being constructed, particularly in the countryside where they are needed most. Today, construction is under way for the 1980 Moscow Olympics, the first ever to be held in a socialist country.

Among the existing first-class facilities in the USSR today are the Central Lenin Stadium in Moscow with 101,000 seats; the Kirov Stadium in Leningrad (100,000 seats); Kiev's Central Stadium (100,000 seats); Moscow's Dynamo Stadium (60,000 seats); the Pakhtakor Stadium in Tashkent (60,000 seats); the Medeo mountain skating rink near Alma-Ata, with 10,500 square meters of artificial ice; a complex of shooting ranges in Minsk and many others. Indoor sports arenas have been built in Moscow, Leningrad, Kiev, Tbilisi, Minsk, Barnaul, Gorki, Riga, Yerevan, Donetsk and other cities. (The Russian word *stadion*—stadium—usually denotes a multi-sport center or complex. The Lenin Stadium in Luzhniki, Moscow, for example, has facilities for swimming, tennis, basketball, *gorodki*, ice hockey, etc.) It is estimated that 10,000 people between 18 and 70 pursue a sport in the Luzhniki sports center *every day*.

The annual state allocations for the building of sports facilities have reached 120 million rubles. Large sums are also allocated for this purpose by enterprises and sports societies.

In all the USSR has more than 3.000 stadiums seating 1,500 people and more, more than 100,000 soccer fields, some 400,000 sports grounds, more than 59,000 gyms, more than 1,200 swimming pools, and many other facilities.

The extent of mass participation in sports in the USSR is demonstrated every four years, in the year preceding the Olympics, by the USSR Games or *Spartakiads*. These are comprehensive multi-stage tournaments held on a nationwide scale in more than 20 sports. Competitions are held in every district, region, town, village and Republic, culminating in finals which are comparable to the Olympics. The First Spartakiad of the Peoples of the USSR was held in 1956 and involved an estimated 23 million people in events leading up to the finals in Moscow. There, over a 10-day period, more than 9,000 athletes took part.

At the last Spartakiad in 1975, six world records were broken as more than 7,000 athletes from all parts of the USSR competed in the finals. The next Spartakiad will be held in 1979. In addition, special children's Spartakiads are held regularly throughout the Soviet Union.

Schoolchildren who excel in sports may attend special sports schools to develop their athletic skills. Today there are more than 260 such schools in the USSR. These schools feature extended periods of physical education classes and specialized coaching, but the students must also meet the same academic standards as their counterparts in regular schools. This provision is strictly enforced and helps to prevent the development of one-sided individuals with no interests outside of their sports specialties. Children attend the sports schools only with the consent of their parents.

The socialist goal of full equality for women is reflected in the achievements of Soviet women athletes and in the widespread participation of women in the mass sports and physical culture movements. In fact, while women's athletic scholarships and the expansion of women's sports programs at US colleges are relatively new phenomena, women students make up a majority in physical education in the USSR: in the 1971-72 academic year, 56 per cent of the students of health, physical culture and sport in higher education, and 87 per cent in special secondary education, were women. (In the USSR, of course, there are no athletic scholarships, as all education is free.)

Today the men and women athletes of the USSR maintain regular contact with athletes in 87 countries. Each year they take part in some 2,000 sports events. International sports contacts help to promote friendship and understanding between peoples. During the 1960s, for example, when the US and USSR first began exchanges in track and field, the friendly competitions between high jumpers John Thomas and Valery Brumel and long jumpers Phil Shinnick and Igor Ter-Ovanesyan helped to ease cold war tensions.

In recent years hundreds of Soviet coaches have visited and worked in developing countries of Asia, Africa and Latin America, helping in the growth of their national sports movements. Many athletes and coaches from these countries are studying in the USSR. In 1975 the Soviet Union was visited by 1,048 sports delegations from other countries. The USSR hosted seven European and World championships, and many other international meets and tournaments.

Soviet athletes are represented in 53 world and 11 European federations, associations and unions.

USSR athletes and sports federations have no ties, however, with the sports organizations of repressive regimes such as South Africa and Chile. Soviet sports representatives have played an important role in promoting the international boycotts against South Africa and Chile, arguing that their governments have made a mockery of the ideals of sport.

It would be naive to suggest that the development of sports and physical culture in the USSR has proceeded smoothly and free of difficulties since 1917. Soviet sport has had its share of problems, conflict and even an occasional scandal. Over the years, there have been changes and modifications in emphasis and organization.

While shortcomings and problems continue to exist, it is impossible to make a study of Soviet sports without reaching a positive assessment. "Whatever the interpretation of past events or the perspectives for future development, there can certainly, however, be no doubt about the absolute positive material gains of the population of the old Russian Empire in the sphere of recreation since 1917," James Riordan, a British Sovietologist, grudgingly concedes at the conclusion of his book, *Sport in the USSR*. "It is also in many ways better off in this respect than the public in many Western countries. Most of the urban population can today pursue the sport of their choice, using facilities largely free of charge through their trade union sports society. Sports are not, as they were before the Revolution, in the hands of foreigners, commercial promoters, circus entrepreneurs or private clubs with restricted entrance. Unlike some Western sports clubs, Soviet sports societies do not discriminate in regard to membership on the basis of sex, nationality, income or social background. Even sports involving expensive equipment are open to anyone who shows natural ability and inclination.

"The Soviet Union could hardly have become what it is today—the world's leading all-round competitive sporting power—without a genuinely wide base—virtually universal access to the means of practicing sports. Lastly, there has been, too, an undeniable consistent aspiration and effort in the USSR to make sport culturally uplifting, aesthetically satisfying and morally reputable which, given all necessary qualifications, has set a tone of altruism and devotion in its sport in which there is much which cannot but be admires." □

25

HOWARD L. PARSONS

The New Person in the Soviet Union: Sixty Years of Progress Toward Human Fulfillment

In ancient class societies humanistic prophets and seers dreamed of a time to come when human personality and society would be fulfilled—when individual persons would be compassionate, cooperative, intelligent, esthetic, and fully realized in all their human powers, and when just and prosperous social arrangements would encourage and enable persons to be so. The Jewish prophets proclaimed peace among all nations. Plato in *The Republic* wrote of "the education of our heroes," and the author of The Revelation to John wrote that he "saw a new heaven and a new earth" as a voice from heaven declared that God "shall wipe away all tears" and "death shall be no more" (21:1, 4). But these dreams proved fruitless so long as societies remained class societies dominated by small groups ruling over slaves, serfs, or wage laborers. In October of 1917 in Russia the first successful socialist revolution smashed class rule there once and for all; and for the first time in history the people of a society organized themselves and their resources to set out on the grand experiment of creating "heroes" and "a new earth"—a society of abundance, equality, and human fulfillment, and a world of peace.

Have the people of the Soviet Union succeeded in their struggle to create "a new person"? I believe so. Not completely, of course; for such creation is never fully finished. But they are far enough along the way so that we can see a distinctive kind of personality emerging in large numbers and clearly differentiated from the kinds living in class societies past and present.

I want to examine briefly four ingredients in their success: collectivism, equality, the affirmation of human life, and the full development of human potentialities. In this examination I have necessarily passed over the com-

HOWARD L. PARSONS is Professor and Chairman in the Department of Philosophy, University of Bridgeport. He has long been active in the causes of American-Soviet friendship and world peace.

plexities of a 60-year history and the problems yet to be solved. That there are such problems the Soviet people, the CPSU, and the leaders are well aware.

Collectivism. The collective philosophy, attitude, and practice is the primary distinguishing feature of Soviet socialist society. Socialism means that individual personality is profoundly social both as fact and value, as actuality and possibility. Dating from Neolithic society or earlier, the *theory* of personality as social found expression in many of civilization's ancient philosophies and religions. In modern times the great utopians articulated it, and Marx defined the human being as "the total unity of his primary interpersonal relations." But only in socialist societies have people really applied this theory to social conditions to create and discover its truth in living human practice.

From the earliest age in the Soviet Union, "mine is ours; ours is mine" is the rule. Blocks are built so that children *must* engage the help of others in order to move them. Children are nurtured not only by their parents; relatives, teachers, older children, and strangers in general look after them (so that strictly speaking the "stranger" is usually the unknown friend). Urie Bronfenbrenner, in his *Two Worlds of Childhood: U.S. and U.S.S.R.*, reports the following incident:

> Our youngest son—then four—was walking briskly a pace or two ahead of us when from the opposite direction there came a company of teenage boys. The first one no sooner spied Stevie than he opened his arms wide and, calling *"Ai Malysh!"* [Hey, little one!], scooped him up, hugged him, kissed him resoundingly, and passed him on to the rest of the company, who did likewise, and then began a merry children's dance, as they caressed him with words and gestures.

In addition to his or her nurtured and responsible role in the close-knit Soviet family, every schoolchild participates in a series of collectives to which he is responsible: his row of double-seated desks, his classroom, and his school organization as a whole *(druzhina)*. Each classroom functions as a unit of the Octobrists (ages 7 to 9) and the Pioneers (ages 10 to 15). The Komsomol (Young Communist League), consisting of more than half of those eligible from age 16 to 28, includes both high school youth and graduates. To participate in such collectives is for the child and youth to be and to become quite a different person from one who lives in the individualistic society of capitalism. It is to grow up into a truly *socialized* person.

Every adult, moreover, continues to participate in collectives, with their corresponding rights and duties. Work, expected and required of all able-bodied Soviet citizens, is the principal way in which the Soviet adult person contributes to and receives from others. From his membership in a collective at his place of work, every adult derives housing rights, travel rights, recreational opportunities, insurance, educational advantages, nursery school privileges for children, and other benefits. Besides the one or more families to which the

Soviet adult belongs, he participates in many other collective activities—political groups, recreational and library clubs, artistic societies, etc.

Unlike the worker in capitalist society, the Soviet worker does not work principally to "make money" and thereby to survive and help his family to survive. He works principally to express his own life, to cooperate with others, to provide his share of wealth for the collective good, and to receive in turn as he has worked. This reciprocity is possible because the classless Soviet society has long since wiped away the antagonism of worker and worker, of worker and owner, and of citizen and government which characterizes capitalist society. The workers' sense that this factory, this farm, belongs to *them* induces a feeling of willing engagement and a sense of meaningful activity in life: the worker feels that his work counts, that it makes a difference, that it is his own contribution to the collective good, material and moral, to which he belongs. The alienation endemic to workers under capitalism is gone.

The fraternal spirit that imbues the family and working unit extends throughout the nation and into international relations. The Soviet Union is a multinational state uniting a rich diversity of ethnic, racial, cultural, and linguistic traditions. This in itself is a signal achievement in a century in which the disease of racism has reached a peak in fascist states like Nazi Germany and in the imperialism of the US. The Soviet fraternal attitude reaches beyond the borders of the Soviet Union to embrace the peoples of many other nations throughout the world.

Because bourgeois analysts presuppose an inherent antagonism between individual personality and society, the relation of these two in the Soviet Union is usually a puzzle to them. The "priority of social interests" for them means a suppression of individual interests and personality. But in Soviet theory and practice the individual personality is not something *apart* from society. The personality is *defined* by social relations, beginning with the family and work unit and reaching out to the whole of society and its relations with the nonhuman ecological order. This dynamic interdependence wherein individuals strengthen and create one another, society, and nature is both an ultimate fact and a supreme value. It calls for a whole code of ethics that in its form and application is really new in human history. We can say that to the extent that people are socialized in this sense, they become truly moral; for to be moral is in the original and fundamental sense to help as many people as possible, including oneself, to live and to live well.

Soviet society demands of each individual person the development, exertion, and contribution of his abilities to the social fund of goods, services, and gifts of character. This places a large burden on each personality, calling him or her to do his share for the good of the whole. From the outside this looks like a heavy weight for individual conscience to bear. The stated objectives of education, for example, the rules for the various youth organizations, and the code of the builders of communism are very demanding. But from an early age children receive from people generally repeated encouragement for doing their duties and self-discipline in responding to the demands of the collective becomes second nature.

One Soviet philosopher tells me he thinks Soviet people are puritanical, inclined to obey social duty rather than individual pleasure. But I doubt that this is a defect. Moreover, anyone who knows Soviet persons individually knows that they have as strong a sense of the private as most Westerners. Private tastes, feelings, preferences, and activities are respected. And this respect has grown with the growth of the social material base for privacy: ample housing, adequate income, leisure time, improved education, and increased facilities and opportunities for the development of private interests.

Soviet society generates in its children and adults a great deal of security, both economic and psychological, as well as a great outward and inward sense of peace. When I first arrived in the Soviet Union in 1964 I experienced a very strong impression of a people sure of themselves and their station on this earth, a people busy, serious, and happy, a people certain they had a firm hold on their life and their future, a people who knew they could do and would do what they set out to do, a people whose deep sense of security with themselves gave them the strength to reach out to other people and nations for the collective security in the world that their government had striven for so patiently for so many decades. During my subsequent half dozen visits to the Soviet Union this impression of security has recurred with the same vividness.

In the past half-century crime has declined by 71.5 per cent while the population has increased by 117 million. A society that has reduced this rate to one of the lowest levels in the modern world, has no organized crime, no profit-making crime (as in the sale of arms, drugs, bets), and no profiteering by individuals and the media by the depiction of crime (via TV, radio, newspaper, journal, fiction, science, cinema, comics, etc.), that has banished prostitution and pornography, and has eradicated the social crimes of racism and illiteracy, must surely be creating "the new person" in large numbers.

Soviet people, as compared with people in western capitalist countries, seem to me to be less egocentric and more sociocentric, to have a keener sense of their moral obligations to others, society, and nature, to be more solicitous about children, the disadvantaged, and the elderly, to be less obsessed with the acquistion and accumulation of material goods, to be more peaceful in handling the conflicts in their interpersonal lives, and to be less interested in money. Many whom I have met, especially young people, seem remarkably indifferent to money. Why? In capitalist society money is the all-powerful god, since survival itself depends on the individual's getting it by hook or crook, by job or rob. Under Soviet socialism the state guarantees a job, subsidized food and housing prices, socialized medical care, state-supported education, and an ample pension. Why worry about survival in such a society? So as a rule Soviet people don't.

The Soviet people *do* worry about one thing: the threat to human survival posed by the arms race and weapons of mass destruction. They worry because they have lost more by war than any other people. They have struggled mightily to build it back again, they are well on the way to winning a world of "the new person" both for themselves and all others, and they are loath to lose it all in the most stupid crime and irrevocable folly.

Soviet society presupposes a "general will" or common interest which unites all individual persons and in which, as Rousseau put it, "each necessarily submits to the conditions which he imposes on others—an admirable union of interest and justice." In the more concrete formulation of Marxism-Leninism, what binds people together is their working class interest in survival and development. That generic human interest, which always expresses itself in social form, gives rise to particular and individual interests that become interlocked with other particular interests. While there is no pre-established harmony of particular interests in Soviet society, the prevailing disposition is to presume that such harmony is more or less possible and to drive toward it. This drive is a collective drive. Both goal and method are collective.

Unlike our own, this society is unified and inspired by a single pervasive philosophy—communism, taught implicitly and explicitly. Every secondary school student in his or her last year must study a full course of economics, philosophy, and scientific communism and must pass an examination in dialectical and historical materialism. As one Soviet philosopher, Professor Yuri Konstantinovich Melvil, said, "In the Soviet Union philosophy is essential to education; each person must understand *what* he does and *why* he does it."

To understand in the full sense is to be *scientific*. Communism is scientific communism, both theoretical and applied. What is science? Broadly speaking, it is good sense in living—the application of observation, reflection (logic, disciplined imagination), and practice in making and carrying out decisions. Soviet society is one of the most rational in the world. Not only is it rationally planned as a whole; but also one meets a striking number of persons who are well trained in some science and whose general mien is one of good sense in personal and social life. These persons are able to restrain their immediate desires in favor of consideration of the consequences for other persons now and in the future, to look beyond the particular object, person, or situation to the universal, and to curb the impulse toward the short-range goal by steadfast attention to the long-range goals and values. Their massive dedication to the goals of the Soviet Union for 60 years and their herculean accomplishments during that time are evidence of this rational spirit among the Soviet people.

The method of human rationality is the dialectical method of intersubjective theory and practice—*i.e.*, discussion, argument, criticism and self-criticism, brainstorming, mutual challenge and check and double-check of ideas; and repetition and variation of experiment by different persons, confirmation, disconfirmation, and revision of theory. This, of course, is the method that the various sciences from fire-making to nuclear physics fashioned in their laborious evolution through human history. What is novel about it in the Soviet Union is the extent of its adoption among the general population, its widespread institutionalization, and above all the employment of the collective scientific method in determining the ideals, plans, and decisions of the whole society. Before 1917 no other society on earth did this or seriously considered doing it. And between 1917 and 1977 no other society has done it so extensively in space and time.

Under Marxist-Leninist theory, each person in principle holds an equal right in the collective power and value of society. That society is in fact defined by the linkage of all individual wills regulating each other. Correspondingly, each person submits himself to the rule of the whole body politic. All rights pertaining to the individual are derived from and are conditioned by the right of the society to exist and develop. The rights of the individual person to the free exercise of religion, and freedom of speech, press, and assembly—which in the Constitution of the United States are beyond the power of the Congress to abridge—are not absolute under Soviet socialism. The right to life for all citizens as it is guaranteed by the Soviet state is the ultimate right, preceding and undergirding all other rights. In their very bones the Soviet people know this from their life-and-death struggle to survive. War and war-mongering are intolerable. No person has the right to advocate the reversion of a socialist state to a capitalist one, or to preach racism. No one has the right to propose or practice the destruction of the people's sovereignty, self-determination, peace, and social ownership of the means of production. The Soviet people accept this definition of rights. They accept the new Constitution's prescription of social duty for all citizens.

Equality. The sense of equality among the Soviet people is widespread. One can observe this in the homes, factories, offices, shops, streets, buses, and trains, where people speak to each other and defend their rights as equals. The sense of rank and status so common in countries like England and France is absent in the Soviet Union. A young research worker in psychology once told me that from time to time he would see Khrushchev in his neighborhood, where the former Premier then lived after his retirement. I expressed some surprise at the casual way in which he reported this fact, and his reply was that no one in the neighborhood took special note of him. He was one of the Soviet masses—no better, no worse. When American journalists, hypocritically expressing sympathy for Khrushchev, complained that Soviet society should pay more respect to their retired leaders, they not only failed to understand the thought and values of the Soviet people; they betrayed their own class snootiness.

Once, about one o'clock in the morning, a group of us were returning home from a party in Moscow and found Vernadsky Prospekt, a very wide avenue, standing in our way. Crossing it on foot at that point was forbidden; underpasses were provided for pedestrians. But the nearest underpass was at some distance, so desiring to save time and energy, and seeing at that time very little traffic, we crossed over on foot. A young policeman stopped us. In the conversation that ensued, the persons I was with were not deferential nor was the policeman overbearing. The relation was immediately serious, but friendly. My friends stated without hesitation what they were about, the policeman issued a firm reminder and warning, and that was the end of it.

Much has been made of how Soviet "bureaucracy" crushes individuality and equality. Of course every government or institution of any size requires bureaus with routinized procedures of administration (i.e., a bureaucracy); and every bureaucracy is infected with some inefficiency, rigidity, looseness, personal whim and arbitrariness, "influence," and unfairness. I have not found the bureaucracies in the Soviet Union worse in these respects than those in capitalist countries. And there one finds resistance to and criticism of inefficient bureaucracy. The criticism is of bureaucracy and not of socialism, and it is made from a sense of loyalty to Soviet society and socialism. The Soviet people view bureaucracy as "our" problem, and scientists interpret it as a stage in the evolution of the management of social affairs that will be superseded as automation takes over such management.

Economic equality in a society where wage differentials remain is enhanced by the "public consumption funds," which constitute that portion taken from the national income to be "distributed among members of society as gratuitous material benefits and services and as money allowances of various kinds." Through such funds, which comprise more than one-third of the aggregate revenue of the average industrial worker family, people obtain free medical help, free education and advanced training, diverse benefits, pensions, scholarships, paid leaves, and free or subsidized accommodation at sanatoriums and holiday homes for adults and at kindergartens and nursery schools for children. Also, two-thirds of the cost of maintaining dwellings, libraries, clubs, etc. comes from such funds. The proportion of these consumer benefits for those in lower income brackets is three times as high as for those in upper income brackets. In this way the inequities of income are reduced.

The principle of equality means that access to resources and assumption of obligations apply indifferently to all people, including those who are limited by mental retardation and physical defects. Thus it follows that, generally speaking, social recognition is a function of talent and not of power or rank, though these latter often come as a result of the successful exercise of talent. In capitalist society social recognition is ordinarily a function of power, economic and political, which very often is a function of the possession of money or some other form of wealth—or of methods which have nothing to do with real humanizing talent. The Soviet Union, in contrast, is perhaps the most successful meritocracy in history, given its short life of 60 years.

The Affirmation of Human Life. In opposition to the anxiety, pessimism, obsession with death, and escapism of much of bourgeois society, Soviet society is optimistic and life-affirming. For it, all significance for us is created by us *in this life* here and now—and by others in human history, workers past and future, who are linked to us by common struggle, labor, thought, love, art, and play. Human beings and their development—within the congenial environment of society and nature—are taken as final values.

Soviet socialism is inspired by daring ideals, and this daring is grounded in a hard-headed realism to match that and make it creative, effecting powerful changes in the material and social world. Theory and practice confirm the facts that (1) human beings have the possibilities for healthy, constructive development in creative interaction with others and nonhuman nature, and (2) that these possibilities *can* and *will* be realized in the course of human history.

The Soviet conviction in progress is grounded in their own 60-year historical experience as well as in their observation of and solidarity with struggles of workers and peasants in many countries. To win the civil war and the war of intervention (losing 13,000,000 people); to combat famine; to construct, from a poorly developed capitalist base, the foundation for a modern society in industry, agriculture, and other spheres of applied science and technology; to beat back the forces of fascism in the Great Patriotic War; to reconstruct the country which had lost over 20,000,000 people and one-third its industrial base—all that was almost superhuman. No people have had to struggle against so much and for so much in such a short time. Only an indomitable love of life—of their own persons, their families, their soil, their communities, their Socialist Motherland—would impel them to do so. While bourgeois nations elicited patriotic heroism from their soldiers and citizens in the war against fascism, the heroism of the Soviet people in that war reached a scale without parallel in human history.

Not only in their collective exertion to build a better material world do the Soviet people express their love of life. They express it also in their sports and recreation, in their appetite for travel and new experiences, and perhaps most of all in their hearty personal relations with one another and with people of other countries. Scientists, taxi drivers, elevator operators, hotel floor supervisors—they all love to converse, to find out about strangers and their families, to tell them about their families. They are the kind who make good neighbors—ready to give a hand in trouble, lending a sympathetic ear, tender and protective toward children. (A babe-in-arms in an elevator or shop is likely to create a minor sensation, as women of all ages cluster and buzz around to have a look, and, most of all, to hold it and play with it.) As much as any people, perhaps more, they love a good party, where food and drink, stories and jokes, talk and toasts, singing and dancing, bring people together in a union of feeling that complements and celebrates the union of common endeavor.

The Soviet love of people is carried out in acts that objectively help people to live and to fulfill themselves. I have already referred to the large network of collective institutions at home that do this. In foreign relations, we observe comparable objective activity in material and moral aid to national liberation movements and in the 60-year-old political movement for peaceful coexistence, disarmament, and detente. I recently thanked a prominent Soviet sociologist for organizing an international symposium on philosophy and social progress and for the expenditure of time and money on it. He spontaneously replied: "What is money compared to the cause of peace and the saving of mankind?"

The love of life and the longing for peace among the Soviet people reflects a new level of material and moral development in human history. Normally all peoples love life and long for peace. But when social and individual existence rise to the point where the great mass of people in a nation experience day by day in their family living, in their work, and in their national life as a whole the joy of collective work and fulfillment, that love and longing rise to a qualitatively new level. "The new person" exists in such large numbers in the Soviet Union that, taken together, they compose a powerful new social force among the 150 nations on our planet. That is a force that demands peace as a necessary condition for the life of all people, and that demands human life and its fulfillment as the final reason and value of why we are here.

The Full Development of Human Potentialities. Socialist society proceeds by concentrating on constructing an economy that will satisfy all survival needs— the needs for food, water, clothing, shelter, sanitation, medical care, safety, etc.—and at the same time assembling institutions that will provide resources and opportunities for people to fulfill distinctively human needs. These latter are the needs for interpersonal relations enjoyed for their own sake (friendship, love), for rest and relaxation, for esthetic creation and experience, for cognition, for play, for dreaming and meditation, for sensuous enjoyment, for selfless surrender, for gaiety. As work becomes more efficient through improved tools and machines, these needs with their corresponding values can be cultivated.

Thus we can see in Soviet history for the past 60 years a whole social organism developing, a whole ecological system, with first the ground being cleared of a rotten social system of poverty and oppression, then a physical basis laid down for modern technology, then a more and more easy and comfortable physical life for people, and gradually and simultaneously the release of human energies from social production into the domain of personal fulfillment.

Take two of the most elementary things, food and literacy. Food for *everyone!* That achievement is the Soviet people's own answer to their deep, desperate cry of "Peace, bread, and land!" 60 years ago. That achievement is unprecedented in human history. When I tell my American students this, they don't seem impressed, and the main reason, I think, is that they have never been hungry and don't vividly foresee they might be. But the hungry masses of the world have been impressed, and almost one-third of them have followed the lead of the Soviet Union into socialism—in their own ways, of course, as Lenin anticipated.

The first step to developed culture, after the care and the feeding of the body, is literacy. The Soviet people, between the two world wars, "accomplished more to raise the literacy of an entire nation than had ever before been achieved in all recorded history" (Carroll Atkinson and Eugene T. Maleska, *The Story of Education,* p. 179). Literacy opens the door to endless corridors of developed culture, the enrichment of consciousness, community with others, and scientific practice, the mark of developed humanity. That is the way of our true human fulfillment—of our true human history, as Marx called it.

Fulfillment includes not only the satisfaction of all our generic human needs. It is also the fulfillment of these needs in the aggregate and in unison, so as to realize what we call the unique human personality or character. That is the meaning of the communist principle "From each according to his abilities, to each according to his needs."

What happens to talents in the Soviet Union? Have a look. The arts—music, painting, sculpture, theater, dance, literature, architecture; the sciences, theoretical and applied; engineering; philosophy; athletics; military sciences; chess; space exploration; circuses; puppet theater; etc.—virtually all fields testify to the development of talent in such numbers and depth that makes it outstanding. What is notable in the Soviet Union is the scale on which talent is identified and educated. Soviet society is a planned society; hence the development of talent is planned.

In this 60-year-old collective movement toward equality of opportunity and fulfillment, in this affirmation of human life for all, the Soviet people have begun to create simultaneously a new person, a new society, and a new world. As we in all nations work unitedly to consolidate and make irreversible the process of peaceful coexistence and detente; as we eliminate nuclear weapons and other weapons of mass destruction; as we reduce arms and military budgets; as we bring about general and complete disarmament and the renunciation of the use of force in international relations—then we will open the way to create and witness in the next 60 years a still more beautiful flowering of ''the new person,'' not only in the Soviet Union but as well throughout the whole world.   □

SOVIET RUSSIA TODAY

VOL. 1 NO. 1   FEBRUARY   1932

10¢

Published Monthly by the

Friends of the Soviet Union

80 East 11th Street   New York, N. Y.

Subscription $1.00 per year

Part Six
Fragments from the Past

In this final section we present excerpts from New World Review *and its predecessor* Soviet Russia Today, *founded in 1932. The pages at our disposal do not permit covering all the events which have shaken the world in the last sixty years, in the struggle for peace and for a just life for all peoples. We can only present a few samples of the steady growth of Soviet socialist society against greater odds than any country has ever faced. We cannot give the full sweep of the Soviet Union's steady, unceasing, relentless struggle for peace, but have tried to provide enough to show that this struggle will never end until it is won.*

We have omitted coverage of the last decade, for the books Voices of Tomorrow *(1972) and* Building a New Society *(1977), dealing with the 24th and 25th Congresses of the Soviet Communist Party respectively, the special issue of* New World Review, *May-June 1975, commemorating the 30th anniversary of the victory over fascism, and the books* Lenin's Impact on the United States *(1971) and* A Family of Peoples *(1973) continue to be available.*

We hope readers will find that these few pages from the past illuminate some highlights of these years since the October Socialist Revolution, and what these years have meant to the world.

JOHN REED
When Lenin Spoke

I t was just 8:40 on Nov. 8, 1917 when a thundering wave of cheers announced the entrance of the presidium, with Lenin—great Lenin—among them. A short, stocky figure, with a big head set down in his shoulders, bald and bulging. Little, a snubbish nose, wide, generous mouth, and heavy chin; clean-shaven now, but already beginning to bristle with the well-known beard of his past and future. Dressed in shabby clothes, his trousers much too long for him. Unimpressive, to be the idol of a mob, loved and revered as pehaps few leaders in history have been. . . .

Now Lenin, gripping the edge of the reading stand, letting his little winking eyes travel over the crowd as he stood there waiting, apparently oblivious to the long-rolling ovation, which lasted several minutes. When it finished, he said simply, "We shall now proceed to construct the Socialist Order!" Again that overwhelming human roar.

"The first thing is the adoption of practical measures to realize peace. . . . We shall offer peace to the peoples of all the belligerent countries upon the basis of the Soviet terms—no annexations, no indemnities, and the right of self-determination of peoples. . . . The question of War and Peace is so clear that I think that I may, without preamble, read the project of a Proclamation to the Peoples of all the Belligerent Countries. . . ."

His great mouth, seeming to smile, opened wide as he spoke; his voice was hoarse—not unpleasantly so, but as if it had hardened that way after years and years of speaking—and went on monotonously, with the effect of being able to go on forever. . . . For emphasis he bent forward slightly. No gestures. And before him, a thousand simple faces looking up in intent adoration. . . .

When the grave thunder of applause had died away, Lenin spoke again:

"We propose to the Congress to ratify this Declaration. We address ourselves to the Governments as well as to the peoples, for a declaration which would be addressed only to the peoples of the belligerent countries might delay the conclusion of peace. . . .

"The revolution of November 6th and 7th," he ended, "has opened the era of the Social Revolution. . . . The labor movement, in the name of peace and Socialism, shall win, and fulfill its destiny. . . ."

From *Ten Days that Shook the World*
Reprinted in Soviet Russia Today, January 1937

DR. W.E.B. DUBOIS

Russia—An Interpretation

Dr. DuBois begins this article written for Soviet Russia Today *following his return from his third visit to the USSR, by recalling what he wrote on his first visit in 1926:*

I have been in Russia something less than two months. I did not see the Russia of war and blood and rapine. I know nothing of political prisoners, secret police and underground propaganda. My knowledge of the Russian language is sketchy and of this vast land, the largest single country on earth, I have traveled over only a small, a very small part. But I have seen something. I have traveld over two thousand miles and visited four of its largest cities, many of its towns, the Neva, Dnieper, Moscow and Volga Rivers, and stretches of land and village. I have looked into the faces of its races—Jews, Tatars, Gypsies, Caucasians, Armenians and Chinese. I have not done my sightseeing and investigation in groups and crowds, but have in nearly all cases gone alone with one Russian-speaking friend. In this way I have seen schools, universities, factories, stores, printing establishments, government offices, palaces, museums, summer colonies of children, libraries, churches, monasteries, Boyar houses, theaters, moving-picture houses, day nurseries and cooperatives. I have seen some celebrations—self-governing children in a school house of an evening; and 200,000 children and youth marching on Youth Day. I have talked with peasants and laborers, Commissars of the Republic, teachers and children.

I have walked miles of streets in Leningrad, Moscow, Nizhni Novgorod and Kiev at morning, noon and night: I have trafficked on the curb and in the stores; I have watched crowds and audiences. I have gathered some documents and figures, plied officials and teachers with questions and sat still and gazed at this Russia, that the spirit of its life and people might enter my veins.

I stand in astonishment and wonder at the revelation of Russia that has come to me. I may be partially deceived and half-informed. But if what I have seen with my eyes and heard with my ears in Russia is Bolshevism, I am a Bolshevik.

Soviet Russia Today, November 1949

WALTER DURANTY

May Day in Moscow

This selection is from a piece written especially for Soviet Russia Today. *Mr. Duranty was* New York Times *Moscow correspondent for 15 years, winning the Pulitzer Prize for his Moscow dispatches.*

May Day is the symbol of what the Revolution stands for. I mean the victory of the proletariat, the defeat of the bosses and the landlords, the freedom of the workers and peasants to create their own state for themselves, to work for themselves in a country where no individual can profit from their toil.

In the days before the first of May in Moscow the streets ring with shouting—the inhabitants are rehearsing the great parade. One might think they would find this onerous or irksome. They do not, because they are proud of the new Russia, whose motto is "one for all and all for one," they are proud of it and they love it, and are eager and willing to give hours of their leisure for its glory.

Then the parade itself. First the Red Army, the only army in the world whose motto is defense. The others talk about defense, but do they mean it? Do the Japanese mean it? Or the Germans? Or the Italians?

But the USSR has nothing to gain from aggressive action against anyone. What it wants is to defend the Revolution. The Red Army is the concrete expression of Soviet Power, the shield and buckler of the Revolution, and something more than that. It is the outward and visible sign of the success which the USSR has achieved in industrialization.

The Red Army parade, however, is only a small part—an impressive part, if you like—of the May Day celebrations. After the Army has paraded, the people of Moscow surge through Red Square in serried ranks for hours and hours. Upwards of a million men, women and children pass through Red Square on May Day. The main basis on which their demonstration is organized is of course the factories—the workers of Moscow. But in recent years there has been a great and evident growth of a new character. I refer to the sport or games organizations of the "Communist Youth" and the "Young Pioneers," which naturally include both sexes. In my own opinion the most significant feature of the success of the Bolshevik Party in Russia is its appeal to youth. Lenin once said, "Give me four years to train the youngsters and they (our enemies) will never set our clock back." Instead of four years they have had eighteen, and they have trained them, and are training them. It is an obvious axiom that one of the easiest ways in which young people are trained to joint effort—which is, it must not be forgotten, the ideal of the USSR—is by playing games. Therefore, nowadays, Young Russia is games-crazy. Tennis, basketball, hockey, football, rowing—you might almost say, at least for the major cities, they play games as much as in the United States. To Americans this may not seem unusual, but to Russians it is a revolution of habit little less startling than the Revolution itself.

There is another interesting point about the parades nowadays. They have lost not all but a good deal of the atmosphere of hostility which used to prevail. In the early days the floats and banners were directed against Chamberlain or Lord Curzon or the Japanese or Mr. Hoover or Poincaré or capitalists. Now, on the contrary, the banners and floats are little concerned with foreign enemies. There is some of it—for instance, Hitler and Nazi Germany, and the Japanese militarists—but most of the decorations in the May Day parade will typify achievements, the new subway or the latest Soviet automobile and tractor, or any other success of Soviet industry.

Finally, there is something which can only be seen by an eyewitness on the spot. I mean the change in the attitude of the people. If you imagine a million people thronging the streets you can well imagine that there were times when you felt that they did not like you. Today it is quite different. The May Day crowds shout to you in a friendly manner. When you can't get through, they press around and talk. They are cheerful. That perhaps is the surest proof, psychologically speaking, of the success of the Soviet government. I mean that the people are cheerful, the people in the streets, the people of Russia.

Soviet Russia Today, May 1936

THEODORE DREISER

I Am Grateful to Soviet Russia

This is not a greeting but an expression of gratitude on my part for that phase of our social evolution which has brought into being and maintained thus far the Union of Socialist Republics called Russia. Since the "ten days that shook the world" consider the world attention given to the problem of the *have* and the *have nots.* Twenty years of fierce discussion in all lands of all the phases of inequity in government and in life in general in the hope that they may be ameliorated if not entirely abolished and with, in many places outside of Russia as well as in, the determination to ameliorate or abolish these same.

Consider also the present state of the world. It is true that in Italy Mr. Mussolini dictates, but on the plea, you will note, that it is for the best social interest of all Italians —father, mother, child, and not for any fore-ordained and god-established gang of social loafers and nit-wits labeled the royal family. And in Germany although the Kaiser and his royal heirs were unceremoniously swept into the social ash can, and although another would-be Kaiser has succeeded him he has succeeded because of his constant reiteration of the statement that he represents and furthers the interests of all of the people and preferably the masses as against any special class. That the cold blooded bandit war of himself and Mussolini against the properly qualified democratic government of Spain gives the lie to all this, is neither here nor there. The holy war for equity undertaken by Russia in 1917 makes such lies, such genuflections and kowtowings to mass opinion, necessary, And even Japan, if you please, talks of its holy purpose to uplift the masses of China by saving them from the "horrors" of Communism and investing them with the true and democratic privileges of Japan. Well, judge for yourself.

In Mexico, a real social war is on. In Spain, the same. In South America not only armed dictatorship but the suppression of every trace of education for the masses, even the A B C, is necessary to prevent them from turning on their oppressors, the monopolists. Here in the United States—and despite our heritages of freedom, most of which had been undermined by our financiers and their corporations, lawyers and paid representatives, by 1917—we have seen the forty hour week, minimum wages, planned economies in connection with crop distribution as well as crop control, and the necessity for mass earnings in order that there may be mass spendings here in America advocated—and no more palaces and yachts scattered over all the alien lands of our related world. Child labor has become a real issue. Also the national health, state medicine, state and national insurance in connection with old age and periods of unemployment, to say nothing of national planning for mass protection against national disasters in whatever form these may appear, droughts, erosions, scarcity of water, food, and the like, even to rational development of national power resources for the benefit of all.

But why this sudden socialistic flare-up in connection with a democratic nation that before 1914 was about as democratic as Germany or Russia before the war? Your answer? Russia. The "ten days that shook the world." Dear old Dr. Marx with his *Das Kapital* and his self-sacrificing devotion to the idea that labor, agriculture, industry and the resources of the state should be so coordinated as to produce a balanced abundance shared equitably by all. He insisted on that and for his pains has become a *Red* with every little whipper-snapper heir and heiress—their lawyers, bankers, brokers and butlers shivering at his name. But, for all this I am grateful to the Red Marx and the Red Russia and I think, despite the present outlook, that I will live to see the triumph of the Marxian equity where now the anti-socialists of Europe, Asia, Africa and South America strut and threaten and for the time being suppress that innate desire in all for work, a fair economic reward for the same and the decent and simple pleasures and satisfactions that should accompany it.

Soviet Russia Today, November 1937

This Is No Time For Tears!

The heroic women of the Soviet Union addressed this call to the women of the world at the great women's anti-Fascist meeting in Moscow, September, 7, 1941.

Dear sisters, women throughout the world!
Our liberty, the fate of our beloved children, of our brothers, husbands and loved ones, lies in our own hands.
This is no time for tears.
A bitter, relentless fight against fascism until the complete victory is achieved can alone save our nations and our families from slavery and shame. The Red Army is fighting heroically for the liberty and the happiness of the entire human race. The future of the world is being fought out at Smolensk and along the Dnieper.
Women of America and of all freedom-loving countries! Do all in your power to assist the just war of the Soviet Union and Britain, who are fighting not

only for their own liberty but for the liberty and independence of your countries too.

Help to increase war production and supplies to the armies fighting Hitlerism. Expose the Hitlerite agents who are disrupting the united front of the freedom-loving nations fighting against fascism. Send medicaments, warm clothes and gifts to the splendid fighters who are stamping out the fascist hordes.

Women of the world! Build a united front of struggle against bloodthirsty Hitlerism! In our union lies our strength and the pledge of our victory.

Ours is a just cause. The enemy will be routed. We will triumph!

Soviet Russia Today, October 1941

GENEVIEVE TAGGARD

On the 24th Anniversary of The October Revolution

Now the inescapable, one
Complete act: to die, flinging down
The body. First passing
The weapon carefully on
To the brothers stepping up to take the weapon.
In the great family stand the true brothers
All necessary to the weapon.
And the weapon, necessary.
In the name of the weapon, no tears.
In the name of all tears, no tears.
Because of the killing Nazi, the horde, no tears.
Bodies,—no tears.
Endless people, one by one, bodies,
Cluster to take the weapon.
Endless, vertical people, death-ready.
We the declared brothers and sisters of the vast family send
A message, short as war:

> *In your death we die*
> *but we also live.*
> *In your victory*
> *we live even*
> *though we die as you die.*

In the name of all weeping and war, no tears.
In the name of the howling wrongs of ages gone, no tears.

In the name of twenty-four years,
In the name of all years beyond these terrible years
No tears.

Soviet Russia Today, December 1948

JESSICA SMITH

US People's Response to Nazi Invasion of USSR and Formation of US-USSR Alliance

With the Hitler invasion of June 22, 1941, President Roosevelt immediately pledged all possible aid to the Soviet Union. On July 15 Prime Minister Churchill announced the formation of the British-Soviet Alliance. The Japanese Pearl Harbor attack in December brought into existence the alliance of the Big Three against the fascists, making the United States and the Soviet Union full allies in the war—as they should have been allies in averting it.

In addition to the military cooperation of the government, there was mass support from the American people, rallies, medical aid, help of all kinds for the defense of the Soviet Union, which coordinated their efforts through a national organization, Russian War Relief. Practically every city and community of the country became involved in raising money for our Soviet ally. Trade unions organized special weeks to manufacture tanks and other vital necessities for both war front and home front.

But there were also reactionary "America First" and anti-Soviet elements holding back the full support needed and delaying the opening by the United States and Britain of a Second Front in Europe which would have hastened the end of the war and prevented millions of deaths and other casualties. Their efforts had to be defeated. A movement to strengthen American-Soviet friendship was started by such organizations as the American Council on Soviet Relations, the American-Russian Institute and our magazine, *Soviet Russia Today*. We are proud to say SRT played a major role in this movement.

American-Soviet Friendship Congress

A new era was opened by the historic Congress of American-Soviet Friendship held in New York City November 7 and 8, 1942. In this great celebration by the American people both of the twenty-fifth anniversary of the founding of the Soviet Republic, and of the epic grandeur of their struggle against the common foe, the Soviet Union at last received the recognition it deserved as a mighty democratic nation, great in war and great in peace. The Congress forged new bonds of friendship between the two peoples, bonds uniting them in an unbreakable partnership to hasten the victory over the Axis powers and guarantee future world peace and progress.

Sponsoring the Congress and joining in the tributes to the Soviet Union at the various panel sessions of the Congress and its final rally were leaders in every section of American life. Our Government and Congress, the United States Army, officials of city and state, leaders of all the great labor organizations, religious leaders—Protestant, Catholic and Jewish—leaders in the business world, leaders in the arts and science, leaders among women, among Blacks, among youth.

Former Ambassador to the Soviet Union Joseph E. Davies, was Honorary Chairman of the Congress, and Dr. Corliss Lamont, Chairman. Distinguished people in many fields participated in the panel sessions.

The final overflow rally "Salute to our Soviet Ally" was held in New York's Madison Square Garden.

President Roosevelt and General Eisenhower sent greetings. Vice President Henry A. Wallace headed the list of prominent speakers, which included Soviet Ambassador Maxim Litvinov, Mayor Fiorello La Guardia, Governor Herbert H. Lehman, and outstanding labor, religious and cultural leaders. The glory of Paul Robeson's voice and person added special inspiration.

With his speech (already printed widely in the press and soon available in pamphlet form) Vice President Wallace ended forever the already fast disappearing era when the Soviet Union could be regarded as an outcast among the nations. He placed the great Russian Revolution in its true historical place as a milestone in mankind's march toward freedom. He showed that the Soviet Union was on our side through no accident of history but because she is a great democratic nation.

Space permits only a brief excerpt from addresses at the "Salute to Our Soviet Ally" rally. Thomas Lamont, chairman of the Executive Committee, J.P. Morgan and Co., declared:

As a businessman among businessmen in this community for over forty years I am glad to stand up and declare my unequivocal friendship and support for Russia.

Among the less engaging qualities of us Americans is a habit of irresponsible criticism of other nations. We all have that habit more or less and sometimes it penetrates even to our legislative halls in Washington. But when we discuss Russia, it seems to me that however much her social system may differ from our own, that difference has no bearing on the question of our alliance today with the people of Russia who, with their deep-rooted love of their country, have shown sublime resistance against our common enemy.

All the more do I say this because without Russia as our friend in the postwar years, never will a man or woman in this great audience see a peaceful or a stable world. Today the Russian nation is the only one on the Continent of Europe that can be a great stabilizing influence.

The Volga River may run red with blood. Stalingrad may be in ruins. But whatever happens, that citadel of courage and faith will remain the symbol of Victory. Stalingrad will live to rise again. Down the ages mankind will remember how the Greeks withstood the barbarians at Thermopylae and the Russians at Stalingrad!

Similar meetings were held in dozens of other cities.

Out of these events grew the National Council of American-Soviet Friendship, organized in February 1943. During the war it campaigned vigorously for the opening of a Second Front and promoted cooperation and exchange between our countries.

Soviet Russia Today, 1942 and 1943

The National Council of American-Soviet Friendship has continued this work of education and exchange all through the postwar period under the direction of Richard Morford, emphasizing work with youth during recent years, and concentrating on work for detente, disarmament and peace. Hampered in its activities during the McCarthy and cold war period, it is now in process of expansion with local societies in a dozen cities coming together in a coordinated national organization. All the affiliated societies participated through meetings, exhibits and other means in celebrating the 60th Anniversary of the Socialist Revolution and making the Soviet Union's achievements and peace policies better known to the American people, and thus promoting detente.

THEODORE BAYER
Jews in the USSR

Theodore Bayer was for many years manager of Soviet Russia Today *and* New World Review, *and later administrative secretary of the National Council of American-Soviet Friendship.*

The Jewish situation in the USSR as well as all over Europe must be projected against the background of the war. Almost four-fifths of the Jewish population of the USSR lived in the war area. Almost three million Soviet Jews lived in the Ukraine and Byelorussia which were occupied by the Germans and another million lived in the Baltic countries, Bessarabia and the Crimea and other parts of the RSFSR reached by the Germans.

Realizing the special danger facing the Jews under the German yoke, Soviet authorities put the task of evacuating them second only to the evacuation of women and children. Thus, with superhuman effort, often running the risk of death, the Red Army men and offiers and civil authorities managed to evacuate about fifty per cent of Russian Jews as well as Jews who fled from Poland into Russian territory.

While the Jews in the occupied areas were suffering frightful atrocities at the hands of the Germans, the Jews in the unoccupied regions were helping to win the war. In the course of their work in industry, in agriculture and other pursuits, they were becoming more than ever integrated into the economy of the USSR, and have diversified their occupations more than ever before. The number of Jews in heavy industry, in transportation, communications, mines, agriculture, has risen and Jewish craftsmen and artisans have, with government help, organized producing cooperatives in large numbers.

In the USSR the Jews have found complete equality. Anti-Semitism was made an offense against the state.

Soviet Russia Today, November 1944

JESSICA SMITH

Victory and Beyond

The triumphant events of the past few weeks are too immense to compress into words, too overpowering for our minds and emotions to encompass. When the generals' and statesmen's papers are gathered, when the historians and novelists have written their commentaries, the poets their songs, the musicians their symphonies, the true meaning of these mighty days will begin to find worthy expression.

But however inadequate our words, we must not fail in our understanding of what victory means and what we are still called upon to do. Above all else, there is this one searing truth burned into our consciousness that we cannot escape. We have seen the awful face of fascism. We have probed the full depths of its obscene degradation. If the stories from the conquered countries and from the Soviet Union failed to convince us, no one who has read the papers or seen the newsreels of the Nazi atrocity camps in these past weeks can any longer escape the full knowledge of what fascism really is. Now at last we know there can be no peace or sanity for the human race until every vestige of fascism is wiped out forever—not only in Germany, and the lands it has befouled, not only in Japan, but wherever it appears in any form.

Mussolini is gone, and Hitler. The invincible goose-stepping armies have marched to their own doom. The ghastly murder camps are idle. The enslaved peoples unbend their backs and stretch toward the sun. Mothers carry their infants under bright skies unafraid. In Europe at last the guns and bombs that have blasted to dust so many million precious human lives and blown to bits the treasures wrought by generations of men's minds and hands, are still. The empire of a thousand years has crumbled in less than a thousand days. We have seen evil beyond anything we could imagine in bestial men who tried to drag down the whole human race into the festering jungle that was their habitat. And we have seen glory beyond anything we could dream in the millions who have struggled and died to save us from that jungle. We have learned again the simple and great truth that the love of freedom burns so brightly in the human heart that it can never be extinguished. Let the human ráce never forget either the evil or the glory of those years.

Soviet Russia Today, June 1945

GLEB KRZHIZHANOVSKY
Lenin's Great Plan Lives

A close comrade of Lenin, Krzhizhanovsky was the noted Soviet engineer in charge of GOELRO, the State Plan for the Electrification of Russia and first chairman of Gosplan, the State Planning Commission.

I know that there is a day in every man's life which is most memorable and precious to him and of which even in his old age he cannot speak without lively emotion. That day for me was the day in December 1920, when, in the Bolshoy Theater in Moscow, we presented our plan for the electrification of Russia.

I recall every detail—the gilt of the boxes gleaming in the dimly lit auditorium (what effort it cost us to turn on electricity for that meeting!); the clouds of vapor formed by the breath of the assembly, for the theater had not been heated for a long time; the tense faces of our audience and the machine-gun belts girdling those who had just arrived from the front and who, as soon as the meeting ended, would return to forward positions. I recall the skeptical smiles and intermittent bursts of jeering laughter and cries of "Fantastic!", "Sheer nonsense!" which came from the rows where the Mensheviks were grouped. And I recall the calm and more than ordinarily stern look of Vladimir Lenin and his encouraging "Never mind, continue," and his friendly nod as though to say, "Everything is going fine."

A huge map of Russia on the stage was marked here and there with dots where the future power stations were to be. And there beyond the walls of the theater our native land stretched for thousands upon thousands of unmeasured miles, roadless and immersed in darkness.

When our report was over, the hall was filled with hubbub and commotion. Lenin raised the pamphlet containing the plan of GOELRO high above his head and shook it vigorously as he confidently cried to the excited assembly: "This is one of the foundations of the program for the building of our new state."

A quarter of a century has passed. How Lenin's great warm heart would glow if he were among us today and could see how the peoples of new Russia, faithful to his behests, are proceeding unswervingly along the path he projected. He would rejoice exceedingly to know that his first state plan for the electrification of Russia had long ago been carried out, as have been other and far grander plans for electrification of the Soviet land.

Our great teacher and friend would have experienced deep pride in his people from the knowledge that the Union of Soviet Socialist Republics has become one of the foremost industrial powers in the world, that the Soviet people have built their own powerful metallurgical industry, their own heavy machine building industry, and their own electro-chemical industry; that there are no more poverty-stricken and God-forsaken villages in the country and that their place has been taken by mechanized collective farms; that we now possess an army of half a million students and thirty million school children and that we Soviet people of both the older and younger generations have justified his faith in the mighty creative power of a free people.

"You have now had the opportunity to convince yourselves, by your own experience," he would have said, "of that accelerating and creative process which I had in mind when I spoke of the extraordinary capacity of the human mind and of human energy when freed from oppression."

Twenty-one years ago the heart of the great Lenin was stilled forever. But his name will be immortal through the ages, as immortal as the lofty idea of love and respect for human beings, for the triumph of which Soviet soldiers, the finest sons of their country, men of a new mold brought up in the spirit of Lenin's behests, are today fighting.

New World Review, March 1954
(The statement dates from 1945.)

REID ROBINSON

Report of the First Official Trade Union Delegation to the USSR

Soon after V-E Day trade union leaders of the allied countries met to form the World Federation of Trade Unions, the first all-inclusive world labor organization. Following a visit to the US by representatives of the Soviet All-Union Central Council of Trade Unions, a group of CIO delegates attended the first WFTU congress in Paris, and then went to the USSR as guests of AUCCTU. The following is from the report of the visit by Reid Robinson, President of the Mine, Mill and Smelter Workers Union, CIO.

O f special interest to us as trade unionists was the procedure by which Soviet unions handle the relationships between workers and management of the plants. We saw how the unions work, from the shop committee in the plant right up to the top commissariats of the industries.

Foundation of the union work is the shop steward setup, which provides one steward elected on secret ballot for every 20 workers. Above this group is the plant committee, which corresponds to our local unions. On top of this is the industry-wide union, corresponding to our internationals, and finally the AU-CCTU.

Grievance procedure is simple, starting with the shop steward (where almost all "beefs" are settled) and going on up, if necessary, to the top. When an operation in a plant is being planned, wage rates are included in the data submitted to the industry commissariat. Before going to the commissariat, the wages rates are worked out with the rank and file in the plant.

In addition to the job of setting wages and working conditions in the plant, unions administer the USSR's social security system directly. Recreation, rest homes, "parks of culture and rest," nurseries, and the like are all run by the unions. In Leningrad, for example, we visited a huge union cultural center that had under one roof a movie, a theater, a big library with thousands of volumes, a dance hall, gymnasium and scores of classrooms for subjects ranging from sewing to economic theory. The building was about as big as the entire Labor Department building in Washington, D.C., and was owned and managed entirely by the union.

Hostile people—including some in the unions in this country, notably the AFL—like to say that Soviet trade unions are controlled by the government, and hence are not "free" unions as we know them. It would be a good deal closer to the truth to say that the unions in the USSR have a big say in "controlling" the government, since they have a voice in so much of the life of the country.

It is noticeable, for example, that almost all the members of the Supreme Soviet of the USSR are also members of trade unions.

Everywhere we went in the Soviet Union we saw evidence that the people were sure of the direction in which they were going, were sure of themselves and the future of their country. That is why the peoples of the USSR fought like lions to save their country from the Nazis. And that is why they will reach their goal of a secure and happy life, despite all obstacles.

Soviet Russia Today, January 1946

HELEN KELLER

A Message

Although we are advanced but a short distance towards peace, yet there are solid grounds for faith to celebrate the 29th anniversary of the USSR. May its founding ever be hailed as a new day-star of healing influences dawning upon man's strife-blurred vision!

Upon American-Soviet friendship rests one of our best chances to pilot a course between the Scylla of self-centered nationalism and the Charybdis of crushing empire absolutism. Its labors of enlightenment are vital in undeceiving those among the American people who think our only safety is to keep half the globe formidably armed during peace, and in rending apart the dreadful weirs of imperialistic greed, fear and misunderstanding towards which we and other nations are apparently heading as fish for atomic bomb slaughter. For the first time in history war aggression has been placed before all men on the code of ethics as an inexpiable crime, and I tremble under the searchlight turned upon America with its huge military budget, its undeniable bomb stockpiles and the effort to multiply its air bases even among countries that are friendly.

Confidence is what human nature needs for ennoblement, and confidence is what modern nations need to accomplish genuine democracy and deliver earth from want, terror and ignorance. The issue is so crucial now—"One world or none"—that it calls forth a million tongues in a voice of steel, reverberating with the penalties which will be visited upon the spokesmen on either side that violate their mission of well-doing unto all peoples. Only by fostering mutual trust can America and Russia achieve a common principle of action to meet this inescapable responsibility.

What touches us here is not subordinate boundary issues or even the practice of daily provocation along the frontiers of Europe and Asia. What concerns us is rather the recoil of opinion in the commonwealth of letters and history if the future must record that during America's greatest glory a ruthless, dictatorial foreign policy was pursued against an Ally who, all authorities admit, underwent the most appalling sacrifice of lives and property, tearing open its breast, so to speak, to save its own and other peoples, as the pelican does when unable to find food for its young. It is precisely because Russia has assumed a colossal role, beset by grievous temptations and the blunders to which the wisdom of mortals is liable, that it can worthily be accorded forbearance. No undertaking to secure cooperation and confidence between us and other nations is beyond our courage when we remember that we are judged by what we do unto them, and not merely by the principles that we advocate.

American-Soviet friendship is a priceless means to lift disputes of two powerful, high-mettled races to a higher ground and test them by an ungainsayable verity—the safety of each land in the working fellowship of all. Therefore it should have the heartiest support in its endeavors to promote conciliation with the USSR and a beneficent intergovernment administration of human affairs.

Soviet Russia Today, November 1946

AMY SCHECHTER

Paul Robeson's Soviet Journey:
An Interview

" I saw in the USSR what a way of life can do. I say it without question—I saw a new type of human being created. Everything is moving. The warmth, the sureness, the knowledge that they are a great people building a new life.

"I never saw such a beautiful city as Moscow today," he continued. "The correspondents—the turn-coats," there was deep disgust in his voice. "I don't see how they have the nerve to lie about the Soviet Union the way they do. How can you find a great people you love and then suddenly turn against them?

"It's just staggering to see the wealth in the Soviet Union," continued Robeson the artist and man of broad culture. "The level of art in the Soviet Union is far away from anything we can possibly see in this country that we can't begin to compare it, so I don't want to hear any more nonsense about the freedom of the artist.

"And the singers!" he said. "At one of our concerts, at the last moment, a singer came in from a factory, a young girl. She had this pure Ukrainian folk voice, but still a voice that knows what it's doing . . . in the middle of all those opera singers.

"Here was a typical instance of Soviet democratic culture in action, the young factory girl, singing for a great audience at a gala concert of top Soviet professional musicians, not as a curiosity, but as an artist among artists, perfectly at home in the middle of all those opera singers."

The status of the national minorities in the Soviet Union has always been of special interest to Robeson, from the angle of the Negro people here and in Africa and of other colonial peoples.

While he was in Moscow, a huge Kazakh Art Festival was held; writers, artists, musicians as well as folk singers, brought fruits of their cultural achievements to the Soviet capital.

"I talked to anthropologists in London and New York about the peoples of Africa. They said: 'It'll be a thousand years before you can do anything.' And I saw the Kazakhs in Moscow. It's a tremendous thing that these people could be there with their literature, music, theater—not after a thousand years, but in hardly one generation. One of the Kazakh artists sang at my concert. There was special feeling among the audience when I embraced this woman from Kazakhstan."

One of the arguments of persons who are anti-Soviet, but are unable to deny the existence of complete racial equality in the Soviet Union, is that there are only a handful of Negroes in the whole land anyway, so equality has no meaning.

Robeson put the finger on this argument. There are of course tens of millions of dark peoples there.

"Take the peoples of Georgia," he said. "The people you see in Tbilisi; they are very dark, like the Puerto Ricans and Mexicans; and there are millions of yellow people—I have seen how the Chinese are treated in San Francisco.

"These Kazakh people, for example, had the same problems as the Negroes in the South today. But in the Soviet Union everything has been done for the development of these nationalities. That is one of the greatest contributions of the Soviet Union. Here, capitalism would like to use the colonial peoples to prop up its declining years, while there they show proudly the level that can be reached in one generation."

Soviet Russia Today, **August 1949**

ESLANDA ROBESON

What the Soviet Union Means to the Negro People

Eslanda Robeson, distinguished anthropologist and lecturer, was for many years New World Review's Editorial Consultant on Negro and Colonial Affairs, and its correspondent at the United Nations.

The present position of world power and influence of the Soviet Union should be of peculiar interest, importance and significance to all so-called "backward" peoples, because the peoples of Russia were certainly regarded as "backward" in the past.

The spectacular rise of the Soviet Union, with its practical, practicing, successful socialist way of life has challenged and destroyed once and for all, the long cherished theory of superiority of certain people because of color, sex, religion, and previous background upon which the Western way of life was built and is maintained.

The successful experience of the multinational Soviet Union has exposed this white supremacy theory as pure myth and wishful thinking, supported not by facts nor science, but by organized propaganda, colonial armies, and force and violence.

Under great handicaps and in spite of world opposition, the Soviet peoples have demonstrated beyond all doubt that so-called "backward" people are backward only because they have been deliberately kept back, are ignorant only because they have been carefully denied education, are poor only because their rightful wealth has been systematically stolen.

The Soviet Government has proved further that these crimes against whole sections of people can be corrected within a generation by a government organized and determined to correct them.

Women, Orientals, Jews, Moslems, peasants, national minority groups, traditionally despised and discriminated against in Old Russia, now live and work as equal Soviet citizens, universally accepted and respected according to the fulfillment of their responsibilities and obligations as citizens, and contribution to their country.

These facts about the Soviet Union, the Soviet people, and their successful socialist way of life are of profound and immediate practical interest to the Negro people and colored peoples everywhere.

Especially so today, because this is a very critical time for the Negro and colored peoples. They are definitely not free in the "Free World," and the governments of the "free nations" have made it clear that they have no intention of allowing them to achieve freedom, equality, independence, and the benefits of democracy. On the contrary these governments are now fighting small wars, and preparing for a world war to preserve their way of life.

We Negroes know that Un-Americans who resist accepting us as equals in the American Family, prefer to fight, lynch and kill us, to sacrifice the economy, morale, and security of our country rather than grant us our Constitutional rights.

We should therefore be the first to recognize that these Un-Americans and their colleagues abroad who resist accepting the Soviet Union, the Eastern Democracies and the New China as equals in the United Nations, the world family, prefer to fight and kill them rather than admit their right to choose their own way of life, for themselves, in their own countries.

As a Negro, as a colored person, as a woman—one of the so-called "backward" people, I hail the progress of the former "backward" Russian people to the present forward Soviet people; I congratulate them upon the success of their new socialist way of life which has brought them to world leadership and power in a few short years.

New World Review, November 1951

CORLISS LAMONT

Basic Principles of Soviet Foreign Policy

The Soviet Republic, standing forthright for international peace since its first day of existence, is generally depicted at present in America and the West as a nation bent on aggression and on plotting the military conquest of other countries. This wretched falsehood undermines the rational bases for international amity and cooperation.

First and foremost, the Soviet Union wants peace above all else in its international relations. Since its founding in 1917, the Soviet Republic has twice gone through the terrible ordeal of invasion of hostile states. The first time was during the civil war and intervention from 1918 to 1922; the second during the four years of struggle to the death with the Nazis, from 1941 to 1945. In both of these periods Soviet Russia lost many millions in dead and suffered economic destruction amounting to tens of billions of dollars.

The Soviets are most desirous of enduring peace, so that their people can live in security and happiness and put their full efforts into the building of socialism and communism. The dictates of simple self-preservation and sheer self-interest, as well as its special concern for the welfare of workers and peasants everywhere, cause the Soviet Union steadfastly to oppose international war.

True enough, the Soviet Communists are eager to see communist or socialist regimes established throughout the earth. But Marxist theory predicts the eventual collapse of capitalism through its own internal social-economic contradictions and has never suggested that Communist countries should seek by conquest to impose their system on capitalistic countries.

Another major goal in Soviet foreign policy is universal disarmament, including the abolition of atomic weapons and far-reaching international controls for atomic energy.

The Soviet record on disarmament has been a notable one. At the Genoa Conference of 1922, the first international conference which Soviet Russia attended, the Soviet Foreign Minister, G.V. Chicherin, proposed a general reduction of armaments. At the meeting of the Preparatory Commission of the Disarmament Conference at Geneva in 1927 the Soviet delegate, Maxim Litvinov, surprised the world by his proposal for general and complete disarmament.

After the formation of the United Nations the Soviet delegation urged, in 1946, a general reduction of armaments and prohibition of the production and utilization of atomic energy for war purposes. In 1948, when the cold war was well under way, the Soviet Government put forward a plan at the UN to reduce the armaments and armed forces of the Great Powers by one-third within a year.

As recently as November 1951, Soviet Foreign Minister Vyshinsky repeated this proposal at a meeting of the United Nations in Paris. The Western Powers treated Mr. Vyshinsky's scheme primarily as propaganda; and, indeed, the tendency of the non-Soviet world from 1917 on has been to sneer at Soviet disarmament proposals as insincere and designed to deceive. This attitude I am convinced is completely unjustified.

Soviet Russia has upheld the goal of disarmament in order to lessen international fears and frictions, decrease the danger of war and save for constructive economic purposes the colossal sums and energies which go into the manufacture of armaments.

The absence of unemployment and the general stability of the Soviet economic system is not contingent on the armaments industry, but is based on socialist ownership and country-wide planning. The Soviets consider armaments production an economic waste. Nonetheless, the very real menace of foreign aggression has compelled them to develop a great defense industry and to maintain a large army. It was fortunate for America and the rest of the democratic world that Soviet Russia was so well prepared when Hitler struck in World War II.

New World Review, Feburary 1952

HARRY F. WARD

The Long Battle for Peace

The following is a portion of an article honoring the 35th anniversary of the October Revolution, Dr. Ward was a noted theology professor and one of the most important peace leaders in the US. He wrote frequently for Soviet Russia Today *and* New World Review.

From the earliest days to the present, the record shows that Soviet foreign policy has sought continuously to implement the principle: "Underlying our foreign policy is the idea of peace." This means peace in the larger sense of ending war.

The interpretation of Soviet peace policy given our people by their government completely ignores this record, as though it had never been read, let alone analyzed. Our leaders deal with Soviet proposals as though they were, like their own intervention in the Korean war by our officials' own admission, a tactic improvised in a crisis to gain advantage over an adversary. When the Soviet Union proposed immediate outlawry of the A-bomb our people were told, and especially the religious groups which might have responded favorably, that this was an attempt to deprive us of our most effective weapon. Yet on the record it was an expression of a Soviet policy made known to the world in 1922.

When millions the world around united in support of the Soviet position, and a new force entered history in the first worldwide conscious movement to end war, our State Department proclaimed that the World Council for Peace was communist-inspired and dominated, and that Soviet proposals for peace were "deceptive propaganda."

Outside of Alice in Wonderland could anything be more fantastic? That a nation, while becoming the second great power, should appear on the international stage continuously for 30 years to attempt a monumental deception on the vital issue of war or peace! And finally gain the support of increasing millions in many lands, of all races, for its basic principles and the essential measures to carry them out! Hitler, with his Big Lie, never attempted anything as impossible as that.

New World Review, November 1952

RICHARD MORFORD

Tour of Five Cities

Amonth's tour of five cities—Moscow, Leningrad, Riga, Kiev and Tashkent—and the near countryside, provides little basis for major conclusions about Soviet life. Yet, as guests of the Society for Friendship and Cultural Relations, Mrs. Morford and I enjoyed extraordinary opportunities. We saw many institutions not on the tourists' sightseeing list; we talked with many leaders and people.

First, about children and young people. We went to a New Year's Party in the Kremlin in St. George's Hall—the most beautiful hall, I think, I ever saw. Perhaps 2,000 children—the younger ones that day—grades 2, 3, 4, 5—what a beautiful sight—lined both sides of the hall—a great tree in the center. Then at both ends of the hall simultaneous pageants—gorgeous costumes, eager faces and great pride for all these selected participants in a program arranged by the Komsomol. The climax came in a child's pinning a red star on the face of the moon rising high (30 feet perhaps) at the end of the hall. And then as the program concluded the master of ceremonies announced the presence of foreign guests and the Morfords got pulled into the center by the great tree to be introduced and presented with gifts. A complete surprise! Just us. And I made my best two-sentence speech into the hand microphone, telling the children how happy I was to be there. Indeed, we saw children—children—children all through that holiday period, the best possible introduction to the Soviet Union and one that filled us with present satisfaction and gave supreme confidence concerning the future.

New World Review, April 1960

JESSICA SMITH

New Soviet Disarmament Proposals

In the all-important question of disarmament now under discussion in the Political Committee due to US efforts to defeat Khrushchev's proposal that it be taken up directly in the General Assembly, the general feeling among UN delegates seems to be that no important decisions will be taken until the new US Administration takes office.

Before the UN are the USSR and US resolutions which reflect the deep-going differences betwen the two countries on this question. The USSR resolution calls for complete and universal disarmament within four years with, it must be understood, a complete control organization under the UN setup as soon as the treaty comes into effect, and inspection measures for every stage. With all the US talk about "dangers of surprise attack," it should be emphasized that the first stage of the Soviet proposals, which have taken positions of the West into consideration, provides for eliminating the retaliatory systems of both sides, through scrapping all means of delivering nuclear weapons to their targets, and simultaneous elimination of all military bases of any nation on foreign soil. It also calls for reduction of conventional armed forces in the first stage.

New World Review, December 1960

JESSICA SMITH

For a New Foreign Policy: The Debate Begins

The need and desire of the American people for a change in our foreign policies is seen in the debate stirred by recent speeches of Senator J. William Fulbright (D.-Ark.), chairman of the Senate Foreign Relations Committee.

In his speech in the Senate March 25, Senator Fulbright called for a new foreign policy based not on the myths of the past but on the realities of the postwar world. He proposed that we start thinking "unthinkable thoughts" about the cold war and East-West relations.

One myth is that "the devil resides immutably in Moscow." The master myth of the cold war, he said, "is that the Communist bloc is a monolith composed of governments which are not really governments at all but organized conspiracies, divided among themselves perhaps in certain matters of tactics, but all equally resolute and implacable in their determination to destroy the free world."

The Senator suggested that one way to make a beginning would be to overcome the myth that "trade with Communist countries is a compact with the devil," and to recognize that on the contrary, trade can serve as an effective and honorable means of advancing both peace and human welfare. He declared that trade restrictions should be ended because the United States had failed completely in its efforts to prevent its allies from trading with the Communist block countries, who had proved to be reliable customers, and that a "moderate volume of trade in non-strategic items" could be "an instrument for reducing world tensions and strengthening the foundations of world peace."

Fulbright criticized "inflexible" US policies in Asia. He said that reduced tensions in the Far East "might make it possible to strengthen world peace by drawing mainland China into existing East-West agreements in such fields as disarmament, trade, and educational exchange."

New World Review, May 1964

OSSIE DAVIS

A Black Man's Salute

I F ALL THE great and bragged-about benefits of the capitalist system were true beyond cavil, it would, from the viewpoint of us who are its historic victims, still stand condemned. It is a system to which we, the Black people of the United States, have never belonged save as the degraded means to somebody else's end. First as slaves, then as sources of cheap labor. Now as a seemingly endless supply of cannon-fodder for the needs of that system in its attempt to swallow up the world as it is now trying to do in Vietnam.

To the Black man capitalism has always been something not to be enjoyed—because we have always known that its benefits were not meant for us—but something somehow to be survived. It did not destroy us—no thanks to it—but it most certainly did not set us free. *Because it cannot.*

The Black man's mightiest expectations have always been in the alternative which, though nowhere present, he dreamed about as a part of the future. A future he frequently placed beyond the bounds of this world, where he would surely receive his reward, not down here on the earth—but up there in heaven. But the dream of heaven is real only to the degree to which it can be made to come true on earth. And since our religion counseled us always to look both ways—"Thy will be done on earth as it is in Heaven"—we searched each passing day for signs and portents.

Thus fifty years ago when the good news came out of Russia that men there had decided to abandon capitalism and attempt to construct, here, "on earth," a system in which no man would be the hereditary victim of other men because of the color of his skin, a system of true equality ultimately to be formulated as "from each according to his ability, to each according to his needs," it was only natural that Black men should associate their own hopes and their own expectations with the promises of socialism.

And so it is natural that today Black men should salute that country and that people who fifty years ago turned their backs on the past and struck out boldly to build a wholly different kind of society. Just as it is natural for us to find in the example of the Russian people enduring solace for all of our struggles ahead, and a constant reminder that *"what men have done, men can do."*

New World Review, November 1967

Our photos: Page 7: a view of Tashkent, capital city of Uzbekistan, reconstructed after the 1966 earthquake. Page 12: Red Square, Moscow, November 7, 1977, celebrating the 60th Anniversary. Page 56, from top: women's suffrage demonstration, Petrograd, 1917; V.I. Lenin and Red Army Commanders reviewing the troops in Red Square, May 25, 1919; the first Soviet tractor, "Fordson Putilovsky," Petrograd, 1924. Page 116, from top: students at a technical institute in Dushanbe, Tadzhikistan; a vocal ensemble, Tuvan Autonomous Soviet Socialist Republic. Page 138, from top: voting for candidates for the Supreme Soviet, Sverdlovsk; workers at the construction site of an atomic power station, Soviet Armenia; miners celebrating a production victory. Page 182: students of the Leningrad Polytechnic Institute. Page 240: the front cover of Volume 1, Number 1 of *Soviet Russia Today,* the predecessor of *New World Review*.